Identity Politics
in George Lucas' *Star Wars*

ALSO BY JOHN C. MCDOWELL

*The Politics of Big Fantasy: The Ideologies of* Star Wars, The Matrix *and* The Avengers (McFarland, 2014)

# Identity Politics in George Lucas' *Star Wars*

John C. McDowell

McFarland & Company, Inc., Publishers
*Jefferson, North Carolina*

ISBN (print) 978-1-4766-6286-2
ISBN (ebook) 978-1-4766-2450-1

LIBRARY OF CONGRESS CATALOGUING DATA ARE AVAILABLE

BRITISH LIBRARY CATALOGUING DATA ARE AVAILABLE

© 2016 John C. McDowell. All rights reserved

*No part of this book may be reproduced or transmitted in any form or by any means, electronic or mechanical, including photocopying or recording, or by any information storage and retrieval system, without permission in writing from the publisher.*

Front cover illustration from a photograph by Brendan Hunter (iStock)

Printed in the United States of America

*McFarland & Company, Inc., Publishers
Box 611, Jefferson, North Carolina 28640
www.mcfarlandpub.com*

To my father and mother,
John and Elizabeth McDowell

To Sandra and my children,
Archie, Jonathan, Joseph,
Margaret (Meg), and Robert

# Table of Contents

*Acknowledgments* — ix
*Preface* — 1
*Abbreviations* — 9

1. "Man your ships, and may the Force be with you": *Star Wars* and Mythically Sanitized Violence — 11

2. "Wars not make one great": Redeeming the *Star Wars* Mythos from the Myth of Redemptive Violence — 42

3. "There'll be no escape for the Princess this time": Re-Gendering the Patriarchal *Star Wars* Texts — 78

4. "We don't serve *their* kind here!" *Star Wars* and the Politics of Difference — 116

*Chapter Notes* — 155
*Bibliography* — 177
*Index* — 191

# Acknowledgments

Among my many faults is that of being unable to turn down invitations. Given the number of research projects I have been working on over recent years and the plans for developing my critical reflections on narratives of hope, and hopefully into a Gifford Lecture series, I had decided that *Star Wars* would not be a series of texts that I would intellectually return to any time soon. However, on the second invitation to consider composing a book on George Lucas' *magnum opus* the seeds of this present set of studies began to take shape, especially since I hoped to tackle the material prior to its impending Disneyfication (I have ignored, for example, the new animated series *Star Wars Rebels*). As much as J.J. Abrams has been successful in directing entertaining spectacles, I tend to find his movies quite philosophically uninteresting. My renewed attention to Lucas' version of the saga has permitted me to develop further the kind of critical intellectual reflection that between 2005 and 2007 resulted in my *The Gospel According to Star Wars*, but to do so now without the potential for bemusing an audience that purchased the book in order to hear "the [Christian] Gospel" through the *Star Wars* saga. My apologies to those who readers who simply bought the wrong book, and were consequently caught in the intricacies of discussions of appeals to myth in modernity, of the burgeoning of forms of religious pluralism in the mid to late twentieth century, of Manichaean politics, of the nature of the good life, of theological reflection and argument, and so on.

I am grateful for the opportunity to make research connections with my new colleagues at the University of Divinity. It is quite a relief to work again in a supportive environment, one in which the appeal to *excellence* in intellectual work appropriately remains a virtue rather than a tool of marketing rhetoric, over which there persists some excitement, and in which the "public impact" of one's work is taken seriously beyond the rhetoric encouraged by corporate power. It has become easier in Melbourne to answer the pressing question "what are universities for?" in terms that are not self-referential or financial but involve "impact" factors, community accountability, and academic responsibility. This book might be considered a celebration of the work of all those who risk their personal security in order to steal the plans to the "ultimate power in the universe." Despite my serious concerns over both the intellectual ecology and the rhetorical masking of not only pervasive academic ordinariness but instances of serious unprofessionalism elsewhere, I still miss conversing with Dr. Fergus King, Prof. Mario Manichello and Dr. Chris Falzon. Drs. Scott Kirkland and Ashley Moyse have emerged as humble, enthusiastic and distinctly high quality and intellectually ambitious scholars who have stood out from those around them. Regular conversations with them have been invigorating, and they have particularly kept me stimulated with regard to reflecting in some depth on products of popular culture. They continually resist the lure of the Sith. I already greatly miss those football clubs with whom I have been involved for almost six years, Lambton Jaffas and St. Johns Football Clubs, especially the lads of the 14/1s for whom I have had the honor of coaching for the past three seasons. Go Invincibles!

It is, however, with sorrow that two friends are now to be acknowledged *in memorium*, Drs. Mike Purcell and Jason Wardley. Jason was a source of valuable information when I first turned to writing on popular culture at Edinburgh in 2005, and Mike was instrumental in enabling me to settle into my new working environment there some five years earlier. Both are sorely missed and very warmly remembered. I would also like to thank the two anonymous readers of my first draft for their thoroughness and useful suggestions.

Once more, however, it is the support of my family for which I am most grateful: my wife Sandra, and children Archie, Jonathan, Joseph, Meg (Margaret) and Robert; my gracious in-laws, John and Margaret Carrick; and my parents, John and Elizabeth McDowell. My maternal grandfather Thomas Manson passed away late in 2013. He had been a tremendous inspiration to me, and I hope that in everything I do I will honor the legacy of this self-deprecating man.

Chapters 1 and 2 substantially expand and redevelop the argument from

- John C. McDowell, "'Wars Not Make One Great': Redeeming the *Star Wars* Mythos from Redemptive Violence," *Journal of Religion and Popular Culture* 22.1 (2010), http://www.usask.ca/relst/jrpc/art22(1)-WarsNotGreat.html and

- John C. McDowell, *The Gospel According to Star Wars: Faith, Hope and the Force* Louisville, KY: Westminster John Knox Press, 2007, ch. 6.

I thank the respective publishers for their permission to use and redevelop the materials.

# Preface

Prefaces to works on popular culture, particularly those focused on the cinema, occasionally begin with nostalgic reflection. I did the same in *The Politics of Big Fantasy*. As Gilbert Perez observes, we "respond to the movies of our youth with something like the feelings of first love," and it is frequently to these that one turns when doing critical work on cinema.[1] However, the danger is that such an approach might suggest that the intellectual work being done in this area is not of a serious and rigorous kind. Indeed, it remains the case that those engaged in studying popular culture in many academic institutions feel pressure to justify themselves in ways not shared by those working with more culturally "classic" texts, such as those my doctoral work considered (tragic drama and hope in the theology of Karl Barth). Moreover, the nostalgic mood is not a particularly useful catalyst for generating important socio-political analysis with some moral urgency. Consequently, this present Preface will take a markedly different direction in order to better ground the ethico-political concerns that provoke the studies undertaken in this book.

• • •

In *The Politics of Big Fantasy* I explained that there were two main reasons for studying the three sets of movies under consideration there in the way I did. This current set of studies is focused more particularly on Lucas' *Star Wars* saga, but it emerges out of a similar sensibility to that animating my 2014 study, and it continues the intellectual labor undertaken there. Firstly, I indicated in the earlier volume that it is important to illuminate the political ideologies of the movies studied, while simultaneously being attentive to any possible folds that the material may provide. The studies in the present book derive from, among other things, a sense that there remains a real political need to exact representations of identity, and the ideological framing for even the very consideration of what identity is and means, to modest critical analysis for the future of hope and planning in the project of human flourishing. As critics rightly observe, *Star Wars* enacts a particular type of meditation on identity and otherness. Of course, this is common to science-fiction literature and film. George Lucas, after all, makes some rather grand claims about not only the pedagogical role of the cinema but also about his own work as being conducted through a "moral megaphone." So, he asserts, "Somebody has to tell young people what we think is a good person. I mean, we should be doing it all the time. That's what the Iliad and the Odyssey are about— 'This is what a good person is; this is who we aspire to be.' You need that in a society. It's the basic job of mythology."[2] In an interview, the creator of the *Star Wars* saga pronounces that there is a quite specific connection between his movies and moral education. After Vietnam, he claims, "there was not a lot of mythology in our society—the kind of stories we tell ourselves and our children, which is the way our heritage is passed down. Westerns used to provide that, but there weren't Westerns anymore. ... I wanted it [viz., *Star Wars*] to be traditional moral study, to have palpable precepts ... that children could understand. ... Traditionally we get them from the church, the family, and in the modern world we get them form the media—from movies."[3] Consequently, Dale Pollock, Lucas' biographer, claims that "Lucas offers more than just escapist entertainment; he gives us a vision of what should be."[4] The question of exactly what Lucas' materials for moral formation involve has been a significant source of contention among cultural and political commentators. What is it that *Star Wars*' audiences are being educated in? Asking just such a question is, in Carl Silvio and Tony M. Vinci's words, "a necessary and progressive step toward exploring how *Star Wars* simultaneously codes and decodes a conflicting matrix of values, beliefs, and understandings that make up contemporary global culture."[5]

More constructively, the current set of studies is driven by a desire to denaturalize, to use Grace Jantzen's key critical category, "necrophilia" in order to affirm responsible life-enhancing possibilities, or what she names from Hannah Arendt "natality." Her analysis exposes a "violent habitus" running through the Western imagination, one that has distinctly disturbing socio-political effects.[6] She has hope that with such an ideological exposure a contribution may be made to enhancing the process of relating to one another without violence. Thereby one may resist the pressures that encourage the emergence of destructiveness of nothingness, and the self-interestedness and attendant relational conflictuality that drive it, as the only available option for regulating political performance. In the comic movie *Nothing* conflictuality is seen to lead to meaninglessness, and eventually the nothingness of non-being.

A second concern that connects the 2014 set of studies with this one has to do with difficulties with the critical scholarship on the movies under consideration. Responding to Theodor Adorno's critique of Stravinsky, Milan Kundera writes:

> What irritates me in Adorno is his short-circuit method that, with a fearsome facility, links works of art to political (sociological) causes, consequences, or meanings; extremely nuanced ideas (Adorno's musicological knowledge is admirable) thereby lead to extremely impoverished conclusions; in fact, given that an era's political tendencies are always reducible to just two opposing tendencies, a work of art necessarily ends up being classified as either progressive or reactionary; and since reaction is evil, the inquisition can start the trial proceedings.[7]

Several scholars have certainly done much to encourage more penetrating analyses of the *Star Wars* saga than had been the case with the lazy appeals to *Star Wars* as modern "myth"—the latter had, for instance, been largely perpetuated without any politically astute ideological critique. For my part, however, I remain distinctly unconvinced by a considerable set of commentary on Lucas' most influential cinematic labor, in particular the dominant trend mentioned above that locates these cinematic texts too neatly, dualistically and dismissively in the development of a neoconservative temperament in American political culture from the late 1970s onwards. Christine Cornea observes that "traditional American values and confidence were definitely shaken to the core during the early 1970s: America's involvement in Vietnam did not end in any recognizable victory and, following the Watergate scandal, Nixon announced his resignation in 1974. It became harder to establish just who were 'us' and who were 'them,' hard and fast dichotomies appeared to be breaking down in the 1970s, which is partly reflected in the bleaker and more ambivalent stance of these later films."[8] It is into this nostalgia for Manichaean-like values and identity representations that numerous commentators locate Lucas' *Star Wars*. So Jonathan Rosenbaum argued in the autumn of the year of the movie's release that *Star Wars Episode IV: A New Hope* (as it has since become known) was a politically reactionary and nostalgic text. It "doesn't seem to *mean* anything other than what it unabashedly is: a well-crafted, dehumanized update of FLASH GORDON with better production values, no ironic overtones, and a battery of special effects."[9] In fact, *Star Wars* has frequently been lambasted for what Lawrence and Jewett describe as pop fascism.[10] Much of this commentary, which is now so familiar and repeated that it has become almost entrenched as a received orthodoxy, appears too superficially sweeping and simplistic in the claims it makes. Worse still, some of it unfortunately is distinctly indolent with regards to its failing to provide any careful listening to texts and contexts, especially failing to consider *Star Wars* in the light of *THX 1138* (although substantial reflections on this earlier movie will have to await a later study I am currently planning). This raises all kinds of moral questions regarding the hegemonic imposition of a reading lens on the texts that results in a failure to begin with attentiveness, regard, and care to their own contextual voice.

A quite different reading is possible because of, and is in fact necessitated by, certain features of these movies as texts. The *Star Wars* movie first released in 1977, later renamed *Star Wars: Episode IV: A New Hope*, does tend to simplify the presentation of self and other. On the other hand, and this is certainly not insignificant, there is much in the movies—even in *A New Hope* itself—to suggest that something more interesting is going on, something, in fact, that can even subvert a reading of them as promoting a clear "identity politics." Accordingly, the *Star Wars* movies of George Lucas can be appreciated as being a politically more complicated set of texts. It is consequently arguable that they are considerably less dehumanizing in any straightforward fashion than certain commentators want to maintain, even if the dramatic categories these movies use are insufficient for enacting a critical hominizing pedagogy since they cannot, in the end, provide a post-essentialist account of moral subjectivity. *Star Wars Episode VII: The Force Awakens* is notably a very different case altogether.

• • •

George Steiner regards the critic as a parasite, and yet if Paolo Freire has been able to successfully make and sustain a case for the role of teachers in the process of transformative learning, a quite significant way of construing cultural analysis and criticism becomes necessary: that of the "teacher as cultural worker," identifying and transforming pedagogies that undemocratically oppress and dehumanize as a result of the vested power "interests of the oppressors."[11] I want to attend to Lucas's space operatic texts under this latter humanizing guise. In order to see what is at stake in such 'humanizing' study it helps to switch the image to another one provided by Grace Jantzen. She characterizes "the west as [being caught] in the grip of a cultural neurosis of which its death-dealing structures are symptoms." This entails, "then, [that] the task of the intellectual can be likened to that of a therapist who seeks by patient listening to bring the repressed dimensions of history to the fore and to release the springs of wellbeing."[12] This therapy, of course, involves considerably more than argument. So Jantzen recognizes that one can treat the troubles of the contemporary West "as an obsession or psychic disorder of the social realm, then it will not be changed by arguing against it."[13] The problems, depicted as neuroses, are far too deeply learned and conditioning for that to be the case. "Appeals to rationality will not bring about the desired change, any more than it would help to tell a person in the grip of a neurosis what it is that they are repressing. Such strategies only bring out stronger resistance, ever more clever rationalizations, deeper anger and control." In contrast, she maintains, bringing "about human flourishing ... requires substantial change in material as well as discursive conditions, changes in behaviour as well as in thought."[14] However, lest the cultural commentator despair at the magnitude of the task of criticism and properly transformative repair, Jantzen indicates the need for "patient investigation and analysis" over the shape and content of the beliefs that form or enculturate our sensibilities and that thereafter regulative our imaginations and practical judgments.[15]

> What we can learn from the therapeutic model is that to the extent that the problems of post/modernity are consequences of acting upon a destructive cultural symbolic, strategies and policies to change behaviour are unlikely to be effective unless the underlying patterns of thought are changed. Moreover for this to happen it is necessary to bring those patterns, the cultural symbolic, to consciousness, and this, in therapy, means probing its sources and history. Once the contours of the symbolic become clearer it becomes easier to see what is involved in its transformation and why it is necessary to go through the massive process of tracing its past in order to redeem the present.[16]

The cultural symbolic of Western societies and the options for social order that are made possible as a consequence require observation, analysis, and critique. The aim is not to simply "understand," as if knowledge is separate from hope and planning, or in order to achieve some nebulous "cultural/media literacy." After all, as Stanley Aronowitz argues, "without agency there can be no history except an automatic kind."[17] The key to practices of transformative pedagogy is to resist the loss of agency, and therefore the reduction of hope. In that way, academic reflection and critical thought has to serve human flourishing and not become a self-referential substitute for socio-political engagement for constructive change.

Reading George Lucas' *Star Wars* through such a politically significant lens takes the form of four chapters constructed as two sets of thematically overlapping pairs. Chapters 1 and 2 belong together as elements of a single argument written in the light of the kinds of questions concerning social responsibility and defining dehumanizing ideologies raised by the pop cultural phenomenon that appeared from within these conditions. They belong particularly closely together as two parts of one substantially extended study, lengthened largely by virtue of the considerable critical work they have to do. They tackle populist approaches to issues of the cultural relation between the *Star Wars* (a largely American) saga and questions of violence, in particular attending to its possible performance of the so-called "myth of redemptive violence." The contention is that the presentation of violence in the sets of narratives is not a simple one since this multi-part cultural product offers several forms of it. These forms range from something akin to a "holy violence," through more a sense of "just war," to an ethical philosophy approaching a full-blown redemptive "non-violence." In fact, there may well be in the performance of the last theme vital potential for even subverting the very "myth of redemptive violence" itself and likewise its discourse of "a good war."

Chapter 2's reading in particular aims to provoke not an indecision over meaning but rather an "undecision" over the grain of the most commonly heard connection of *Star Wars* with a mythically violent ethos, and this is done largely in order to open up a liberative reading of the saga. It is argued that although Lucas' *Star Wars* takes the child-friendly and entertaining mega-form it does that nonetheless, it is conceived of as a *morally pedagogical* text, one that displays Lucas' own discomfort with the Nixon government and the Vietnam War. Although this will have to remain a study for another day, it would be fruitful to read the 1977 *Star Wars* movie carefully in the light of Lucas' earlier dystopian socio-political protest movie *THX 1138*.

Chapters 3 and 4 extend questions of violence and an emancipatory politics as the result of a set of critical claims that identify crucial difficulties in the shaping of the representation of Otherness in Lucas' saga. The nature of the way otherness is construed enacts violence against those excluded from power by being "othered," made "alien." According to Patricia Melzer, "Many descriptions of aliens in traditional science fiction narratives are limited to representing either warring opponents, who resist colonization of their planet by the heroes or terrorize a sector of the universe; or gentle, often dumb creatures, who, as 'sympathetic aliens' …, shyly shake the hero's hand in farewell."[18] Paul Verhoeven, for instance, the director of *Starship Troopers*, exemplifies the former when he asserts that "the US is desperate for a new enemy. ... Critics' Alien sci-fi gives us a terrifying enemy that's politically correct. They're bad. They're evil. And they're not even human."[19] Verhoeven's lack of irony in using the phrase "politically correct" with regard to such a use of terms for the alien such as "enemy" and "evil" is revealing of a powerful strand in American political culture. It is here that *Star Wars*, a culturally pervasive set of texts, requires critical attention. Matthew Kapell, for instance, argues that *Star Wars* uses categories of "race," and other critics argue "gender," in order "to reinforce ideas of difference and to reinforce discriminatory practices."[20] The question is not so much one of why there is a paucity of non-white human characters or significant female characters in the saga, although those in themselves are important matters and may well be bound up with larger racist and sexist tendencies in American culture, but "whether the effects of ... [Lucas'] cinematic representations perpetuate racist discourse and practices in the wider society."[21]

It is worth indicating again that the following critical studies are interested in *George Lucas'* space opera, and therefore they do not address the most recent cinematic addition to the franchise, *Star Wars Episode VII: The Force Awakens*. While it would take some time to make this case, and I will do so at a later date with a second edition of *The Gospel According to Star Wars*, the two sets of movies (I–VI and VII) have a quite different political vision, and the newest installment almost has the feel of being an expensive and much hyped element more from the Expanded Universe. There is another reason for focusing on I–VI. The crucial fact is that the Disney owned and produced version trilogy is incomplete at my time of writing, with the final movie in the series currently scheduled for late 2019. Given the critical purchase that Episodes V and VI, not to mention I–III, brought to much of the political sensibility of the *Star Wars* movie that was eventually given the numerical value of Episode IV, it makes sense for critical hindsight to await the saga's completion before making grand scholarly claims concerning it. The studies in this particular book will, therefore, continue on as if Disney had not happened to Lucasfilm.

# Abbreviations

| | |
|---|---|
| *ANH* | *A New Hope* |
| *AOTC* | *Attack of the Clones* |
| *ESB* | *Empire Strikes Back* |
| *ROTJ* | *Return of the Jedi* |
| *ROTS* | *Revenge of the Sith* |
| *SW* | *Star Wars* |
| *TPM* | *The Phantom Menace* |

# 1

# "Man your ships, and may the force be with you"
## Star Wars and Mythically Sanitized Violence

## Why Does Violence Please?

Several year ago D. Daiches Raphael, in his book *The Paradox of Tragedy*, asked the stark question "Why does Tragedy please?"[1] After some discussion of the meaning of the term "pleasure," arriving instead at something closer to the sense of audience "satisfaction," he refers to the setting of the question in Aristotle's determinative depiction of the mimetic art of tragic drama. In this classic and superlative text the Athenian had made the claim that Tragedy effects through fear and pity a *catharsis* or purging of the emotions. Numerous commentators have exercised considerable anguish in attempting to understand what Aristotle could have meant by this, ranging from emotionally restorative exhilaration,[2] to medicinal purgation,[3] to an ennobling vision of humanity at its most noble in the face of the extremity of suffering,[4] to provoking "compassion" and "distress."[5] One particular version of a cathartic sensibility is expressed in Friedrich Nietzsche's *Birth of Tragedy* in which both the Dionysian music and the cathartic *Stimmung* (mood/atmosphere) virtually appear to bury plot and character, for the purpose of the spectatorial affirmation of life.[6] George Steiner, in response, laments paucity of philosophical approaches to Tragedy, which he regards as "of course, of the essence," and by this he means philosophical approaches that are markedly different from Nietzsche's use of the dramatic genre for the purposes of affirming life.[7] In contrast, he offers a claim about the possibility of art's "interrogation" of life, since it functions, in an important sense, as "a sharply political gesture, a value-statement of the most evident ethical import."[8] This means, he maintains, that art "purposes change," or at least it can do (he has plenty to say about why *kitsch* is, therefore, not art).⁹ To take pleasure in the tragic in any less of a sense would be to approach it in an excessively sanguine fashion and, indeed, even in a form of "high-flown sadism," according to Terry Eagleton.¹⁰ Accordingly, Eagleton is prompted to morally protest, "The doctrine of *catharsis* that there is indeed something edifying and enjoyable about the experience of tragedy, but 'inexpressible satisfaction,' with Cordelia dead in her father's arms, borders on the positively sadistic."¹¹

The question of what screened violence, in particular, is good for, and therefore in what sense it *pleases* or *satisfies* its audiences, has long been an equally contentious matter. Is it good for the sake of some kind of simple entertainment, perhaps functioning to provide a form of distraction from the chores or sufferings of the mundane and the everyday? Or can it even operate as a cathartic moment, purging violent instincts through the safe spectacle? Stanley Kubrick, for instance, defended his *A Clockwork Orange* from much of the criticism it attracted by announcing that "any kind of violence in films serves a useful purpose by allowing people a means of vicariously freeing themselves from the pent-up aggressive emotions which are best expressed in dreams, or the dreamlike state of watching a film."¹² Or are matters more complicated than that? For instance, do the imagined and the lived realities overlap in disturbing ways that involve the latter coming to mimetically perform the former? This possibility of the copycatting of screen violence has been debated at some length, both by intellectuals and in the public forum. In his *Media Ethics Goes to the Movies*, Howard Good explains that from the considerable number of studies on media violence since the 1960s the overwhelming finding has been that "repeated exposure to violent programming produces health risks, particularly to children and adolescents."¹³ Good's study then appeals to Seneca to reveal some of what is at stake.¹⁴ The Roman statesman had complained that the spectacle of gladiators fighting to the death or criminals being thrown to the lions actually brutalized and desensitized the Romans. It made them *"crudelior et inhumanior"* ("more cruel and more inhumane"). Their pleasure in observing violence as willing participants in encouraging the spectacle not only undercut what Seneca took to be central task of life—to grow in spirit, understanding, and self-control—but also actually reversed the development. It, in other words, destroyed the various audiences' *humanitas*. Violence, in this vein, is offered as an *entertaining* spectacle for the titillation of consumptive viewers. One can observe the intensification of the brutalizing spectacle over recent years—for instance, in the likes of Quentin Tarantino's aestheticized trivialization of the violence of vengeance, the heavily stylized and eminently blood-soaked cinematic adaptation of Frank Miller's *300* or *Sin City*, and the ostentatious violence offered to viewers' amusement by the Star Channel's multiple seasons of *Spartacus*. So Good colorfully declares that "a society that finds violence entertaining, and that even allows the entertainment industry to target children and adolescents with violent fare, may be lost in its own sort of moral morass. Prolonged exposure to media violence has been shown in study after study to desensitize viewers. And a desensitized viewer is one less likely to recognize the rights and feelings of others or to think ethically about human relationships. The symbolic violence spreading like a toxic spill in our midst may not actually destroy life, but neither does it promote the love and joy we need to live."[15]

However, there is a further, and deeper, issue than that of whether or not there is violence portrayed onscreen, or whether there is or is not a correlation between the amount of screened violence and that possibly mimetically realized in the real world. After all, anti-war movies like *Apocalypse Now* have a high body count, as do *Schindler's List, Shooting Dogs* and *Hotel Rwanda*, or *All Quiet on the Western Front*. A clue to the more significant question, however, emerges from Seneca's reference to the viewers' *humanitas*: what *values* are being assumed in the violent filmed fiction? The question, then, has to do with how the violence is portrayed within a value system. In particular, what are the ideological operations in the cultural symbolic? In an interview conducted in 1991 Julia Kristeva claimed that "the media propagate the death instinct. Look at the films people like to watch after a long tiring day: a thriller or a horror film, anything less is considered boring. We are attracted to this violence. So the great moral work which grapples with the problem of identity also grapples with this contemporary experience of death, violence and hate."[16] This, she explained, expresses itself in extremist forms of identity politics: "Nationalisms, like fundamentalisms, are screens in front of this violence, fragile screens, see-through screens, because they only displace that hatred, sending it to the other, to the neighbour, to the rival ethnic group. The big work of our civilization is to try to fight this hatred." The mention of hatred here is important. Violence does not come from nowhere. On the contrary, it is a sort of "communication ... of hatred, fear, or contempt."[17] Even if it is not the provocative action of one seeking to assert herself it may well be the response to another's self-asserting, of another's fear and loathing.[18]

Violence becomes a spectacle of entertainment, a commodifiable framing of the popular imagination. It is the value system inherent in this screened agonism or conflictuality that movies like *God Bless America* and *Apocalypse Now*, among others, take issue with. According to Kurtz in the latter: "We train young men to drop fire on people. But their commanders won't allow them to write 'fuck' on their airplanes because it's obscene." If this is what is at stake, then, Jane Mills believes, perhaps the operations of censorship can even, in the end, deflect attention away from "understanding where the real roots of violence lie."[19]

Even if this is so, there remains a question over the nature of the representation of violence—is violence a singular matter, or is it a considerably more complex affair? Ridley Scott, for instance, makes an interesting, albeit a rather grand and glib, claim that every war movie is an antiwar movie.[20] In the Wachowskis' cinematic adaptation of the comic book series *V for Vendetta* there is a moment in which the title character V claims that "violence can be used for good, for justice!" This suggests that there are bad forms of violence as well, and that not all forms of violence can be lumped in together. The significant conversation in Christopher Nolan's *Batman Begins* between Bruce Wayne and Rā's al Ghūl on the nature of justice and its relation to violence suggests something similar.

This chapter tackles the issue of violence in the *SW* saga, in particular in relation to the classic trilogy, Episodes IV-VI. Recently the screening of a new animated series entitled *Star Wars Rebels*, and prior to that George Lucas' approved animation series, *Clone Wars*, has rekindled the imaginations of the youngest generation to immerse itself in not merely the excitement of the Lucas-inspired visual materials, but also in the expensive consumption of a wide-range of merchandise. Aggressive lightsaber battles can again be seen taking place on the streets, and consequently concerns about the relation of this saga and violence are worth raising once more. According to Mathew Alford, "Science fiction can accommodate rather simplistic narratives depicting morally unambiguous fights between the US and space aliens, from *War of the Worlds* (1953, 2005) to the Pentagon-assisted *Invaders from Mars* (1986), as well as numerous installments of Buck Rogers and Flash Gordon."[21] However, this chapter and the following one assume that the pop philosophy of the *SW* movies possesses certain kinds of resources to enable them to be recognized as a multi-volume set of publicly ethical texts. Primarily the chapter at hand tackles populist approaches to issues of the cultural relation between this (largely American) saga and questions of violence, in particular attending to *SW*'s possible performance of the so-called "myth of redemptive violence," "the myth of a Good War," to use Trevor

McCrisken and Andrew Pepper's terms. This is a myth that Susan Sontag regards as being prevalent in the morally unproblematic presentation of armed conflict and the "righteous bellicosity" against monstrous enemies that is common to the genre of science fiction.[22] (Here, one might observe, reflections on violence turn specifically to war, or "state-sponsored" violence.) According to Robin Wood, it is "unlikely" that people engage in multiple readings of movies like Lucas' in order to "discover new meanings, new complexities, ambiguities, possibilities, and possibilities of interpretation."[23] While this would be entirely understandable in terms of the kind of audience that the saga tends to particularly attract (children, adolescents, and the adult "fanboy") it would be culturally unfortunate and would intellectually stabilize problematic receptions. Over the course of the next two chapters, then, the contention will be that the presentation of violence in the sets of narratives is not a simple one since this multi-part cultural product offers several forms of it. These arrangements of violence can be argued to array from something akin to a "holy violence," through a sense more of the enactment of a "just war" approach, to an ethical philosophy that approaches a full-blown redemptive need for "non-violence." In fact, there may well even be in the performance of the last theme vital potential for subverting the very "myth of redemptive violence" itself and likewise its discourse of "a good war." This first chapter's reading, as the initial part of a double study on the issues, aims to provoke not an indecision over meaning but rather an "undecision" over the grain of the most commonly heard connection of *SW* with a mythically violent ethos. This is done largely in order to open up a liberative reading of the saga with regard to what Judith Butler terms "the pecarity of life."[24]

• • •

## *"You may fire when ready" (Grand Moff Tarkin, ANH): A Violent Mythos*

All human artifacts are culturally and contextually produced. Mythologies, for instance, express, through their judicious symbolic depiction of "archetypal" forms of living, the cultural (Latin, *cultura*) conditions that mark their location or setting. However, they also possess a certain transcendental quality which enables them to re-cultivate or transfigure, either subtly or radically, perspectives of their cultural instantiation by offering imaginative alternatives which themselves can become effective through their ritualistic telling and retelling. What these claims do is argue that mythological stories can provide powerful unconscious forces for the motivation and justification of the collective behavior of those various cultures in which they are told and retold as being existentially meaningful narratives. Put another way, they are formed within discursive webs of significance that determine what we learn to value, although one should be careful not to overplay the determination that has plagued the analysis of, for example, Theodor Adorno on "the culture industry" and "mass culture."[25] Thereby, through their mediations, these ritualised story-telling performances significantly contribute to "socializing" us. It is precisely "because culture matters so much," Ben Agger claims, that "it deserves full critical attention."[26] Speaking specifically of the hegemonic role of the cinema, a particular form of the power of cultural production, Margaret Miles and S. Brent Plate argue that "in just over one hundred years, film has become a powerful force in modern life that changes the way we think about, interpret, and live in the world. Because of this alteration of the ways we literally see the world, critical attention to film becomes a vital task for those engaged with issues of religion and ethics, and concerned with more equitable social arrangements."[27]

Yet, because this process occurs more often than not in largely *unseen* ways the emotive matter of the relation between screen violence and social crime, for instance, can only at best be *superficially* dealt with through reflection on whether there is a *direct* influence of fictional violence on, a *conscious* appropriation or repetitious simulation of, actual violence. Given the way mythologies help shape cultural dispositions, identity and discourse, the values and dispositions portrayed in the violent piece become "internalized" and "naturalized" in the cultural unconscious. Richard Mollica, director of Harvard's program in refugee trauma, announces that "people who commit murder find it very easy to rationalize ... and come to terms with it."[28] Partly this can be explained by the psychological need for emotional "survival" after traumatic incidents. But it is also the product of the way in which the belief system that one is inculcated into itself requires the rationalization of certain forms of inflicting fatality on "others." As Carl Silvio and Tony Vinci maintain, "To speak of popular mythology, then, is to speak of politics, economics, identity formation, and ideology to the extent that our relationships to these categories are thoroughly mediated by popular narratives."[29] These values are assumed to be the way things are, and are, in René Girard's term, "learned" through the mimesis of imaginative repetition (and the sheer amount of screen violence suggests that the repetition has made us familiar, all too familiar, with these assumptions).³⁰ This entails that in the undoubtedly complex process of the social construction of reality "the power of the media," if we can even speak meaningfully of that in a culturally porous set of interpenetrating cultures, lies more fully at the level of the *unconscious*. It can provide resources for the forming of discourse and of persons and persons' imaginations, for the construction of identity and understanding.

What may initially appear to be simple and child-friendly entertainment in the youth-market of novels, comic-books, movies and television programs may actually be simultaneously an ideology full of unquestioned assumptions.³¹ As George Orwell claimed soon after the Second World War, "no book is genuinely free from political bias."³² His own interest in politics, he explained, involved the "desire to push the world in a certain direction, to alter other people's idea of society that they should strive after." It has only been relatively recently that scholars have turned their attention away from appeals to *SW* as a "new myth," wherein myth is portrayed ahistorically in terms of trans-cultural and trans-temporal forms of human meaning, to concerns with the specific shape of the cultural mythologies or hidden value-presuppositions that are determinative in this six-volume saga of George Lucas. Veronica Wilson, for instance, maintains the need for *deep* study of the texts: "Scholars have discussed at length how George Lucas drew inspiration from Joseph Campbell's ideological analyses and from Jungian archetypes when crafting characters and situations for his *Star Wars* saga. Few, however, have analyzed ways in which Lucas's characters and narratives apparently reflect other sorts of cultural and authorial attitudes as well—assumptions so deeply embedded that they are logically unexamined, unconscious, and perhaps wholly unintentional."³³ In other words, identifying the nature of the particular Campbell-inspired use of a mythic form in *SW*, or in any other mythic text, is not the end of the process of studying myth—it is only the start of the questions about "myth" that can be employed. In fact, according to Kevin Wetmore, the myth-study approach might even serve to mask the operative ideological assumptions and therefore "much myth criticism ignores the complicity of myth in establishing and maintaining social dominance and power structures. Many myths are created in order to explain why those in power are in power and why those who are oppressed or dominated are (and should be) oppressed and dominated."³⁴ Therefore, Wilson argues, "To dismiss the *Star Wars* films out of hand as lowbrow adventure-romance films that cannot support any meaningful analysis, as some commentators have done, is erroneous and perhaps irresponsible.

Given the saga's immense popularity, its potential cultural and psychological impact upon millions of viewers ... should not be underestimated."[35] We may observe with Silvio and Vinci, then, that *SW* is an important "site of cultural investment that both reflects and shapes late twentieth and early twenty-first century global culture."[36]

When critical attention is refocused on the sense of the movies as culturally reflective one can perceive the myriad of ways in which Lucas' movies, in Wetmore's words, "are not so much 'mythic,' as some have argued, as an 'ideological mirror.'"[37] The distinction Wetmore makes here, as is likewise made by several of the contributors to Silvio and Vinci's volume, between myth-study and ideology-critique is somewhat overdetermined—the two should work together as a deep study of myth, of the mythological intentions and the cultural myths that unwittingly influence the movies. The problem is more that when separated, "myth" tends to be studied acontextually as is evidenced by the work of Andrew Gordon, Mary Henderson, and John Shelton Lawrence (Henderson, in spite of the "myth-focus" of her reading, does at least recognize that the portrayal of good and evil shifts over Episodes IV-VI).[38] However, as Dan Rubey observes, this approach to *SW* in the form of a myth-study overlooks the cultural specificities and contextualities of mythologies, and the multiplicity of these stories and their cultural meanings in their differences.[39] Moreover, "mythologies" have not only more culturally specific but also more political meanings than the myth-study approach to *SW* has taken time to notice. As Silvio and Vinci maintain, if a myth is the story told by a culture that expresses its understanding of the world and the relations between persons then the myth becomes an expression that also conditions, or socializes, each generation within that culture. "To speak of popular mythology, then, is to speak of politics, economics, identity formation, and ideology to the extent that our relationships to these categories are thoroughly mediated by popular narratives."[40] Recognizing Lucas' indebtedness to Joseph Campbell requires less complaint and certainly not avoidance in one's provision of an ideology-critical analysis, but more a better cultural-politically specified reading of both Campbell and of Lucas than has tended to be offered by readers.[41] Nonetheless, Wetmore's point is a good one insofar as it is the job of "ideology criticism" to uncover hidden ideological dynamics and to put them on display for critical testing and possibly contesting. So, for instance, scholars have been asking how far there is an indication of 1970s' American patriarchalism,[42] racism,[43] capitalism,[44] homophobia,[45] individualism,[46] or American supremacism[47] driving the *SW* texts. In this way the movies are properly perceived to be culturally *expressive*, or at least expressive of a particular strand of culture. This is, of course, one of the reasons for their success—their well packaged, glamorous, action-packed and fast-paced adventure resonated in meaningful ways with a mass audience. A sense of the cultural appeal of the movies is suggested by Liam Neeson, the actor portraying Qui-Gon Jinn in *TPM*, but only as his analysis slips again into the decontexted eternalizing of mythology as mythic: "George's tales, the *Star Wars* tales, have really tapped into the psyche and mood that popular modern culture has never done before. For me that says yes these films are incredibly well made, but also it's tapping into a void which we have as human beings that we have kind of lost something. And George provides ... the great story-telling sense of myth."[48]

The difficulty with, and even naïveté of, several critical studies of the ideological values of Lucas' products, however, is that they fail to make an appropriate distinction between the values that *unconsciously* shape this *auteur*'s performance and those that he intentionally attempts to promote. Consequently, these critiques are open not only to a logical flattening of potential complexity, but to the possible counter-claim regarding Lucas' own political values, should they be different. Dan Rubey's analysis is particularly prone to this when he speaks of "Lucas' conservative ideological bias."[49] After all, Lucas *critically* reworks important political aspects of Campbell's monomyth. Silvio and Vinci's book a little more promisingly, at least, aspires to explore "how *Star Wars* simultaneously codes and decodes a conflicting matrix of values, beliefs, and understandings that make up contemporary global culture."[50] However, as Wetmore argues in a more appropriately sophisticated way, it makes sense not to argue that Lucas is consciously, for instance, racist or sexist.

> Yet, as Stuart Hall argues, "an ideological discourse does *not* depend on the conscious intentions of those who formulate statements within it." What Henry A. Giroux asks of Larry Clark, I ask of George Lucas: The "pertinent question" is not whether Lucas is racist, but rather "whether the effects of his cinematic representations perpetuate racist discourse and practices in the wider society."[51]

A question frequently raised over the mythology offered by the saga, a pop myth of monstrous popularity, crucially has to do with matters of (macho) militarism and systemic violence. The claim is not due to the *amount* of violence in *SW*, for as mentioned earlier, movies like *Schindler's List*, *Hotel Rwanda*, and *Shooting Dogs* are full of violence. Yet these particular movies design the visual texture of violence in such a way that it disturbs us into moral reflection, remorse, and watchfulness against the pressures to violate other people in our own lifetime. Instead, the issue is of the *function* of the violence, and their relation to what Slavoj Žižek calls violence as "purely 'objective,' synchronic, anonymous."[52]

Certain critics particularly identify in *SW* what biblical scholar Walter Wink calls the "myth of redemptive violence." Wink rather grandly identifies this as "the real religion of America," and in fact "of the modern world," or the culture of death and violence that Grace Jantzen even more imposingly claims lies pathologically at the heart of Western philosophy.[53] In this regard, then, according to L. Gregory Jones, "It may be impossible to unlearn violence because it is inscribed in the way things are, in the very nature of the world."[54] Wink explains what he means by the myth of redemptive violence: it "enshrines the belief that violence saves, that war brings peace, that might makes right. ... The belief that violence 'saves' is so successful because it doesn't seem to be mythic in the least. Violence simply appears to be the nature of the things. It's what works. It seems inevitable, the last and often, the first resort in conflicts."[55] This may even amount to a justification of pre-emptive violence as a survivalist means of self-protection, such as that which Jonathan Wolfe locates in the influential political philosophy of the seventeenth century thinker Thomas Hobbes: "As pre-emption is a form of defence, invading others can often be seen as the most rational form of self-protection."[56] Such a soteriologically ordered ideology of instrumental violence (or violence towards the end of peace) is markedly different from that identifiably directing numerous computer games, according to Wink. "What we find here [in the latter] is the sadistic enjoyment of evil pure and simple. Redemptive violence gives way to violence as an end in itself. It is no longer a religion that uses violence in the pursuit of order and salvation, but one in which violence has become an aphrodisiac, sheer titillation, an addictive high, a substitute for relationships. Violence is no longer the means to a higher good, namely order; violence becomes the end."[57]

Critics feel they do not have to work terribly hard to expose this supposedly American myth in the saga. So, for instance, Bryan Stone argues that "the ultimate victory of good over evil finally boils down to firing laser-blasters, detonating bombs, or slicing through one's enemies with a light saber."[58] Despite the Jedi Masters Yoda and Obi-Wan Kenobi counseling Luke Skywalker not to succumb to the Dark Side of "anger, fear ... aggression ... hate," the question is whether the films on the whole serve to justify violence, or at least a certain kind of violence—the *redemptive violence* of the Rebel's and Jedi's causes.[59] Does the *SW* saga tap into and reinforce (in both either consciously or unconsciously) the violent American fascination with, and celebration of, the hero who overcomes all odds to dispense true justice himself, what Robert Jewett and John Shelton Lawrence call "the Captain America complex"?[60] Simply, as "space opera" *SW* belongs to, to use the words of one commentator on the genre, "a literature of conflicts, usually with violent resolutions."[61]

As mentioned earlier, underlying this chapter and the succeeding one is the sense that *SW*, a supposed example of morality diverting popcorn culture with wide sphere of influence, possesses resources to be read as a multi-volume set of a publicly ethical texts.[62] The main feature driving the study has to do with the issue of the relation between this saga and violence. The contention is that violence takes several forms in these movies, and these range from something akin to a "holy violence," through a sense of "just war," to an ethical philosophy approaching a full-blown redemptive "non-violence." Certainly it is true that *SW* is a polymorphic set of visual texts that generates multiple interpretations. Yet, there may well be in the performance of the theme of "the redemptive" vital potential for subverting the so-called "myth of redemptive violence," or the talk of "a good war," itself, and for the presentation of differentiations in the acts of violence that open up to questions of otherness, difference and good relations *beyond* violence. Consequently, *Star Wars*' creator George Lucas, then, exhibits in his cinematic product something of the complex historical arrangements that make the cultural environment of the U.S. something recognizably more diverse than associating America with the myth of redemptive violence might suggest. Thus, when discouraging hasty and ill-informed readings of it as mythologizing violence and violent aesthetic voyeurism, the saga can perhaps surprisingly invite the re-imagination and re-cultivation of the moral vision for the flourishing of responsible agency. Lucas complained in 1981: "A lot of articles either are wrong about things or they make up things. And when it's *Time* or *Fortune* everybody takes it as the gospel truth. Suddenly it becomes 'resource material' and keeps cropping up over and over again."[63] Unfortunately a considerable amount of academic reflection is problematic for a similar reason—it tends to take shortcuts and makes judgments on the basis of a small amount of the available resources, and the superficial plausibility of the claims subsequently seep into the scholarly and popular imaginations in such a way as to ossify what was a little tenuous and uninformed in the first place. Even if my somewhat grand critical claims remain unconvincing to readers in the end, my pair of chapters suggest that at the very least one must recognize that matters are not as simple as most readings of *SW* as a violent set of texts would like to assume.

There is something else that needs to be stated in advance of launching into the detailed argument, and this has been developed more substantially in *The Gospel According to Star Wars: Faith, Hope and the Force*. The saga is, of course, two sets of trilogies, and these are separated by over a decade and a half. There are observable differences in context, style, mood, and so on. Where I perceive these differences to be important I will provide an indication. Yet my first and second chapters equally advocate that better attention needs to be paid by cultural scholarship of the saga to the differences and continuities than has generally been the case.[64]

It is worth pausing a little longer at this point to provide a further clarifying parenthesis. It is noticeable that many studies of *SW* slip interchangeably from talk of "violence" to that of "war," and one should be careful in doing this. They are not the same thing, especially since "war" is often presented as involving more moral innocence for those involved in enacting the state sanctioned violence. On the other hand, it is nonetheless important to recognize the overlap, and therefore the way in which "war" becomes an expression of an underlying violent instinct. As Jantzen explains, "it is not war, worrying though that is, upon which I think our attention should be focused. Many thoughtful people deplore war—sometimes all wars, sometimes specific wars as unjustifiable morally or tactically—and would hold that the values of western society are and should be fundamentally peaceable. But if I am anywhere near right, war is no more than an explosive symptom of the systemic violence which spreads its underground tentacles throughout our cultural habitus."[65] Likewise, Susanne Kappeler puts this point starkly: "War does not suddenly break out in a peaceful society; sexual violence is not the disturbance of otherwise equal gender relations. Racist attacks do not shoot like lightning out of a non-racist sky, and the sexual exploitation of children is no solitary problem in a world otherwise just to children. The violence of our most commonsense everyday thinking, and especially our personal will to violence, constitute the conceptual preparation, the ideological armament and the intellectual mobilization which make the 'outbreak' of war, of sexual violence, of racist attacks, of murder and destruction possible at all."[66]

## "So this is how liberty dies—with thunderous applause" (Padmé, ROTS): The Will to Specular Violence

Martin Luther King's sermonic meditation on the words of the Jesus dying on the cross—"Father, forgive them, for they know not what they do"—understands them to be the expression of someone refusing to retributively respond to violence with vengeance. But there is more to Jesus' prayer than that—the reference is to the self-deception of his executors for "they know not what they do." The Fourth Gospel's ironic use of the *ecce homo*, for instance, holds up a mirror to the agency of the authorities, driven as they are by the dream of the sovereign kingdom of Rome or a god that cannot recognize the presence of Jesus as the proclaimer of the true Kingdom, the *basileia* (rule) of God. King's reflections lead him to claim that "the ultimate measure of a man is not where he stands in moments of comfort and convenience, but where he stands at times of challenge and controversy."[67] While this may appeal to the typically modern Western reduction of the ethical to the limit- or extreme-situation, the point is that these moments of discord are more revealing of who we are and the values that determine us than the relatively "quieter" moments are. In other words, it is important to attend to the structuring dynamics of human consciousness and agency, to the cultivating of instincts that form and direct decision-making at its deepest level.

John Shelton Lawrence and Robert Jewett attempt to do just this at a very particular point when developing their own version of Joseph Campbell's claim about an identifiable American "monomyth," the story that sustains as well as best illuminates and expresses the cardinal values shared by many Americans.[68] It is this that makes the character of Kurtz in *Apocalypse Now* a chilling expression of, rather than a sheer monstrosity, the national war-machine as it performs its deadly dealings in South East Asia. While Lawrence and Jewett's use of the term echoes Campbell, the latter is concerned more with Jungian archetypes especially in relation to the individual, whereas this pair of commentators is more interested in the politics of ideologies in relation to the formation of communities'/nations' self-understandings. Their studies on the theme attempt to penetrate below shallow crisis-ethics which asks questions about decision-making without paying attention to the types of things that influence the formation of moral judgment. Rather than focus on high-cultural expressions or politicians' explicit claims this scholarly pair tackles the matrix of popular-culture-as-identity-cultivating, or in Tom Beaudoin's terms that cultural discourse which is the primary medium through which younger Americans tend to develop their self-consciousness. Therein they trace the monomyth through numerous pop cultural moments.[69] They claim that the prevalence of this monomyth as they perceive it generates an ideological structure of violence, responsive vengeance, and so on, webs of significance themselves spinning the process of learning ideologies of death and violence. As Nicholas Jackson O'Shaughnessy claims in his study of propaganda, "We have no inherited predisposition to kill. We do it because we have been persuaded to, because our deepest emotions have been colonised by something else. The murderers going about their work in Kosovo were not monsters but normal men. Yet their barbarism is incomprehensible unless it is placed in the context that explains it, years of saturation propaganda at once sentimental, self-pitying, vindictive and xenophobic."[70]

In Lawrence and Jewett's identification and critique of the myth of the American (super)hero there are numerous points of politically significant argument: firstly, in particular they uncover a prevalent undemocratic ethic; secondly, they claim that the myth resists admitting moral complexity; and, thirdly, they maintain that this myth assumes a sense of American purity that is largely an expression of a Manichaean-like "us-versus-them" type framework.[71] Kapell and Lawrence, for instance, proclaim, that "This valorized violence, sanctioned by deities, runs deep in all cultures that have imagined themselves representing higher powers who authorize them to slaughter others in battle."[72] This notion of the sacralization of conflictuality and the aggression required to sustain it, whether in self-protective defensive or self-aggrandizing expansionist mode, echoes Wink's claim that it is "This Myth of Redemptive Violence ..., not Judaism or Islam, [that] is the dominant religion in our society today."[73] So Jantzen observes the process of internalization that occurs, and its political effectiveness:

> It is inescapable that the habitus of the west is violent, and that western history, including its most recent history, is a reenactment of this violence which has been internalised to such an extent that in any situation requiring response violence seems natural, the only alternative. Violence has so colonized our habitus that we have collectively lost the capacity to imagine other sorts of response. In the global context this is regularly expressed in military terms: from the Gulf War to Bosnia, from Kosovo to Afghanistan and Iraq, the alternatives are presented as either "doing nothing" or military bombardment. Since there is a felt moral and political need to do something, the west, claiming God and goodness on our side, goes to war.[74]

Nonetheless, it is the link between the hero and a good violence that is worth testing in relation to one of the examples Wink provides: the *SW* saga.[75] Thus while the *SW* movies are more concerned with, in the words of Lawrence, "the American monomythic tale of redemption by reluctant, selfless superheroes," the explicit connection of this myth with themes of "peacemaking through holy war," the "selfless muscular hero," and both "the mystique of violence ... [and] the obsession with victory" significantly echoes Wink's talk of the "myth of redemptive violence."[76] This, then, seemingly proves to be an example of "the belief that violence saves, that war brings peace, that might makes right." The mythic nature of this claim is, however, masked and difficult to perceive for what it is. Accordingly, Wink observes, "The belief that violence 'saves' is so successful because it doesn't seem to be mythic in the least. Violence simply appears to be the nature of the things. It's what works. It seems inevitable, the last and often, the first resort in conflicts."[77] Violence is, apparently, not only inevitable but effective. "In short," Wink argues, "the Myth of Redemptive Violence is the story of the victory of order over chaos by means of violence. It is the ideology of conquest, the original religion of the status quo. The gods favor those who conquer. Conversely, whoever conquers must have the favor of the gods."[78] One might imagine Bob Dylan's mid–1960s protest song "With God on Our Side" being played as Wink shapes his critical reflections here.

The implications of this for reading George Lucas' saga are consequently pronounced. Of course, Wink's work was published in the 1990s and Jewett and Lawrence published their own two major studies on this in 2002 and 2003. As the next chapter will suggest, it is not insignificant that *TPM* was released in 1999 after Wink's reflections, and *ROTS* (2005) had not been released by the time of Jewett and Lawrence. In fact, the critical writings of the latter even seem to have occurred without knowledge of *AOTC* (2002). Lawrence, however, has continued to maintain the trajectory of this reading in a more recent paper.[79] Their joint perspective on the set of *SW* movies characterizes it as firmly "captive to the American [heroic] monomyth" and thus to the myth of redemptive violence, most noticeably presenting "the spiritual innocence [and redemptiveness] of ... violence."[80]

The account provided by Jewett and Lawrence and by Wink in making such an assessment of Lucas' movies has become rather commonplace. Predominantly critics have come to identify in *ANH* especially the operation of a kind of "good" violence, a type of "holy war." This interpretation tends argue that George Lucas at worst naturalizes violent conflict and contributes to making the violence of war (unavoidably) part of the (proper) way of life. A "good violence" does not transform the "rules" of cultures of violence but conservatively perpetuates them, thereby endlessly impoverishing the ethical imagination of non-reactive and liberating forms of peaceableness and also forming "the solid bedrock on which the Domination system is founded in every society."[81]

In many ways the matter is crystalized by the function and *mise-en-*

*scène* of the closing medal-ceremonial scene of the 1977, the moment that offers the emotional climax of the movie and which is pervaded by important signs, symbols, and references. It is set in the Rebel base on the fourth moon of Yavin, more specifically in the throne room of what looks like an ancient Massassi temple. Does this religious setting in the ancient temple provide a religious halo or justification for the preceding violent action against "evil"? Luke Skywalker, Han Solo and Chewbacca enter the long room and walk up between two massed ranks of Rebel troops. Will Brooker notices that this "sequence is surprising in its coding of Rebel victory as regimented, ritualized, uniform, disciplined and ordered—precisely the qualities the film has previously associated with the Empire."[82] Once the three reach the end of the room they face a select group on a raised platform, composed of Rebel dignitaries and the droids C-3PO and R2-D2. From Princess Leia, Luke and Han receive medals for their actions in the recent victory at the Battle of Yavin.

There are a number of significant issues that emerge in one way or another from this scene. Firstly, the temper is an entirely jubilant one. While this may echo historic events like those witnessed in Trafalgar Square and Times Square after the Victories in Europe and in Japan, *SW* runs roughshod over the cost and the loss in the military conflict. The scene, of course, follows on from what has been a visual and emotional feast with the climactic exhilarating depiction of the dogfight over Yavin. Yet the disastrous and traumatic consequences of the violence are rarely seen.[83] Judith Butler argues for the importance of grievability and the respect for precarious life, radically unsubstitutable life. "Only under conditions in which the loss would matter does the value of life appear. Thus, grievability is a presupposition for the life that matters."[84] A telling sign of what is at stake is the fact that Luke's good childhood friend, Biggs Darklighter, has recently been killed in action, and yet not only is there no mention of this loss after its occurrence, but Luke's mood on returning from the battle is an unreservedly euphoric one that is jubilantly shared with his new Rebel friends. The moment that tempers this, but only a little, occurs when his attention is caught by the damage that been inflicted on his R2 unit during the recent attack on the Death Star. In fact, earlier in the movie Luke perceivably expends very little emotional energy in grieving the brutal loss of his aunt and uncle (does their death come as a bit of a relief to him, since now it *frees* him to begin to realize his longing for adventure?). Likewise, Obi-Wan is less slain by Vader (passive) than sacrifices himself to become an eternally universal presence (active). Narratively speaking, Butler's point would be that the lives of Luke's relations and friends have been instrumentalized and thereby rendered valueless, just as much as those of the stormtroopers who appear simply as the adventure's cannon fodder. As Rubey argues, "when ships or planets blow up, we do not think about the people who presumably die in those explosions."[85] Developing this, Wetmore claims that "a million voices cried out and were silenced all at once when Alderaan was destroyed, ... [although w]e do not feel those million deaths ourselves, nor do we feel anything about it."[86] Moreover, later in *ROTJ* Anakin Skywalker is redeemed by his violent action; and even the terrible slaying of Qui-Gon too in *TPM* somewhat loses its emotional resonance by this film's own version of the subsequent victory-celebration. The audience is therefore denied any view of the consequences of large-scale warfare and the violent overthrow of the galactic civil authority for ordinary citizens. We are distracted from those who live "ordinary lives" by the cameras' immersion in the characterizations of the *grand figures* of the drama. All other characters are rendered largely incidental by being reduced to the background mass that enables the elite figures to function.[87] Of course as a criticism in its own right this is distinctly weak. Narratives, after all, function by way of providing a focused lens, and by providing a range of small scale roles for people who do not feature as the main protagonist(s). Where it has some teeth, however, is in reminding that because none of the main characters are the victims of violent deaths or the subjects of palpable grief (as is, for instance, the mother of *Bambi*) in the classic trilogy, the audience is diverted from the trauma of loss involved in grieving for a valued life.

Rubey's assessment maintains, then, that *SW* "romanticizes war" for a post–Vietnam generation, and presents it, in the words of Michelle Kinnucan, in a "tidy and uncannily bloodless" way.[88] Unfortunately Kinnucan's own account is supported here with a decidedly weak example taken from one of the prequels. She complains that "during a lengthy battle scene in *AOTC* where Anakin has his arm severed at the elbow, we see not a drop of blood leave his body or pool on the ground." This certainly could raise the issue of violence in the saga as largely a game-like spectacle, but this commentator also simply has to bear in mind the fact of the design of the lightsaber in the narrative. This weapon is an energy blade that cuts/burns. It would cauterize the wound so that there would be a clean cut. In fact, if one watches carefully one can see smoke rising from the wound. Arguably, nonetheless, this scene is considerably more brutal in its use of violence and its mood than those from the classic trilogy that tend to form the cornerstone of much ideological critique, especially when focused on *ANH*.

Even if one were to leave aside the critical suspicion of the operative ideology of redemptive conflict, the very packaging of violent images in a child-friendly form still remains a significant problem that requires comment. Violence, *unless shown to have serious moral questionability* (and that, presumably, is something most children could relate to on some level), is rendered everyday, part of the "natural" fabric of existence, and therefore, at the very least, *not a bad thing* while it at most becomes the (only?) path to redemption. As Wink argues, "By making violence pleasurable, fascinating, and entertaining, the Powers are able to delude people into compliance with a system that is cheating them of their very lives."[89] It is entirely possible, then, to identify the problem as lying less at the level of matter than at the level of form. In this account, the way that Lucas pits incomprehensible and existence-threatening evil against manifest good in an inevitably violent conflict renders the violence rather hygienic, so that what results at best aestheticizes the violence. Here the identifiably sanitized and largely and disturbingly bloodless character of the hostilities in the so-called "classic trilogy" is intensified by the nature of the *simulated violence* in *TPM*. The machines of war (of the Trade Federation) and the constructed warriors (of the Republic) create a sense of simulated hyperreality, a violence that is gamed rather than fought and bled in and through. Significantly, while this mechanization is presented as something of a perversion (a perverted *sacramentum* of unreality or unincarnated life, one could argue) of the Jedi Order's values, this simulation nevertheless wins its own reality, its own sense of presence, and thus the Jedi sense of the real disappears behind the map of the moral simulacra. In this visual trajectory the audience is largely distanced from the violence in a way that accentuates the role of audience-as-spectacle-voyeur. So Jonathan Rosenbaum argues that "wiping out entire planets in the Lucas scheme of things is clean, bloodless fun that never threatens the camaraderie between fuzzy creatures and humans—who trade affectionate wisecracks while zapping enemies from afar—even when this all gets ennobled by mythical conceits derived from Joseph Campbell."[90] It is this role that John Milbank regards as "actually more violent than participating in violence—that to be violent *is* actually to survey in a detailed, uninvolved fashion a scene of suffering."[91]

Secondly, the form of Han Solo's garb provides significant clues as to why the final scene of *ANH* possesses the celebratory tone that it does towards the victory at the Battle of Yavin. Solo's costume is designed in the style of the Westerns' archetypal gunslinger, *High Noon* without the Stetsons, and this alludes to the violent frontier myth of America that, among other things, skirts over the moral problems with the late nineteenth century appeal to "Manifest Destiny" in settling the American west. The genre of the Western trades on the notion of meeting out "instant, summary justice. ... In short, we need a messiah, an armed redeemer, someone who has the strength of character and conviction to transcend the legal constraints of democratic institutions and save us from our enemies."[92] As Wink explains, Western mythologies are, then, shaped by the dynamics inducing violence—"Life is combat. ... [I]t is a theatre of perpetual conflict in which the prize goes to the strong. Peace through war; security through strength."[93] *SW*, critics argue, displays a vigilantist suspiciousness of authority, and thus the gunslinger's being a law-unto-himself. Violence seems to be celebrated as a way of repairing many of the ills of society. After all, the sensibility of the closing scene of *ANH* is largely that that of the achievement of resolution. Evil has been defeated, even though the content of the previous scenes has left enough unresolved to support a sequel, most notably the escape of Darth Vader.

Thirdly, the celebratory mood is significant for another reason, and that has to do with the way it develops a contrast between the heroic figures and their cause, and those in the Imperial order they rebel against. In *ANH* evil is rather obvious and it has its personification in flatly dark characters such as Darth Vader, and later in Darth Sidious (*ROTJ*) and Darth Maul (*TPM*). This reference to "evil" here is significant. Soon after its release Michael Pye and Linda Myles, among others, were claiming that *ANH* "offers the ultimate escape, withdrawal from complex questions of morality, and a display of magnificent fireworks as a bonus. It is a holiday from thought."[94] This sensibility is reinforced by the suggestion that in *SW* evil is rather obvious and metaphysically distinct from "the good." As Rubey argues, *ANH* "makes Darth Vader and Grand Moff Tarkin as evil as they are *in order to* justify the violent actions of Luke and his comrades."[95] At the point of the second draft of *SW* in 1975 there was no backstory granting Vader a more complex psychology. And even when he does finally appear, early on in the movie, he exhibits nothing but power and he offers nothing more than the presence of menace to be fought against by the heroic characters of the story. "From the moment that Darth Vader first appeared on screen in 1977—a nightmarish demon in black striding down a spaceship corridor—he became an instant icon of evil."[96] While there is at least a small hint of something more complex when Obi-Wan Kenobi reveals that Darth Vader had been "a young Jedi Knight," the potential impact of this note remains distinctly and noticeably underplayed and underdeveloped in *ANH*. Vader's costume itself is symbolic, combining a

Nazi reference (the *Stahlhelm* shaped helmet in SS black), medieval monastic robes, a samurai girdle (and even the helmet as well, reminiscent in shape of the Japanese *kabuto*), the black knight (the black armour), and Jack Kirby's Darkseid and Doctor Doom.[97] Equally, Emperor Palpatine (Darth Sidious is his Sith name) is presented less as a person than as a metaphysical principle, as "evil incarnate." Ian McDiarmid, for instance, the actor portraying Darth Sidious describes his cinematic character as "the blackest of the black. ... He's a solid block of evil [with n]o redeeming features."[98] Perhaps this is why he tends to make only brief appearances in the saga, particularly in the "classic trilogy"; he is the mythological mover behind the events of the story, just like the gods who manipulate things behind the scenes of the *Iliad*. McDiarmid interestingly uses the devilish-image to depict his role, announcing that in *ROTS* he is "revealed, finally, in all his satanic glory," although he also suggests something even more sinister: that Sidious "is more evil than the devil. At least Satan fell— he has a history."[99] Similarly, Executive Producer Rick McCallum describes "the guy who's truly evil is Palpatine. He has manipulated this whole saga."[100] Significantly, in a densely referential scene towards the end of *ROTS* the Emperor's black Sith robed apparel, contrasting with his illuminated skin tones, gives him the appearance of Death in a visual echo of Ingmar Bergman's *Seventh Seal*. So Tim Rayment asserts that "Star Wars is not subtle: good characters are good, bad characters are evil, and if the actors smile it means they are happy. In Return of the Jedi you know which side a person is on because the good live in an environment of warm, earthy colours and the bad live in harsh black and white."[101] The educational consequences of such a portrayal are unpacked by Wink: "Once children have been indoctrinated into the expectations of a dominator society, they may never outgrow the need to locate all evil outside themselves. Even as adults they tend to scapegoat others (like the commies, the Americans, the gays, the straights, the blacks, the whites, the liberals, the conservatives) for all that is wrong in the world. They continue to depend on group identification and the upholding of social norms for a sense of well-being."[102]

George Lucas' ancient and distantly situated galaxy supposedly tells the mythical story of the conflict *between* good and evil, and thus speaks precisely within this particular process of objectification. However, he does not offer a creation theme, a notion of the originality and ultimacy of the good such as J.R.R. Tolkien does in *The Simarillion* (although it is important to observe that his *Lord of the Rings* trilogy throws the reader into the midst of apocalyptic conflict). This fact, combined with much of the imagery in *SW*, contributes to a common understanding of the relation of good and evil that perceives the ultimacy of the *conflict between two eternal principles*, and therefore is seen to be essentially akin to Manichaean inspired dualistic philosophies. Lucas himself gives some weight to just such a reading: "The idea of a positive and negative, that there are two sides to an entity, a push and pull, a yin and a yang, and the struggle between the two sides are issues of nature that I wanted to include in the film."[103] Is this why "the Force" is spoken of as having a "dark-side" and of the messianic figure coming to "bring balance to the Force"? Lucas himself makes a dualistic-type comment about his movies in the feature entitled *The Making of Episode I*: "The overriding philosophy in *Episode I*—and in all the Star Wars movies, for that matter—is the balance between good and evil. The Force itself breaks into two sides: the living Force and a greater cosmic Force."[104] Intriguingly, however, a moment in the novelization of *ROTS* is perhaps less evocative of an ultimate ontological dualism that justifies the presence of evil within the life-system than of an evolutionary monism. Mace Windu admits to Yoda and Obi-Wan, "Jedi create the light, but the Lords of the Sith do not create darkness.[105] They merely use the darkness that is always there."[106] The "always there" comment is revealing. It would resonate with dualistic motifs but for his next comment. For Windu, articulating what could be called an evolutionary ethic, "Greed and jealousy, aggression and lust and fear—these are all natural to sentient beings. The legacy of the jungle. Our inheritance from the dark."

The moral implications of a reading of *SW* as a Manichaeanly regulated ideological performance are undoubtedly pronounced. For instance, and this is the third political implication that can be drawn from Lawrence and Jewett's reading, the Manichaean tendency is pre-eminently expressed as an unself-critical ideology that pits "us against them," and thereby predicates a kind of difficult to test assumption of the purity of the moral agents aligned with "us." Such a sensibility generates a self-congratulatory self-image of claiming to know just "how good we are," and a pure projection of evil onto the "other" in its "universe of innocence" that constitutes an "infantilising [of the] cinema again."[107] Consequently, dualistic ontologies open up the possibility for temptations to not interrogate or reflect morally on one's own self or behavior. The mythologist Joseph Campbell, one of Lucas' influences, once argued that "one may invent a false, finally justified, image of oneself as an exceptional phenomenon in the world, not guilty as others are, but justified in one's inevitable sinning because one represents the good. Such self-righteousness leads to a misunderstanding, not only of oneself but of the nature of man and the cosmos."[108]

Evil is out there—among, in, or even identified as "them" and not "us," vampiristically attempting to feed off "us." As Orson Scott Card sarcastically asks, "Isn't it grand to be on the side of Truth and Justice? Especially when we never have to explore exactly what is true and who is just."[109] *ANH* in particular, critics argue, is a product of a particular American politico-cultural environment of the type that one commentator describes as the landscape of "narcissism and fear of the Other."[110]

The saga, it would seem, reinforces the idea that Campbell claims to be a "basic idea" in the mythologies of war—"that the enemy is a monster and that in killing him one is protecting the only truly valuable order of human life ... one's own people."[111] This survivalist mythology and the larger and longer standing mythologies of redemptive violence keep people chained to war as a way of life. They infuse individuals, national political and military leaders, and societies with deep attraction to both imaginary and real violence.[112] Accordingly, "no premium is put on reasoning, persuasion, negotiation, or diplomacy. There can be no compromise with an absolute evil. Evil must be totally annihilated or totally converted."[113] This means that there are dangerous explanatory shortcuts that direct one away from substantive and honest reflection on what makes "evil people" and "evil deeds." Mary Henderson, curator of the Smithsonian's *Star Wars: The Magic of Myth* exhibition makes an interesting observation: "There is no crossover between the two forces; when the Death Star is destroyed along with everyone on it, it is a clear-cut victory of good over irredeemable evil."[114]

Kinnucan's citation of the killing of the stormtroopers in support of her claim concerning redemptive violence is worth considering at this point. She claims that "the imperial soldiers are human but dehumanized," and cites Koenraad Kuiper for supplementary effect: "they are pawns who die in large numbers. Their inhumanity is clear from the fact that their faces, if they have any, are never visible."[115] This somewhat echoes a claim of Henderson who asserts that in *SW*, "there is no point in attempting to 'save' any of the Imperial troops."[116] They are, quite simply, beyond hope. Unfortunately, this particular example from the saga actually subverts Kinnucan's and Henderson's argument. In the late 1970s Lucas began to develop a backstory that resulted in the stormtroopers being conceived as being clones. Of course, that was not fully established in the original trilogy, and given that science-fiction like *Blade Runner* had asked the question concerning the personhood of those cloned it is at least excusable that Kuiper and Henderson continued to ask the question of the guiltless destruction of these armored figures. However, Kinnucan's paper appears after the cinematic release of *ROTS* (although the lack of references to this last piece in the saga suggests it is unknown when she is writing). Of course, the irredeemability of the stormtroopers, in a sense at least, is explained particularly by *AOTC*, and to a lesser degree *ROTS*—they are presented as not being fully human, a consequence of the deliberate constraining of their individuality in the cloning process. They become more like biologically material machines, constructed through an instrumentalizing of life that denies them their own potential for becoming free and equal subjects in their own right. As the Kaminoan Prime Minister Lama Su admits to Obi-Wan, "They are totally obedient, taking any order without question. We modified their genetic structure to make them less independent than their original host." They are in that respect "docile." The cloning and biotechnological processes are, in other words, that practice of relational corruption made manifest, so that lives are created (and with Grievous and Vader, *recreated*) solely for their usefulness as *machines of death*. What makes the biomechanical clones play an *important symbolic role*, and one which undermines the force of Kinnucan's argument, is the dual fact that the shadowy origins of the clone army appears to have the stamp of the manipulations of Darth Sidious, and also that they are instrumental in destroying the Jedi Order that is complicit in their existence and *use*. The symbolism associated with the role of the Clone Army should not be missed: the order for them came in mysterious circumstances, but revealed in the back-story to *ROTS* to have been *Sith directed* (Sidious' commission, acting by Dooku directly through Jedi Master Sifo-Dyas); the uniforms of the Clones are significantly a link to the Imperial Stormtroopers in the "classic trilogy"; the clone's Republic cruisers are distinctly precursors of the powerful Imperial Star Destroyers; but most important is the scene at the end of *AOTC* when the Clones, departing for war, move off with the *Imperial March* theme being clearly and boldly performed. The point of Episodes II-III, in this instance, is that the violent order and the instrumentalization of life contribute to the catastrophic fall of the Republic and its so-called keepers of the peace. Padmé alone seems to be well-equipped to remain interrogative and suspicious of the swift drive to war.

Crucially critics also cite the way in which even the redemptive moment is portrayed in the climactic battle of the saga (*ROTJ*). As Kinnucan observes, the Emperor is slain and the mortally wounded Darth Vader dies just before the Rebel Alliance triumphs by destroying the second Death Star.[117] Consequently, through the presentation of this conflict the audience is arguably treated to a kind of cathartic experience in which any feelings of guilt are expiated by the overwhelming feeling of rightness of action.

However, as will be explained in the next chapter, there is considerable room for a response that recognizes the way *ESB*, through the characterization of Luke's training in the ways of the Jedi, comes to simultaneously *interiorize* evil. Dramatically he is tempted by those things that Jedi Master Yoda warns are the pathways "to the dark side"—hate, anger, and fear (which he explains are the way of un-Jedi-like possessive attachment in the prequel trilogy). It is this refusal to implicate considerations of good and evil in a distinctly problematic *exteriorized* form that is handled well in the prequels' portrayal of "the tragedy of Anakin Skywalker."

Fourthly, the various references to Nazism, in many ways, support this emotionally charged ideology of redemptive violence. Lucas broadly imagined, for instance, *many* of the lines of the process behind Palpatine's emergence from being a senator of a relatively unimportant star system to Galactic Emperor in the vein of the coming of Hitler to power in and through the manipulation of public fears and resentments as well as violence. Roz Kaveney, however, protests about the portrayal of the political machinations of the saga's prequel trilogy, specifically claiming that "the politics of the first film makes little sense."[118] Her main reason for disassociating Palpatine and Hitler, and for regarding the prequels as narratively problematic, is that the politician from Naboo is a powerful member of the occult Sith. Of course, this, as with other aspects of the movies (and several of those Kaveney is more positive about) is a feature of multi-extra-textuality, or Lucas' expansive visual and conceptual borrowings. Moreover, it is of symbolic significance in that Palpatine, as Sidious, is something of a figural intensification or representation of wickedness, and Kaveney herself does, at least, recognize that Sidious is like those depicted as wicked in Tolkien's Middle Earth narratives. Moreover, the design of the officer-class Imperials' costumes, complete with knee high black boots, does not require them to goosestep down the corridors in formation to suggest the National Socialists. Equally suggestive are the following observations: that the shock-troopers of Episodes II-III are renamed for Episodes IV-VI as "stormtroopers"; the fact that the space-battles are clearly modeled on World War II aerial dog-fights; that the Great Jedi Purge with Order 66 in *ROTS* is Night of the Long Knives–like; that Palpatine declares the need for "a strong Chancellor" who will "bring peace and prosperity back to the Republic," resulting in a call for a vote of no confidence in Chancellor Valorum, and cleverly manufacturing a crisis to enable the senator from Naboo seizing of power (*TPM*) with popular approval, and his subsequent securing of power through engineering a war (*AOTC-ROTS*).[119]

The element of guilt that exists in moving to war is eliminated in the *SW* fantasy since the Galactic Empire (a phrase taken from Isaac Asimov's *Foundation Trilogy*, and echoing the rise of Roman tyranny) is conveniently and *consistently* evil, blowing up entire planets with defenseless people like Alderaan. Non-resistance to such an Empire would be seemingly ethically unthinkable, and thus the shroud of the dark-side covering the Imperials starkly contrasts with the enlightened purity of the Rebels' motives and means of action. The violent rebellion against this totalitarian oppressor (conceived after the form of the Roman Empire/Third Reich) is thereby relieved of its moral burden, so associated as the Empire is with evil in the American imagination.[120] For instance, the difference between the Rebels' *mass* destruction of all those on the Death Star and the Imperials' annihilation of Alderaan is simply one of mood and attitude, so that the latter is to be seen as an aggressive and wicked act of those who are "evil," whereas the former is a necessary act of moral virtue and heroism.[121] According to Lawrence in an article on *The Matrix* the "classic" *SW* trilogy speaks of "Luke Skywalker [as] a man who with an utterly clear conscience ... destroys the Death Star with a Force-guided nuclear missile—a moment in cultural history that helped restore a nuclear pleasure earlier dampened by the grim awareness that hundreds of thousands of Japanese were incinerated at Hiroshima and Nagasaki."[122]

It is possibly this connection with Nazism that molds *ANH*'s "bad guys" largely into single dimensional icons of evil, on screen as the vehicle for the celebration of the heroism of the Rebels, and whose deaths are to be celebrated in a moment of cathartic release. *SW*, therefore, becomes as much a "revenge narrative" as a quest and rescue story.[123] The apparent simplicity of what is "taught" here chimes with the mood of Reagan's 1980 presidential victory—the celebratory wave of strong values and confident moral and political self-presentation.[124] In such a mood, the vague and imminently threatening "Other" has, in a sense, no face (the iconic "Darth Vader" and his "Stormtroopers" are masked) but is given a name, the "evil Empire." One is encouraged to identify with those who are evidently heroic, and classify the "other" as evil, a projective move of externalizing of evil that creates a mood conducive to a self-secure "us vs. them" scheme and narcissistic self-perfecting. According to the macho absolutist political rhetoric and simplistically clear-cut pantomime politics of Reagan's infamous "Evil Empire" of March 8, 1983, speech, taking the right side in this conflict (crusade) against evil Soviet Communism was nothing less than the holy Christian duty of the American people. So Jonathan Rosenbaum assesses this war-spirit in *SW* by arguing that "one would probably have to go back to the 40s, as Lucas did, to find such a guiltless celebration of unlimited warfare."[125] The movie series, in such an account, would then fulfill Wink's identification of the myth of redemptive violence in the sense that "when the good guy finally wins, viewers are then able to reassert control over their own inner tendencies, repress them, and re-establish a sense of goodness without coming to any insight about their own inner evil. The villain's punishment provides catharsis; one forswears the villain's ways and heaps condemnation on him in a guilt-free orgy of aggression. Salvation is found through identification with the hero."[126]

A humorous take on this issue is provided by a debate in Kevin Smith's movie *Clerks* concerning the nuclear destruction of the second Death Star from *ROTJ*. A speculative exchange over the merits and demerits of 1983's third movie in the *SW* series makes an interesting point in this regard. In an attempt to defend *ESB* as the superior movie against his friend Dante's preference for *ROTJ* Randall turns attention to a moral problem involved in the destruction of the second Death Star:

> The first Death Star was manned by the Imperial army-storm troopers, dignitaries—the only people onboard were Imperials. ... So when they blew it up, no prob. Evil is punished. ... The second time around, it wasn't even finished yet. They were still under construction. ... A construction job of that magnitude would require a helluva lot more manpower than the Imperial army had to offer. I'll bet there were independent contractors working on that thing: plumbers, aluminum siders, roofers. ... In order to get it built quickly and quietly they'd hire anybody who could do the job. Do you think the average storm trooper knows how to install a toilet main? All they know is killing and white Uniforms. ... All those innocent contractors hired to do a job were killed—casualties of a war they had nothing to do with.

Dante is suitably confused at this point and on noticing this Randall attempts to further explain the nature of the problem: "All right, look-you're a roofer, and some juicy government contract comes your way; you got the wife and kids and the two-story in suburbia—this is a government contract, which means all sorts of benefits. All of a sudden these left-wing militants [viz. the Rebel Alliance] blast you with lasers and wipe out everyone within a three-mile radius. You didn't ask for that. You have no personal politics. You're just trying to scrape out a living."

On the other hand, the references to Nazism are ambiguous at the point of the final scene. As mentioned earlier, Will Brooker has expressed surprise at the sudden regimentation of the Rebel Alliance's military ranks. But the very visual form of this mass gathering is suggestive of something that a number of critics find particularly disturbing. Controversially, the Rebel medal-presentation ceremony distinctly and substantially visually echoes two moments from Leni Riefenstahl's Nazi propaganda movie of 1934 *The Triumph of the Will*.[127] Does this equate the Rebels' victory with the politics of central European fascism? Lawrence and Jewett's talk of a form of "Fascist faith in the *Star Wars* universe"[128] had been predated some years earlier by Rubey and Michael Moorcock whose assessment had been published soon the movie's theatrical release. Rubey commented that an "implicit conservative and reactionary strain is present in *Star Wars*, and undercuts the film's tone of youthful rebelliousness."[129] One of the indications of this, emerging quite seamlessly, is the Riefenstahl visual reference, the "totalitarian, fascist overtones [that] grows so naturally out of the rest of the film's fantasies and images."[130] In a damning assessment, Rubey announces that "in the end, *Star Wars* embraces by implication all the things it pretends to oppose. The Nuremberg rally scene is a fitting conclusion coherent with the film's fascination with speed, size, and violence, and with the mysticism that cloaks the film's patriarchal structures."[131] According to Lucas, however, the Riefenstahlian echoes were entirely unintentional at this point, and he further admits to having planned instead to use a set of Riefenstahl inspired images in order to depict "the Emperor on the Empire planet."[132] Nonetheless, this, would, of course, not solve the criticisms of violence in these movies since it would simply return the reader to the interpretive category of "holy rebellion."

## *Conclusion*

ANH was conceived in the aftermath of the Vietnam War, and, as Stephen McVeigh suggests, the saga is "a unique commentary on America's understandings of war over a thirty-year period ... dealing with traumatic transitions and events."[133] Lucas' engagement with the consequent traumatic suffering of guilt in the American soul was, of course, indirect. "Rather than detailing the horrors, he [viz., Lucas] decided to offer a balm, to try to reinvigorate American mythic tropes, remap the mythic landscape that had been so badly traumatized by American involvement in the war in Southeast Asia."[134] The question is what kind of "balm" Lucas offered, and how it relates to issues of a violent soteriology. James Gibson, for instance, argues that the late 1970s fantasies of "New War" redevelop the "archaic warrior myths" and thereby "attempt to reaffirm the national identity" and perpetuate the ideological matrix of the code of attraction to violence.[135] In this context, not only is the violence against "evil" entirely legitimate, but the spectating of it "serves as catharsis."[136]

One might attempt to mount a defense at this point in the form of suggesting that the *SW* movies are designed for children, and consequently any portrayal of the notion that "war is hell" would be inappropriately too gruesome and emotionally disturbing for such adolescents. A comment by an interviewer of Lucas suggests as much: "Lucas defends his simplicities by saying that Star Wars is aimed at the young. There is an importance to stating that the wicked witch is bad, he says, and that the prince embodies everything to which we aspire."[137] But this defensive strategy is weakened by at least two factors. Firstly, it displaces Lucas' own intention to generate a popular mythology that would have educational effect. "Somebody has to tell young people what we think is a good person," he claims. "I mean, we should be doing it all the time. That's what the Iliad and the Odyssey are about—'This is what a good person is; this is who we aspire to be.' You need that in a society. It's the basic job of mythology."[138] After Vietnam, Lucas claims, "there was not a lot of mythology in our society— the kind of stories we tell ourselves and our children, which is the way our heritage is passed down. Westerns used to provide that, but there weren't Westerns anymore. ... I wanted it [viz., *Star Wars*] to be traditional moral study, to have palpable precepts ... that children could understand. ... Traditionally we get them from the church, the family, and in the modern world we get them form the media—from movies."[139] Secondly, and more seriously, it is simply a glib response that appears to be grounded in a naïve assumption that persons are unencumbered creative agents. This is precisely the supposition that is appealed to by Palpatine in the novelization of *ROTS* as he tempts Anakin to challenge Jedi philosophy: "Do the one thing the Jedi fear most: make up your *own* mind. Follow your own *conscience*. Do what *you* think is right. I know that *you* have been longing for a life greater than that of an ordinary Jedi. *Commit* to that life."[140] The assumption crucially fails to acknowledge the issue of ideologies that are enculturated and considered "normal," and that help form moral-agents within their framework. It is thus reductive of the contributions of any and every moment of culture to the formation of public discourse.[141] This significant lack may itself reveal that late-capitalist societies have reduced the formation of selfhood and identity to an ideology of individuation and the self's own creativity. Herein culture is largely reduced to the apoliticized and therapeutic indulgence of the self, thus valued for its affective intensification and limited to aestheticization and catharsis for those pleasured by being entertained in supposedly "innocent" ways.[142] This is a "vision of a video-culture of mass passivity [that] represents a disastrous diminution of imagination and creative intelligence and responsibility."[143]

Critics often point to the concept of "the Force" as a religious one, and one that divides reality into *both* good *and* evil.[144] Luke may have used "the Force" to help him select the appropriate moment to fire his torpedo into the Death Star reactor shaft, but the second occasion in the movie that "the Force" is mentioned (and it is important that the moment in the Death Star Conference Room *immediately* follows the scene in which it is first mentioned by Obi-Wan) is quite different. According to Kinnucan, for instance, "when Vader tells Luke at the conclusion of *Return of the Jedi* that the inexplicably and monstrously evil Sith Lord, Emperor Palpatine, 'will show you the true nature of the Force.' That is, violence and its repetition, whether perpetuated by the 'good' Jedi or the complementary 'bad' Sith, is the 'true nature' of [the] Force." However, couched in this way this critical claim simply does not pay attention to the distinctiveness of the *use* of the Force by the Sith and the Jedi. The question of violence, then, takes a different form from what Kinnucan suggests, and it is indeed given a religious sanction in relation to the violence of the Jedi and all who fight for their cause. The fact that the Jedi are aligned with "the Force," then, provides the most ultimate of sanctions for unself-critical moral agency in the conflict against evil. Suggestively, in the novelization of *ROTS* Obi-Wan's violent confrontation with General Grievous' Magna Guards on Utapau is described in spiritual terms: "Obi-Wan wasn't even fighting. He was only a vessel, emptied of self. The Force, shaped by his skill and guided by his clarity of mind, fought through him."[145] "The righteous," one writer starkly maintains, "are called by God's law to exercise a holy 'violence' against certain of the wicked, thereby manifesting God's wrath."[146] According to Frank Allnut, "The galactic wars in the movies are really religious wars. The people of the Alliance, who believe in and follow the ways of the Force, are pitted against the satanic emperor Palpatine, Darth Vader and all the other 'fallen stars' of the Old Republic. The Bible tells us that there is bitter conflict raging throughout the spiritual universe, and it's no secret to anyone that a fierce battle between the forces of good and the forces of evil is being fought on planet earth today."[147] Allnut sees the church in terms of that "small band of Rebel forces led by Luke, Han, and Princess Leia on the mission to restore the former glory of the Alliance."[148] He continues, in the spiritual "star wars" "Jesus has an even deadlier sword ... to strike down all the ungodly nations of the world."[149]

If the broad critical set of readings described in this chapter can be sustained, then *SW* becomes an ethically problematic text that is imbued with an ideological "Manichaean quality," a governing clarity in its depiction of "good" and "evil" which nonetheless displays a morally simplistic and nostalgic sensibility.[150] It would be well to construe it, seemingly, as belonging to a broad tradition "in which heroism and traditional values are celebrated."[151] *SW* is infused, it is frequently argued, with the mythology of a "good war," that those who are benevolent fight fairly for a just and positive outcome of peace, and the fact that "the Force" is implicated gives it the ultimate (because divine) sanction. After all, there can be no more absolutely legitimating ideology than that which appeals to "God." According to Frank Castle, himself a victim of horrendous violence, in *The Punisher* of 2004, "Those who do evil to others [are] the killers, the rapists, psychos, sadists." Castle's task, then, in his guise as The Punisher is to exact justice, violent justice, on the wicked. In this, however, is the inscription of violence into the very heart of human relations, and in this there is something particularly troubling, according to Wink. After all, "violence is simply not radical enough, since it generally changes only the rulers but not the rules."[152] The violated who seek restitution become, when the chance arises, themselves violators of their own original abusers.[153] So, drawing on Christian imagery, the myth-scholar Joseph Campbell observes that "the hero of yesterday becomes the tyrant of tomorrow, unless he crucifies *himself* today."[154] In this system victims are made in the image of their enemy, and thus the violence is perpetuated. Commenting on Clint Eastwood's *The Unforgiven*, L. Gregory Jones claims that "habits of sin, and more specifically of violence, are inescapable; they cannot be unlearned. Violence is the inescapable reality that persistently tears at the fabric of people's lives until everyone is diminished, if not destroyed by it."[155]

But there is more to reflecting on violence in any given society than this cycle of vengeful retribution, and it has to do with the very ideology or way of understanding the world we learn and indwell. We are not merely born into violent action, and its never-ending cycle in reaction,[156] habituated in it, but it has been "naturalized"—the very way we see and understand the world maintains systems of violence. *The Unforgiven*, for instance, is set within a context in which the West could only have been "tamed" through violence, the *Wild* West as it has been called. Even the way that most Westerns are filmed testifies to the grip that ideology of "good violence" has on society's imagination. Eastwood's movie deconstructs those Westerns by climaxing not in the "happy ending" or sense of resolution, good done, but with the sense of emptiness in the destruction. To adapt a point made by Stanley Hauerwas, the reason violence and war seems to be *inevitable*, and therefore the *only* alternative in certain situations, is largely because of the kind of society in which we live and the kind of people we are—and that has to do with the types of ideologies that shape us.[157]

# 2

# "Wars not make one great"
## *Redeeming the* Star Wars *Mythos from the Myth of Redemptive Violence*

Following the shimmering appearance of "Lucasfilm" in glorious emerald letters on the silver screen, John Williams' triumphant orchestral theme resounds. The audience of *ANH* at that point is greeted with a Flash Gordonesque introductory text which begins its fading crawl back into the background. Its reference is to civil war, rebel spaceships, "the evil Galactic Empire" and its "ultimate weapon," a princess, and an imperial pursuit of stolen plans. It does not take long for the camera to descend and focus on the atmosphere above the desert planet of Tatooine, and altogether shattering the briefest moment of calm is the determined pursuit of the little Rebel blockade runner Tantive IV by the hulking Imperial Star Destroyer. Within a few moments of the curtain drawing back audiences the world over have been directed to what is promising to be a thrilling ride in the form of an action-packed space fantasy adventure.

*SW* has been ground-breaking in numerous ways: commercially, it was so successful that it helped shift science-fiction film from the low budget cultural periphery to the mega-blockbuster; it unleashed the culture of movie merchandising in the most expansive of ways; and it became part of the cultural imagination of three generations of fans. Keith Booker explains that

> *Star Wars*, with its groundbreaking special effects and staggering commercial success, may be the most influential science fiction film in history. Its characters became icons of American popular culture, its language became part of the American vernacular, and its simple, but powerful, story became one of the best known in American history. It inspired a string of sequels that together now constitute the most commercially successful franchise in film history. Meanwhile, science fiction film, once a lowbudget genre seeking a

niche audience, was transformed into a genre of big-budget blockbusters, often relying more on spectacular special effects than on thoughtful scenarios, compelling plots, or believable characters.[1]

While it is arguable just how far *SW* can be classified as "science-fiction" rather than, for instance, "space opera" or "space fantasy," Booker's point concerning the cultural fruitfulness of the saga, the way it has penetrated popular culture more generally to the point of being pre-eminently globally recognisable, is an appropriate one. Likewise, Kevin Wetmore claims that "the *Star Wars* series ... is a touchstone that has changed our culture and changed the way in which movies are made, marketed, and seen."[2] In what has now become almost commonplace among cultural commentators both Booker's and Wetmore's ensuing critical evaluations of the saga reduce its metaphysical significance to a form of ontological dualism. So Wetmore argues, "*Star Wars* is family entertainment. Its target audience, as stated by Lucas time and again, is children. It is accessible, inspirational, and offers a clear view of the world, not muddled and weighted down by complexity. Good is good, evil is evil."[3] In other words, the Manichaean tendency is largely the fruit of its political context and the type of cultural wistfulness that direct its own presentation to its youthful target audience. *SW*, Booker declares, "is very much a nostalgia film that looks lovingly back to its predecessors in the science fiction serials of the 1930s," and very much "in the mold of Lucas's own *American Graffiti* (1973)."[4] In fact, "*Star Wars* is, one might say, the sort of science fiction film that filmmakers of the 1930s might have made had they had available to them the special-effects resources (technological and financial) that were available in the late 1970s. ... [It] is an unabashed work of popular culture and that much of the film's success can be attributed to its unpretentious celebration of the kind of simple, straightforward oppositions that had given the pulp fictions of the 1930s their innocent appeal."[5] "This simplicity and innocence helped the film appeal to children," Booker continues, "but Star Wars also had a great appeal for adult audiences in the United States in the late 1970s. After the trying times of Vietnam and Watergate, American audiences were eager for the kind of reassurance provided by simple verities and uncomplicated expressions of the ultimate power of good to defeat evil."[6] Commentators observe what Stephen McVeigh speaks of as *SW*'s being a "controversial and politically engaged" cinematic text.[7] It is what that engagement is seen to involve that has made the saga particularly controversial for commentators concerned about egalitarian relations and radical politics. The conditions for *SW*'s reactionary politics played in to the growing conservative element in American political life. For Booker, then, "its old-fashioned, nostalgic appeal also marked the beginning of a rightward turn in American politics that would lead to the election of Ronald Reagan to the presidency in 1980. Indeed, looking at the Cold War years of the 1950s, then at the late 1970s and early 1980s, some critics have concluded that science fiction film seems particularly to flourish in conservative times, perhaps because of their escapist appeal to audiences appalled by contemporary reality."[8]

Accordingly, the claim is that both the ethos of Lucas' movies and the cultural reception of them overlap with shifting political sensibilities. As with *SW*, Booker maintains, Reagan appealed "for a return to traditional values, its presentation of international politics as a simple opposition between good and evil, and its belief in the fundamental value of free enterprise."[9] "Indeed," he continues, "*Star Wars*, perhaps more than any other single science fiction film served as a harbinger of social change in America. The early 1970s had been marked by dark, dystopian SF films, such as *A Clockwork Orange* (1971), *The Andromeda Strain* (1971), *The Omega Man* (1971), *Silent Running* (1972), and *Soylent Green* (1973), reflecting the pessimistic tenor of late-Vietnam and Watergate era America. The success of *Star Wars* announced a new desire for an optimistic, reassuring message that announced the possibility of a better future, a message also delivered by the Reagan campaign and, later, the Reagan presidency."[10]

In Booker's reading at least, the marshaling of *SW* to depict elements of the Reagan administration was far from arbitrary or illegitimate.[11] And yet the movie scholar is honest enough to admit that "the politics of *Star Wars* are somewhat more complex than they might first appear." It is just such a "minority report" that this chapter intends to move on to offer.

One reading that offers pause for thought, here, is that of Martin Winkler. His account is blighted by sweepingly depicting *SW*'s "theme" in mythological terms as "the struggle of the forces of Good against absolute Evil."[12] However, he at least more aptly regards the Empire as Rome-like as much as Nazi-esque. The parallels he identifies suggest that one of the many cinematic influences on Lucas was Anthony Mann's *The Fall of the Roman Empire* (1964), partly mediated through the "Galactic Empire" of Isaac Asimov's *Foundation* trilogy that was itself dependent on Edward Gibbon's *History of the Decline and Fall of the Roman Empire*.[13] In this context, Palpatine's rise to power significantly involves the overthrow of the old Republic, and this occurs very broadly in the manner of Julius Caesar. In the opening of the Prologue to Lucas' novelization of *ANH* in 1976 comes the following claim: "Aided and abetted by restless, power-hungry individuals within the government, and the massive organs of commerce, the ambitious Senator Palpatine caused himself to be elected President of the Republic. He promised to reunite the disaffected among the people and to restore the remembered glory of the Republic. Once secure in office he declared himself Emperor, shutting himself away from the populace."[14]

Winkler comments, "Lucas's galactic empire has overthrown an earlier republic and, as in Roman history, the new monarchy has preserved the original republican governing body, the senate."[15] "Early in the trilogy's first film," the Professor of Classics continues, "the usurping emperor dissolves the senate. Except for this, the film's senate parallels the history of the imperial Roman senate."[16] Part of the difficulty in identifying political allegory, however, is the fact that Adolf Hitler's overthrow of the Weimar Republic is equally in view, and the National Socialist visual echoes are close to the surface of *ANH*. Moreover, one cannot fail to notice that apart from Vader's voice, the entire Imperial leadership has British (more specifically English) accents, suggesting that there may even be a reference to the American Revolution (in this regard *AOTC* suggestively refers to a "Grand Army of the Republic"). This is certainly how many American moviegoers read the political references at the time. Things become complicated, therefore, by the multiple images and textual references that are involved. Of course, there is something in the fact that the very name "Palpatine" may itself be a play on "palatine," the name of the most central of the seven hills of Rome on which several of the emperors constructed their palaces, although Winkler does not notice this. In *ROTJ* the Imperial shuttle is given a Latin name Tydirium, although Colebatch provides a rather idiosyncratic reading of this: "the name of the shuttle 'Tydirium' seems to suggest 'tide'—an echo of the feeling that a tide is now flowing. ... An echo of the word 'delirium' here also suggests that things are moving out of ordinary control and reality."[17] Winkler notices too that the Governor or the Grand Moff is named Tarkin, echoing the name "of the Tarquins, the last dynasty of Roman kings, which had become synonymous with tyrannical monarchy."[18] There is, moreover, a reference to the organizing of the imperial infantry into "legions" in *ROTJ*.

The mention of Palpatine as "Senator" of course also has implications for understanding this in a more contemporary American political context, and this cannot be underestimated. According to Winkler, "The fundamental similarity between Rome and America is quintessentially American as it is Roman, that of expansionism and the concept of the frontier."[19] However, it remains important to ask what this connection means for understanding what is occurring in the *SW* saga. "The popular American view of the Roman Empire, especially in its reincarnation in the cinema," according to Winkler, "has almost invariably been that of a degenerate totalitarian society characterized by militarism, slavery, religious persecution, bloody games, sexual debauchery, and spiritual emptiness."[20] What this means, then, is that "the American founding fathers had therefore modelled their own government on the Roman republic, not on the empire." What is important is that in this context *SW*'s Rebellion comes to represent the celebration of the politics of the old republic against the corruptions involved in the usurping empire, a political appeal to a form of primitivism that plays a crucial critical and indeed utopian role in identifying problematic patterns with the contemporary political life. In fact, the Rebellion comes to ideologically occupy some of the same territory that the fascination with slave rebellion in the Roman Empire has produced with the various depictions of *Spartacus* (albeit that is a pre-imperial revolt) and *Gladiator*, for instance, with the promotion of civic freedom against the centralization of power in the brutal imperial order. In this context Lucas' claims to likening Palpatine to President Richard Nixon and Darth Vader to Henry Kissinger need to be borne firmly in mind. Keith Booker's reading is instructive here, and it is therefore worth citing at some length:

> To some extent, it is true that the galactic political situation portrayed in the film draws upon the rhetoric of the Cold War, with the Soviet Union replaced by the Galactic Empire. However, Star Wars is hardly a simplistic allegory of individualist Western rebels opposed to totalitarian Eastern despots. Indeed, in many ways the rebels appear more Eastern, while the Empire appears more Western. For one thing, the real empire builders of world history have been Great Britain, France, and the United States, all members of the anti–Soviet Western bloc during the Cold War. Moreover, much of the representation of the heroic rebel alliance seems to draw upon the rhetoric of anticolonial resistance, an historical phenomenon that drew much of its theoretical inspiration from the Marxist critique of global capitalist expansion. It is certainly the case that the forces of the Empire, with its advanced technology and superior resources, clearly have much in common with the capitalist West, while the rebel forces often resemble less well equipped anticolonial forces, such as the Viet Cong in Vietnam or the National Liberation Front of Algeria. ... [T]he underequipped but staunchly determined rebels seem less like the revolutionaries who founded the United States than the anticolonial fighters of the second half of the twentieth century and various Third World resistance movements of today.[21]

Even so, the movies are simply too broad to be read in straightforwardly allegorical terms, and that ambiguity makes singular identifications difficult to sustain: the characters possess too little depth for such unqualified allegorizing specification by virtue of their construction in mythically archetypal ways. Nevertheless, the manner of the ahistorical and archetypal nature of the politics of *SW* can and does encourage paying critical attention to even the most self-proclaimed "democratic" and "free" of political environments (and this is one of the main reasons why reductionist complaints of *ROTS* being anti–Bush allegory cannot be taken too seriously).[22] It is this reading that *AOTC* and more controversially *ROTS* lend some weight to, particularly in an era when talk of the relation of the U.S. and "empire" is becoming increasingly popular after the post–World War II post-colonialist aversion to the term. Read in this context, the *SW* saga displays a moral struggle with the kinds of reactive politics that operates from fear of "the Other," and from the avaricious accumulation and maintenance of power by the few, in contrast to its utopian desire for a humanitarian inclusiveness and a co-operative symbiosis generating mutual care and responsibility. As Patricia Kerslake observes generally, "The ongoing SF fascination with empire and imperialism more accurately reflects the perception that humanity has not resolved its historical nationalistic guilts and responsibilities."[23]

The previous chapter detailed a series of overlapping critiques that emerge from just such an analysis and identify the determination of *SW* by an ideology of "good" or "sacred violence," especially associated with the "us" of the American nation, whether that is through a fascist faith or the guiltlessness of the celebration of the rebels' violent actions. The present chapter continues the examination but does so by suggesting that these readings require significant contestation and subversion. Their main difficulty arises from the fact that they tend to trade on a double abstraction. Firstly, they abstract the first theatrically released *SW* movie, *ANH*, from the succeeding movies in the saga. The movement of each succeeding movie in the series constitutes a "retroactive defamiliarization."[24] Each adds not merely a new narrative layer to the saga, but acts as a reading regeneration. In particular, the tragic sensibility of the more recent prequel trilogy accentuates the earlier movies' own deconstruction of the Manichaean sensibility. Secondly, they abstract their accounts of *ANH* from its historical context (the questioning of American empire). What comes after begins to unpick the simplistic assessments that have been made, whether that be *SW*'s Manichaeism, or the straightforward "myth of redemptive violence," and so on. In particular, it flattens the multiple *forms* of violence that the movies display. The question remains, if *SW* depicts a corrupting and destructive fall into totalitarian government then what does this say not only about its understanding of the United States around the time of the Vietnam War, but of the violence that the nation was engaged in?

## "Don't make me destroy you" (Vader, ESB): "Good war"?

The second version of the broadly construed "good war" sensibility relevant to considering the saga is somewhat reminiscent of an approach most familiar and palatable to many people in the West as "just war," growing as it does largely out of medieval Christian traditions of moral reasoning. This has its most common appeal in the claim of the justifiability of war when performed in self-defense against an aggressor. The mood here is somewhat different from proactive and crusading war-mongering, although the demonizing of the enemy may occasionally continue to play an important role here too, even if it perhaps does so in a somewhat more muted form. After all, it is *the enemy* who is the aggressor, it is *he* who is the victimizer against whom we have to take action for self-defense. So during the Cold War American intellectual Reinhold Niebuhr conducted an appeal to self-protection for the sake of "freedom" against the demonic "other" system when grandly appealing to principles of self-evidence, announcing that "everybody understands the obvious meaning of the world struggle in which we are engaged. We are defending freedom against tyranny and are trying to preserve justice against a system which has, ironically, distilled injustice and cruelty out of its original promise of higher justice."[25] Where this sentiment can be more muted than in the "holy war" reckoning is that the enemy now does *not have* to be portrayed in the darkest shades, and therefore does *not have* to be identified with evil pure and simple. The victimizer may well be understood to be himself a victim in many ways, which is perhaps why he comes to act so aggressively; but the fact that he plays the role of victimizer (*whatever his reasons for doing so*) enables the self-defense of potential victims to be accorded *moral justification*. They are *right* to defend themselves, and it is *good* that they do so.[26]

Given that this is a lengthy chapter in my discussion, it is worth pausing briefly to obtain a conceptual roadmap. The chapter will detail several of the features in the saga that appear to express this sense of violent mood. The second part of that detailing will involve understanding the features that deconstruct the first form of violence, the "holy war" mentality. The discussion shall then very briefly compare *SW* with elements of the Christian traditions.[27] This, in turn, requires a reading of *SW*'s violence within an onto-ethical framework that can be characterized as a *presumption against war*. Finally, the question of what kind of ethical "guidance" on "just war" *SW* provides is considered in the light of a brief explanation of the *tragic sensibility* of the prequels that develop plot hints from the "classic trilogy." The significance of this chapter for the present two-chapter study should be obvious. When *SW* is read as a set of violent texts it is important to be clear just what kind of violence its "good" violence is. Thus there are two versions—the holy war and the just war—and while there may be some conceptual overlaps and convergence at the level of practice their sensibilities are quite different right down to their ontological core.

Mike Alsford, remaining heavily dependent on Campbell's work throughout his study, announces, "It is clearly the case that the hero and the villain have fought their eternal battle across all of human history and imagination. Myths and legends down the ages have told stories of those who fought for good or evil. History is full of instances of heroism and villainy in every field of human endeavour—artists, explorers, scholars, saints and martyrs, for example, have all helped to reveal to us the meaning of heroism."[28] However, something substantially more interesting and culturally transgressive begins to emerge in the saga's succeeding Episodes. By *ESB* Luke, the heroic destroyer of the Death Star, has become a Rebel commander, and his "Force-consciousness" has significantly improved (he "Force-grabs" his lightsaber in the Wampa's cave on Hoth). Yet his learning Jedi character, or we might say wisdom, takes a highly unexpected direction which forces him to learn how to *unlearn* what he has learnt. Indeed, his faith in "the Force" needs to be radically purged of inappropriate conceptions and evaluations; and he has to be forced to become conscious of, confront and test his prejudices and assumptions, and then reconstruct the very way he perceives life, heroic responsibility and the universe around him. Early in the movie a ghostly Obi-Wan Kenobi instructs Luke to go to Dagobah and be trained by Jedi Master Yoda. But in a richly suggestive and important scene what the young man finds on Dagobah is far from what he had expected, and the mirror held up to him is painfully revealing. The planet itself is a murky and swampy world, wholly uncivilized in a way that makes his former home-world—gangster-run Tatooine—appear cultured and sophisticated. It is not the place from which to expect a great Jedi Master. On feeling he is being watched he swings around with blaster drawn only to see something apparently unthreatening—an unarmed diminutive green being with protruding ears. This being acts like a scavenger, uses a strange grammatical syntax, is physically unimpressive, and appears more fool or jester than Jedi Master. But later this seemingly simple-minded and minuscule individual is unexpectedly revealed to be the one the young man has been seeking. The observable shock in the responsive tone, with his surprised rhetorical "Master Yoda?" of the young Jedi-hopeful is telling. The problem for Luke, with his obviously militaristic notions of "power," as with many of Jesus' contemporaries with their own militaristic expectations for the coming Messiah, simply is that the reality did not fit the expectation of what "a great warrior" should look like (Luke, *ESB*). According to Anker, the Jedi-in-becoming "finds ... one who seems to be the very antithesis of power," a significant moment in a Western culture that tends to depict its warriors in terms of intensive male physical power and military might as in the likes of *Conan the Barbarian, Commando, Rambo, Demolition Man, Gladiator, Troy*, and *300*.[29] At any rate, in this event Luke has again to re-evaluate the world beyond the distorted impressions provided by his senses so as to become truly re-ordered toward the Good. This is why Yoda later challenges him with the rhetorical question: "Judge me by my size do you?" Even the Luke who *begins* with a macho sense of the hero-myth has to be brought up short by his Jedi Master. The fact that he can ask "is the dark-side stronger?" indicates just how difficult it is for him to move away from thinking in terms of sheer power, echoing Vader's response to Admiral Motti over "the power of the Force" (*ANH*).

Yoda's initial appearance could not be more contrasting with that of Vader's dramatic entrance in *ANH*. The masked Sith Lord arrives striding over recently slain bodies, exuding a cool and power-full arrogance, distinguished by his menacing warrior dress and with his cape flowing behind him that impressively adds to the threat of his presence. His black clothing is accentuated against the light backdrop of both the stormtroopers and the sterile walls of Tantive IV. His voice and manner reveal that he is one to be obeyed because, imposing in form and character, he is eminently fearsome. Soon after he is seen holding a Rebel commander by the neck a few feet off the ground before the sound of breaking bones can be heard. *The difference between Yoda and Vader has to do with different conceptions of power and the self*—for Vader, power is the power of force and the right of might; for Yoda, power has to do with the virtues of wisdom, self-control, and just living; for Vader, the self is to be exalted, and that at others' expense; while Yoda is a servant of "the Force," and correspondingly a servant of all living things.

So Yoda responds to Luke's talk of a "great warrior" by claiming that "wars not make one great," and later instructs, "A Jedi uses the Force for knowledge and defense, never for attack." Anger, fear, hate, aggression, all those traits that are conducive to generating violence, characterize the dark side. This is why the Jedi who resort to such unrestrained belligerence suffer for their actions. Luke's aggressiveness, for instance, in later cutting his training short in order to rush off to face Vader and save his friends culminates in his losing his right hand in his defeat. In this way the saga begins to seriously expose the problems of appealing to "necessary violence." Lucas had originally planned to name his central protagonist Luke Star*killer* and the change to Skywalker a month into shooting *Star Wars* in 1976 is itself a significant nod towards the Jedi philosophy. Similarly, in the earlier versions of the script Lucas had a major role for a *General* (1 August 1975—"General of the White Legions"), but that character then became the Jedi Knight Obi-Wan who, although there remains a reference to him as having been a general in the Clone Wars, is now given a primary role as mentor to Luke and whose Jedi order is associated more with having been guardians of peace and justice in the old Republic. Lucas himself seems to demonstrate an unlearning of what he had learned!

It is significant, then, that (violent) *defense* against an aggressor is observably the main reason underpinning the violent hostilities in and throughout the saga. So the Jedi defend the lives of the three facing Count Dooku's order for execution in *AOTC*; the defense of the democratic Republic in *AOTC* and *ROTS*, and (although it is never made absolutely clear) presumably the defense of "the Good" against the aggressive tyranny of the Empire in the "classic trilogy." "Defense" is a key notion here, especially given Lucas' designing of the Jedi to be "like negotiators," a group that is "special, and more spiritual, and more intellectual than just a fighter or a superhero or something like that."[30] In the Special Edition of 1997, he even changed the order of firing in a scene in *ANH* to appear defensive. Originally Han Solo is confronted by the Greedo in the cantina in Mos Eisley spaceport, and the Corellian smuggler executes the Rodian bounty hunter with a single shot from under the table. In the updated and released version Greedo opens fire, misses, and Solo self-protectively responds with the fatal blow.

Before moving on it is worth unpacking this particular Cantina scene further. I include the detail not by way of nodding to my extensive fan-knowledge of the saga, but in order to illustrate my argument that Lucas is concerned with construing a "good violence" around the act of self-defense; and to strategically pre-empt the possible response a reviewing critic might (should!) mention. It also functions to provide the kind of detailing that I expect of scholarly work, including academic reflections on popular culture. Many of my critiques of readings of the *SW* saga might be summarized under the claim that too few pay proper attention to the vast range of resources, and thus the depth of erudition, required for a good reading. Many fans have reacted negatively to the various alterations in the Special Edition of the three movies in the classic trilogy, and partly this is because the beloved originals were changed in a way that has stolen the innocent perfection for many reared on, and emotionally attached to, the original theatrical releases of 1977–1983. Intriguingly, there has been considerably less outpouring of "fanboy" angst and rage (and, one might even suggest, grief) over the tinkering with *Blade Runner* or *Alien* and *Aliens*, for instance.[31] While this largely emotively enacted response is distinctly intellectually shallow, the Solo-Greedo modification is at least arguably a genuine mistake, however, and I very much sympathize with the sentiments expressed by the classic trilogy fan tee-shirt that claims "Han shot first." Firstly, in terms of the narrative sequence it is incomprehensible that a professional bounty hunter could miss from such close proximity; and, secondly, it takes one piece away from the quiet (because it is not to detract from the existential "journey" of Luke) "conversion" of Solo from self-concerned and relatively amoral smuggler to team-playing general of the Rebellion against the totalitarian state. Nonetheless, it is crucial to recognize the nature and reason for Lucas' adjustment of the firing sequence, and this reveals much about his moral disposition with regard to the function of the violence in his saga.

This protective disposition, performed less in terms of the machinery of war than as police action, is embodied in the character of Obi-Wan who himself declares that "there are alternatives to fighting" (*ANH*). Even when he is forced into battle it is instructive to see both that the weapon he and his Jedi brethren use, and his very combat-form itself are primarily defensive. (It is Mace Windu's Vaapad combat-Form VII that is dangerously close to the *aggressive stance of a Sith*, whereas Obi-Wan prefers the more deflective and defensive combat-Form III of Ataru and the patient form of Soresu. According to Expanded Universe Clone War literature, only Mace, his former student Depa Billalba, and Sora Bulq have ever mastered Vaapad, though suggestively both Depa and Sora fell to "the dark-side.")[32] Hence when handing Anakin's lightsaber to Luke in *ANH* he describes it as "an elegant weapon for a more civilized age." Of course the identification of "civilization" with any form of violence and similarly alignment of weaponry and "elegance," especially when one compares it to the elegance of, for example, the landscape and architecture of Theed city on Naboo, should be questioned. Nevertheless, the appeal to the lightsaber in these terms places it firmly in the context of chivalrous notions of the knightly-warrior, and thus enables the weapon to be an expression of a *defensive sensibility*, and thus a contrast to the mechanistic violence and assertive aggression symbolized by a blaster, a weapon that can deal death at a distance (although still closer again than, for example, the canon of the Death Star). Accordingly, in the 2004 DVD commentary on *ANH* Lucas speaks of the difference of "a more humane, honorable way of being a warrior as opposed to ... the mechanical, heartless, machine-like approach to killing in battle and war. ... The lightsaber became the symbol of that humane way of conducting your life even in that worst possible way which is protecting yourself by killing someone."[33] Obi-Wan's, it would seem, is a modest vision of violence, and that of a most defensive, limited, emotionally controlled, and restrained conflictuality. Is this why, despite the three recorded victory celebrations, there is no sense of the "good" characters of *SW* reveling in the killing of others? That reserve, of course, is not the Sith way—Palpatine/Sidious seems to express intense delight in unleashing Force-Lightning on Luke (*ROTJ*) and Mace Windu (*ROTS*). In this constrained sense of "just war" as it has been used in Christendom, what Augustine speaks of as *lamenting* "the fact that he is faced with the necessity of waging just wars,"[34] the Jedi appear to echo further the sentiments also of the Tao, "Weapons are the tools of fear," and consequently,

> A decent man will avoid them
> Except in the direst necessity
> And, if compelled, will use them
> Only with the utmost restraint. ...
> His enemies are not demons,
> But human beings like himself.
> He doesn't wish them personal harm.
> Nor does he rejoice in victory.
> How could he rejoice in victory
> And delight in the slaughter of men?
> He enters a battle gravely,
> With sorrow and with great compassion,
> As if he were attending a funeral.[35]

So Yoda's response to a rather glib sounding Obi-Wan in *ATOC* is unmistakably haunting and prescient: "Victory! Victory you say! Master Obi-Wan, not victory. The shroud of the dark side has fallen. Begun the Clone War has." As mentioned above, even the Luke who *begins* with a sense of celebration of the hero-myth has to be brought up short by Yoda (*ESB*). His whole sensibility requires to be "unlearned" and therefore transformed in a conversion of his moral imagination. He has to deconstruct and replace the macho expectation of Jedi as "great warriors."[36]

In this regard, violent conflict can be seen as always a tragic possibility in a morally messy universe. It is a disruption of a prior and original peace as symbolized by the millennial image used in *ANH* for the old Republic. "For a thousand years the Jedi were the guardians of peace and justice, before the dark times, before the Empire" (Obi-Wan to Luke [*ANH*]). As such it perverts and destroys the proper possibilities for that non-abstract peace—a peace defined substantively beyond the mere absence of conflict—of good and non-possessive relations that the Jedi virtue of other-serving self-dispossession exemplifies. As Mace Windu declares of the Jedi Order, "We are keepers of the peace, not soldiers" (*AOTC*). Likewise Anakin announces, "the Jedi are selfless. They only care about others." (*ROTS*) The novelization has Anakin declare to Palpatine that the "Jedi believe in justice and peace."[37] When seen in this context, it is far from insignificant that until the creation of the Grand Army of Clone Troopers (*AOTC*) the Republic had no professional standing army. Similarly, neither did the Naboo (*TPM*) who relied instead on volunteers and a handful of dedicated security personnel instead.

Anger, fear, hate, aggression, those traits that are conducive to generating violence, characterize the "Dark Side of the Force," according to Yoda (*ESB*). And it is noteworthy that the Jedi who resort to such unrestrained belligerence suffer for their actions. So Anakin Skywalker's aggressiveness towards the end of *AOTC* culminates in his losing his right hand to Count Dooku onboard General Grevious' Confederacy flagship *The Invisible Hand*, a fate that similarly befalls Luke in *ESB* when takes the initiative by rushing to battle Vader. In this way the *Star Wars* saga performs a kind of deconstruction of appeals to "necessary violence." After all, war in *TPM* and *AOTC* is depicted as a means to a self-seeking end, created by the self-serving political machinery of the manipulative and dominating Sidious, aided and abetted by the greed motivated profit-seeking big business of the Neimoidian directed Trade Federation. Here is a clear echo of the move by the influential fifth-century Christian writer Augustine, bishop of Hippo, and those who broadly follow his theological perspective, among others, to spend some time attempting to expose the false values and desires that generate warfare.[38]

The reason war seems to be *inevitable*, and therefore the *only* alternative in certain situations, is largely because of the kind of society in which we live and the kind of people we have become. So Amartya Sen argues that "violence is promoted by the cultivation of a sense of inevitability about some allegedly unique—often belligerent—identity that we are supposed to have."[39] This is why theologians Augustine and Karl Barth, for example, spend some time attempting to expose the values and desires that generate warfare (e.g., ambitions for power, the greedy acquisition and protection of material interests, the possession of land and property, even the recovery of stolen land, offence to one's honor, and perhaps most significantly the protection of the existence of the nation-state). Likewise Christian ethicist Stanley Hauerwas associates violence with idolatry: "our violence is correlative to the falseness of the objects we worship, and the more false they are, the greater our stake in maintaining loyalty to them and protecting them through coercion."[40] In this context it is noteworthy to admit that there is rich symbolism in the fact that war in *TPM* and *AOTC* is depicted as a means to a self-seeking end, created by the self-serving political machinery of the manipulative Sidious, aided and abetted by the profit-seeking big business of the Neimoidian directed Trade Federation.

In a profound sense, then, arguably the saga possesses something of a profound *presumption against war*. Actually, this is a rather negative way of expressing the Jedi version of the virtue ethic and the notion of the symbiosis of all life-forms in "the Force" that Qui-Gon witnesses to (*TPM*)—perhaps it is better to say it has a *presumption for peace*. In this way it noticeably echoes the Augustinian inspired "just war" tradition in Western Christian moral reflection. Of course, that is recognizably not the way the broadly "Christian" traditions of "just war" have tended to function, and there are occasions when Augustine himself, the one who greatly influenced its development, can himself make rather glib sounding comments about war. Nonetheless, the theology that drives this preeminent Latin Church Father possesses a profound presumption against war.[41] Violent conflict *can only be understood in the context of a world whose ways with the richly creative God and itself are not "good" as they are created to be, and certainly not the harmonious "good" as they are ultimately called to become. It is, at very best, but a temporary effort to respond to the disruption of peace by a neighbor and therefore always arises out of, and necessarily assumes, a prior injustice.*[42]

The very fact that Yoda and Obi-Wan take the roles of *combatants* during the Clone Wars suggests that they must have felt that, at least on this occasion, there was no alternative to fighting, and therefore that the struggle was the last available possibility once all other possibilities involving non-military intervention had been ruled out. This more "prudential path" to conducting warfare as the last resort, what could be called in Karl Barth's terms the "exceptional case." As sagacious as ever, Yoda admits as much to Mace Windu (*ROTS*) when the only option left was to resist Palpatine/Sidious by arresting him (and possibly having to kill him) and momentarily assume control of the Senate in order to secure a peaceful transition. For him, this is nonetheless a very dark route fraught with all kinds of seen and unseen dangers and intensely tragic possibilities. For the wizened Jedi Master this is a troubling possibility and is to be handled only with the greatest care and sensitivity.[43] So it is patently with a heavy heart that he reluctantly agrees to sanction the "coup" against Palpatine's Chancellorship, and in this his disposition resonates with the spirit of a good Augustinian. Moreover, Anakin intensely struggles when ordered by Palpatine to execute his defeated opponent, Count Dooku, not because he does not have the means to kill but simply because he recognizes the dangerous darkness involved in assassinating even one so dark (*ROTS*). It is this sensibility that we hear something of in Gandalf's warning Frodo in *Lord of the Rings*, "be not too eager to deal out death in the name of justice, fearing for your own safety. Even the wise cannot see all ends." Nor, we should add, can they see the beginning or middle of evil.

The *SW* saga does not provide any clear-cut suggestions of when a war, or in fact any war, can be "just" (even when the matter of that term is properly qualified). Indeed, if we follow the trajectory of the development of Luke, the tragic conflict of the Jedi in the prequels, and "the tragedy of Anakin Skywalker" in *AOTC* and *ROTS*, even the picture of what "justice" means in relation to conflict becomes somewhat complicated, with blindness and bad judgment regulating all the parties involved in various ways. For instance, and crucially, the Jedi Order is unwittingly complicit in its own destruction.[44] Nevertheless, there is a sense that the virtue-tradition of the ethical code and general practice of the Jedi in the service of co-responsibility can suggest that the deathly disruption of the peace of good relations is the only "justifiable" reason for death-dealing military intervention, and only then until peace can be restored and reconciliation made. Thus the saga provides the feeling that the code and general practice of the Jedi can potentially prohibit one commonly heard use of the "just war" tradition in Christendom: that it makes for a "good" war. In other words, there are possibilities here in which the way of Jedi wisdom is in a position to properly ask just what kind of society we would have to live in, and what kind of people we would have to become if we were to relate to each other in peaceful ways. That in turn would demand that "peace" be understood in positive ways, and not in thin terms as the mere absence of conflict, perhaps even the "peace" of consumerist apathy, that which is but the barest type of peace and one that is imposed by the victors).[45] Claiming this is to remember that talk of "just war" cannot be divorced from the deep issues of what makes for just relations. "Reduction of conflict by means of a phony 'peace,'" Wink suggests, "is not a Christian goal. Justice is the goal, and that may require an *acceleration* of conflict as a necessary stage in forcing those in power to bring about genuine change."[46] On these terms, then, given the broader theo-ethical context of the Jedi version of "just war" reflection in the making of the good symbiotic life together in and through "the Force," there is something perverse in using the "just war" criteria to decide flatly on a moment in time without casting one's attentions back to what it is that has led to the terrible point. Among other things, this is to lift "just war" reflection out of its proper theological context—that is as a witness to the God who makes the harmony of peaceable relations so that the wellbeing of creatures is constituted by a flourishing *together*.

It is important to notice the logic of Augustine's theology, and that of those who closely follow the spirit of his lead: God is Peace and Gift; God's relations are then peace-full and gracious; the works of God's hands are only true to their being when they participate in the *peace that God is*, and not the illusory peace of distorted valuations (that is what he means by the *heavenly City of God*); so all unpeaceful conflict is an expression of sin, that which God opposes (this is what he means by the *earthly city*); but the way of the world's relations in conflict may well throw up situations in which engaging in violence is the "lesser of two evils," so to speak, in order to restrain as well as possible the greater one. In this account, therefore, killing can *only* belong to the world as it is *distorted, disrupted, perverted*, and *corrupted* by wickedness, a wickedness that is chosen and therefore alien to the world as it was and should be as God's good creature. If the God of Jesus Christ's way with us is through the gracious making of healthy and peace-full relations then how can God be claimed as the generator or support for our warring? These reflections suggest that even the so-called "just war" tradition emerges from, and thus properly belongs in the context of, the very *character of Christian communities* in peace as well as wartime. As such, it only makes sense as an expression of certain forms of life deeply concerned with the daily hallowing of God's name, acting in witness to the coming of God's dynamic rule, and acting for justice and love of near and distant neighbors. This "means that," according to Daniel Bell, "embodying the just war tradition entails much more than pulling out a social statement with its checklist of criteria on the eve of a state's military mobilisation. Rather, it is about inhabiting certain virtues—

like justice and courage and temperance and prudence—something graciously made possible through the church's liturgy and preaching and teaching and practices of discipleship."[47]

Had the Jedi taken more seriously this presumption for peace in *AOTC* the Clone Wars may have been avoided, for as Republic Senator Padmé Naberrie Amidala from Naboo observes in a deleted scene, "this war represents a failure to listen." All the diplomatic avenues had not to her mind been exhausted (indeed they could not have been, given the manipulation of both the Separatist Confederacy and the Republic by Darth Sidious/Palpatine). Instead, the Jedi Council (and the majority in the Republic Senate), blind to the truth of the conditions that had taken the galaxy to that terrible point, allows itself too easily and uncritically (apart from the brief expressions of regret by Yoda and Mace in *AOTC*) to function almost as Palpatine's "attack dog" in practical support for the Republic's war-cause. And the result? Firstly a notable fall-out among Jedi who actively resist the call to war (as noted in some of the "Expanded Universe" literature covering the Clone Wars), and the near annihilation of the Jedi Order itself. Can one really argue that the maintenance of a political form and style of life, and the resistance to political separatism are causes worthy of killing against or for? How does supporting them compare to commitment to maintaining, and thereby as far as possible resisting taking, the life of any humanoid? The Jedi, even with their more prudential move to war as seemingly a last resort, do not really ask the questions—and this failure significantly aids the unfolding tragedy.

Thus several of the "just war" elements in the *SW* saga go some way to suggesting that there is something fundamentally distorted and distorting in construing it in terms of a "good" or "justifiable" war. Such talk will at the very least rhetorically mask the tragic catastrophe of war, and may even lead further to what Barth calls "the satanic doctrine that war is inevitable and therefore justified" and "good," even "unavoidable."[48] This rhetoric can in turn make for a much less strenuous search for peace by dulling and constraining the imagination to resort all too quickly to military solutions before all other options have been *honestly* exhausted.

## *"I will not turn and you'll be forced to kill me" (Luke,* ROTJ*): Peace Beyond Violence*

In many ways the mood of the third movie to brandish the *Star Wars* name, *ROTJ*, is very like that of the first *SW* film. Lucas appointed Richard

Marquand to direct, and this was partly to guarantee that the movie's creator could have more control over the director, more than he had had with Irvin Kershner, director of *ESB*. Much like the first film, *ROTJ* involves a high octane race to destroy a newly operational Death Star, has a climactic battle scene, and a celebratory end. The climatic conflict is cast, though, in three different settings. Firstly, a Rebel team on the forest moon of Endor, supported by the indigenous Ewok peoples, battles to destroy the shield generator that is protecting the incomplete Second Death Star. Secondly, the Rebel fleet fights to destroy that super-weapon. Finally, in a highly significant scene, on the Second Death Star Luke comes to clash with Darth Vader in front of Emperor Palpatine.

Reflecting on the *character* of Luke Skywalker is crucially important in the context of considering the relation of the saga to mythologies that generate and sustain violence. He is, in fact, slowly transformed in his understanding of the place and nature of violence. Soon after we meet him this whinny, petulant and rather self-absorbed youth surveys the dreadful murderous scene at the Lars homestead and his revealing comment to Obi-Wan (living at this stage under the name of "Ben Kenobi") centers not on the injustice of the stormtroopers' assassinations, or on his grief for the deaths of those who had raised him, but tastelessly on himself: "I want to come with you to Alderaan. There's nothing for me here now. I want to learn the ways of the Force and become a Jedi like my father." This would suggest that Luke's anti-imperial action is undertaken not as a resolve for revenge (he simply makes no mention of his aunt and uncle later in the movie). While he had made the comment to Obi-Wan earlier that "It's not like I like the Empire, I hate it" the real reasons he takes up the cause have to do with a series of accidents and *his longing for excitement and adventure*, as Yoda later reveals in *ESB*. In fact, as Anker perceptively observes, "his dreams stretch no further than the macho ideals that his culture glorifies, and here the filmmaker undertakes a quiet but persistent strain of social criticism. Luke's great ambition in life is to attend fighter-pilot school to become a 'top gun' and then go off to war."[49] Yet in his subsequent training Luke has continually to undergo training *in looking at the world in new ways*, and in having his disordered desires purified. As mentioned earlier, this process of learning the Jedi way takes a highly unexpected direction—he has to learn how to *unlearn* what he has learnt.

Lucas comments that Luke "has the capacity to become Darth Vader simply by using hate and fear and using weapons as opposed to using compassion and caring and kindness."[50] It is this we see displayed in *ROTJ* in a climactic scene on the second Death Star. The visual imagery here is striking—Luke's Jedi clothing is now black, and his prosthetic right hand is an early reflection of his father's mechanized state. He is being urged by the Emperor to succumb to the values of the "dark side" (hate, anger, revenge and self-assertiveness), take revenge on Vader, and replace his nemesis at the Emperor's side. This is a movie that for some time was apparently allocated the title *Revenge of the Jedi*. Yet with the release date looming, the movie was renamed to *Return*. One of the reasons given, recounted by producer Howard Kazanjian and actor Mark Hamill, is that "revenge" is not the business of Jedi.[51]

In a brutally violent moment born of pure rage, the possessive anger of filial protectiveness and reactive sense of retributive justice, Luke attacks Vader. It is only when he gazes at the defeated Vader's fizzling mechanized stump, realizing that his own artificial hand is a sign of Anakin's fall to the wickedness of the Sith, that Luke rejects the temptation of dispensing the violence the Emperor desires. What is and is not being said here is very important, particularly as it is so controversial. One might claim that Vader's violence against Palpatine, for example, refutes my argument. After all, without the violent assault on the shield generator on the forest moon of Endor, the Rebel Alliance fleet's attack on the second Death Star's reactor, and Vader's disposal of Sidious, the celebration of the new found peace at the *ROTJ*'s close could not have occurred. But this is beside the point entirely. As has been indicated, there is no denying the *ambiguity of the movies*, and *the ambiguity is part of the point*. And, as I have argued in the concluding chapter to *The Gospel According to Star Wars*, the closing set of scenes have something of an eschatologically final feel about them. But, in the midst of all that, *Luke simply refuses to continue the violence* and offers himself to Sidious' destructive rage. Here I am speculating as to Lucas' intentions, although it is an idea that works well in the context of these movies. The young man simply and willfully refuses to succumb to the "Sith" values (fear and hate) and his own earlier mood of "reactive justice." He rejects patterning his way in the world on relations molded finally by discord. He refuses to succumb to the Emperor's temptation to kill his most bitter of foes in a fit of angry aggression when he has the chance. Instead he acts *restoratively* in loving compassion for his most bitter of foes. His is ultimately a radically different mode of conflict resolution from the reactive one of simple retributive justice. What kind of conflict can be fought by one who is beyond greed, who does not give free reign to the determination of action by hate, but who does not weakly capitulate under the temptation to self-aggrandizement? Subsequently, he discards his lightsaber, thereby leaving himself defenseless against the

## 2. "Wars not make one great"    61

overpowering gust Emperor's own destructive rage, and refuses to participate any further in the conflict, a conflict that Palpatine/Sidious has in any case specifically engineered to entice Luke to the "dark-side." He is prepared to sacrifice himself rather than do evil. Incidentally, there is a parallel here with his mother (and, to a lesser extent since he is silent in the scene, father) in a deleted scene from *AOTC*. On Geonosis Count Dooku demands that the captured Naboo Senator join the alliance of rebellious Separatist factions or be executed, and the morally upright Padmé self-sacrificially chooses the second option. "In short," Anker argues, "Luke chooses to die because he has at last comprehended the heart of Yoda's teachings: that the universe runs by love and that love should pervade all thought and action."[52] This is a useful claim up to a point. What it fails to notice, however, is that Luke actually adheres to the Jedi philosophy *against the practices of the Jedi themselves*. Anker's book is understandably weakened here by having been written before the prequels were completed, but also by simply being uninformed about the burgeoning back stories Lucas has provided (as well as with the materials of the so-called "Expanded Universe"). There are enough hints in the classic trilogy to suggest this is an even more significant weakness—particularly Luke's move towards resistant non-violence that follows the implications of Yoda's claims about the universal presence of the Force in, to and through all life-forms, and Obi-Wan's claim that "there are alternatives to fighting" (*ANH*). The guidelines Lucas had provided for Expanded Universe materials regarding the period subsequent to *ROTJ* suggest that the New Jedi Order under Luke would be quite different in many ways to that from the period leading up to the fall of the Order during the Clone Wars. For instance, the Jedi are no longer required to be celibate, nor are the younglings taken from their homes at such an early and vulnerable age. Luke, it seems, in *ROTJ* comes to move *against* the Jedi defensive violence with his offer of non-violent resistance to Sidious. Even if the Emperor does succeed in taking his life (which, of course, he does not due to Vader's timely intervention) he cannot in the end take away Luke's obedience to the "ways of the Force" (Obi-Wan to Luke, *ANH*). But more than that, significantly the young Jedi's "non-violent approach" to, and compassion for, Vader actually, in the end, "so stirs the conscience of the opponent that reconciliation becomes a reality."[53] When this moment is linked to the millennial image in *ANH*, among other places, and into the Jedi philosophy, the result is distinctly different from the responses to violence occurring elsewhere. Perhaps the point is precisely to retain a sense of ambiguity in order to echo tragic complexity in a messy world.

In his journey into a "larger world" (Obi-Wan) Luke's whole value system has been deconstructed (or "unlearned," in Yoda's terms) and replaced with a whole new way of seeing the life and interrelations of all things. Towards the end, then, his journey seems to have brought him closer to a "pacifism" that is an active "non-violence," a purposeful action that is beyond a "bare peace."[54] His heroic journey is into a type of "sainthood" rather than into "warrior-heroism." Of course, one cannot overlook the fact that the Empire is defeated only through the violent act (albeit defense-of-another) of Vader/Anakin, the commando attack on the imperial shield bunker, and the torpedo from Lando Calrissian in the Millennium Falcon. Luke's action is just a hint of peace, a moment, but not any less significant for that!

Wink observes that "violence is simply not radical enough, since it generally changes only the rulers but not the rules."[55] Those people who have been violated and seek restitution become, when the chance arises, themselves violators of their abusers. Victims here are made in the image of their enemy and perpetuate the violence through an ethos of revenge, not restitution and reconciliation. And so we hear Padmé urge the Republic's Senators to "wake up. ... If you offer the Separatists violence they can only show violence in return. Many will lose their lives, all will lose their freedom." (*AOTC*, deleted scene) The Jedi training in virtue aims not so much to change the rulers, unless the situation in the end demands that, but more radically to change the way people relate to one another. In other words, it aims to change the people who act with, towards, and against other people. As Joseph Campbell observes using Christian imagery, "The hero of yesterday becomes the tyrant of tomorrow, unless he crucifies *himself* today."[56] This is why Yoda's lessons for knighthood consist not of better swordplay or martial arts, but of training in humility, patience, tolerance, calmness and trustfulness. In this way, the virtues of "the good life" have the capacity primarily to work for peace at an earlier and more proactive phase than merely dealing with the symptoms of conflictual relations (war). They can reveal and subvert the very causes of state and interpersonal conflict.

In the context of those who in post–9/11 America securely wrap themselves against the chill wind in the flag, and powerfully lash out at all those Others who stand in the "nation's" way for a new world order, Lucas' choice of returning to the backstories covering the fall of the Republic and the making of Darth Vader takes on a particular political resonance. By the time of the prequels this suspicion of violence in the name of the Good (or "the Force") comes to look distinctly shrewd. Some so-called politically conservative commentators have expressed their dismay that *ROTS* appears to be so antiwar in ethos, banally saying it was perhaps even rewritten as an anti–Bush diatribe. Lucas himself denies the claim that the movie's content was deliberately shaped with contemporary American foreign policy in mind (or at least he denies this in the sense that its story was composed much earlier than the coming of George W. Bush to the Oval Office). Even so, the important point would stand whether the acting President had been someone other than Bush. Suggestively, then, *SW* producer Rick McCallum claims that "first of all we never thought of Bush ever becoming president, or then 9/11, the Patriot Act, war, weapons of mass destruction. Then suddenly you realize, 'Oh, my God, there's something happening that looks like we're almost prescient.'"[57] Following on from the "classic trilogy" *TPM* arguably is premised on the claim that it is right to overthrow oppressive government, before *ROTS* brings into clearer focus something that is much more discomforting—that the corrupt tyranny referred to may be our own, and that the overthrow of the corrupt may even be the pathway to greater evil, in this instance the pathway to the rule of the Sith.[58] In this complex political life, we see Padmé's diplomatic sensibilities preventing her from rushing in with others to commend the growing militarism in *AOTC* and worrying about the conduct of the war in *ROTS*. Hers is the voice of reason, of diplomacy, and that voice which the revelations in *ROTS* eventually suggest is not only the most insightful into what is transpiring politically but also perhaps the wisest.[59] Moreover, it is a voice from the margins, protesting the death of liberty with the formation of the "First Galactic Empire" which emerges "with thunderous applause" (*ROTS*). Her role here may echo the ethical sensibility that Lucas' early biographer Dale Pollock discovers through interviewing Randall Kleiser, an actor in Lucas' early student film *Freiheit*: "Lucas disliked USC students who felt it necessary to die for one's country to defend democracy."[60] As John Sutherland writes, "He shaped Star Wars as anti–Vietnam allegory."[61] After all, despite the hype of the rhetoric, what is it about democracy in itself that is worth killing for? Are not most Western appeals to "democracy" and "freedom" not themselves devoid of contextual conditioning by constructive considerations of the values of human flourishing, so that they become negative and reactionary?[62] Can the sense underlying their rhetoric not be identified as rather shameless attempts by the powerful to justify the political status quo, and whip up support for the abstract idea of regional boundary-claiming nation-state which tends to become more important than human life, important enough to die for, to kill for? This preparation to die must especially be brought to face just what it is that the one willing to give of one's self to the deathly point of sacrifice is prepared to *live for*. And so, subsequent to his 1973 movie *American Graffiti* Lucas returned to the movie on which he had been working, *Apocalypse Now*. Of it he claims something significant for our purposes: "It's the same argument as *The Wild Bunch*: an anti-violence film. Francis [Ford Coppola] says the way to make an anti-violence film is to have no violence in it, but I feel there should be so much violence in it you're disgusted."[63]

In this context it is both interesting and important, because it sheds light on the Lucas who only a few years later created *SW*, to consider Lucas' award-winning student dystopian film *Electronic Labyrinth: THX 1138:4EB* (1967) which was then expanded into a feature film more simply entitled *THX 1138* (1970). The very broad conceptual background to the distinctly constrained plot of Lucas' "basically existential" movie seems to be Plato's simile of the cave, with the man known as THX 1138 escaping the "chillingly automated society" of the manufactured environment he has been imprisoned by, but escaping alone into sunset with the movie providing no sense of his return to free the other captives.[64] Yet the Vietnam-era context must be borne in mind, and there are several movie references that indicate its importance. One perceives a "massified" society, with the "herd" "giving their lives'" as unnamed (lettered and numbered)[65] fodder for industry, in *Metropolis*-like dehumanizing service of the state; the worker receives the Communist-sounding "Blessings of the State" in response.

This, together with what Ryan and Kellner claim to be the valorization of "the differentiated individual," could sound like the exaltation of American values against the oppressive Communists were it not for two further features at least: the references to consumerism and consumerism-supporting religion.[66] So, as THX 1138 ascends an escalator a voice can be heard exhorting "Buy now. And be happy," a reference to the American consumptivism that appears again later in the *SW* saga with Luke and Leia's criticism of Han Solo (*ANH*), the transformation of the businessman Lando Calrissian (*ESB*), and the portrayal of the commercial sectors in terms of sheer greed and pure self-interest (*TPM* and *AOTC*). As Lucas claimed in 1970, "The terrible thing about this country is that the dollar is valued above the individual. ... In this country, the only thing that speaks is money and you have to have the money in order to have the power to be free."[67]

Soon after this scene, THX 1138 enters a booth with an automated Christ-image that instructs him in ways that indicate that religion here has a consoling, and thus narcotic-like pacifying, effect on the bedraggled worker in the "system." This is an echo of the use of pop-spiritualist Wilbur Mercer in Philip K. Dick's *Do Androids Dream of Electric Sheep?*, and it is used in Terry Gilliam's dystopian movie *Brazil* when what looks like a Salvation Army band is seen carrying a sign announcing it represents "Consumers for Christ." Of course, *SW* treats the religious in a distinctly more positive way than this.[68] Yet the point remains that for Lucas it is *American* society that is largely being explored and critiqued in *THX 1138*. It "was an 'abstraction of 1970,' an appalling vision of a future that is already here."[69] The movies' largely American audience is disturbed from its complacency by having to consider that the United States is involved in generating and sustaining certain systems of dehumanizing conformism that its anti-communist rhetoric and involvement in the Vietnam war "for freedom" would otherwise mask. Lucas admits that THX's society is not "oppressive" as such in the sense that "no one was unhappy."[70] But it is inauthentic. "We are the drugged society and in case anyone thinks we're not go talk to Bristol-Myers." The problem Lucas soon feels afterwards is that America is unprepared for the challenge: "I realized after *THX* that people don't care about the country's being ruined. All that the movie did was to make people more pessimistic, more depressed, and less willing to get involved in trying to make the world better. So I decided that this time I would make a more optimistic film [viz., *American Graffiti*] that makes people feel positive about their fellow human beings."[71]

To return to reflections on *SW*, *ANH* in particular presents in a relatively optimistic vein the hero-myth as Lucas develops it through engagement with Campbell's writing. Yet what emerges from seeing the flow of the movies succeeding *ANH* is something very different, indeed the very deconstruction and transformation of the myth itself and of much of what critics detected as "the moral certainty" in *ANH*.[72] It does this in such a way that one can argue that *SW* displays a self-reflective praxis of reorienting the violence of the fantasy imagination, a very particular portrayal of moral formation and wisdom that responds to Vietnam in a quite different way from what *Apocalypse Now* would have been had Lucas continued with his project.[73] The hero's journey is one into a type of "sainthood" rather than into "warrior-heroism," and here Lucas distinctly echoes Campbell according to whom "the hero is still striving, but for oneness with the cosmos, not for control over it. ... He is, moreover, acting on behalf of others, not for just himself. He is still heroic, for he must still undertake a daring journey to an unknown land, but his heroism is peaceful rather than hostile."[74]

Take the example of Darth Vader, for instance. In *ANH* he simply plays the space-serial part of the archetypal "baddie," dressed up for the occasion in armor and a cape of nobility while wielding a sword, evoking memories of sinister medieval black knights crossed with Japanese samurai warriors and Nazi SS troopers. But by *ESB* he is stunningly revealed to be Luke's father. He is the one whom Obi-Wan had spoken of in such glowingly heroic terms earlier in *ANH*. And by *ROTJ* he himself becomes instrumental in both defeating the Sith and saving his son from death. In other words, as the story develops through the succeeding two episodes, the audience is forced to understand him in a very different fashion. This new emphasis of the subsequently made Episodes I-III transforms *Star Wars* from the heroic "adventures of Luke Skywalker" into the catastrophic *"tragedy of Anakin Skywalker,"* which is presumably why Lucas was reluctant to consider further thoughts of making *Episodes VII-IX*. This move into the tragic drama of the prequels is, of course, a darker version of *Star Wars*, not only dark in its own right as tragic drama but also equally casting a darkening shadow over any watching of the "classic trilogy." We cannot after these read IV-VI in the same way again. It is the tragedy and redemption of Darth Vader that the saga is "really what the story was all about," Lucas declares. Even in the 1970s Lucas had already worked out in quite detailed ways the direction even the later movies would eventually take, and it is important to take this seriously when approaching the saga *as a whole*. So in an interview in 1980 Lucas remarked:

> I wanted to make a fairy tale epic, but this was like *War and Peace*. So I took the script and cut it in half, put the first half aside and decided to write the screenplay from the second half. I was on page 170, and I thought, 'Holy smokes, I need 100 pages, not 500,' but I had these great scenes. So I took that story and cut it into three parts. I took the first part and said, "This will be my script. But no matter what happens, I am going to get these three movies made." ... You have to remember, we're starting in the middle of this whole story. There are six hours' worth of events before *Star Wars*, and in those six hours, the "other" [the "another" referred to by Yoda in *ESB*] becomes quite apparent, and after the third film, the "other" becomes apparent quite a bit.[75]

It is well-known that *ANH* was only part of Lucas' epic script, although presumably self-contained enough that the adventure required no sequel if it did not succeed at the box office—although Lucas here clearly suggests that the making of IV-VI was intended. Where this is significant is in his characterization of Vader: "Darth Vader became such an icon in the first film, *Episode IV*," Lucas reflects lamentingly, "that that icon of evil sort of took over everything, more than I intended. If it had been one movie that wouldn't have happened. ... But now by adding *Episodes I, II* and *III* people begin to see the tragedy of Darth Vader as what it was originally intended to be."[76] Lucas' claim is that the somewhat Manichaean feel of *ANH* was left as it was precisely because of his longer view—at the time that meant more V-VI—and later this could be explored even more radically through I-III. *Star Wars: Episode IV A New Hope*, does tend to simplify the presentation of self and other. On the other hand, there is much in the classic trilogy, even in *ANH*, to suggest that something more interesting is going on, especially with the reference to Vader's fall by Obi-Wan followed by the shocking revelation of his identity to Luke.

However, for audiences whose expectations and moral sensibilities frequently locate justice within a retributive perspective, the distinctly anti–Manichaean sensibility displayed particularly in the "redemption" of Darth Vader in *ROTJ* is an unacceptable and unsatisfying bolt from Lucas' dramatic blue. David Brin is a good example of this when he complains that Lucas is too soft on evil here: "In the Star Wars universe ... [a]ny amount of sin can be forgiven if you repent ... and if you are important enough."[77] The mood circumvents that which drives much of Hollywood's output and the catharsis that a scapegoating culture derives from it, from Tarantino's balletically styled revenge-narratives; to the "torture porn" of the *Saw* series and its derivatives; to "the Othering" displayed in most alien invasion cinema such as, for instance, the various versions of *The Thing* and *War of the Worlds*, the ironically comic take in *Mars Attacks*, as well as *Starship Troopers, Monsters, Battlefield Los Angeles, Independence Day* (although the last also has a mitigating ecological reading),[78] and so on. It is precisely this approach to "evil" that David Fincher's *Se7en*, for instance, effectively challenges in its brutal and unforgiving drama. According to Christopher Sharrett, for instance, the culturo-political issue has to do with the fact that the apocalyptic imaginations of Hollywood cinema (and the examples he gives of its evidence are *Alien, Robocop, Terminator*, and *Predator* cycles) is "endemically ahistorical and reactionary [in a way] that has been part and parcel of American cultural expression since the Puritans, an ideology preferring total annihilation (including self-annihilation) over radical change or even reform."[79]

To return to *ROTJ*, then, as Roy Anker observes, "the very surprise it occasions effectively uncovers the bad manners of contemporary cynicism and hopelessness. ... [T]he effect of ... the unlikely return itself pivots on the audience's usual gullibility about the way the world usually works, which is badly."[80] Furthermore, Lucas' move to "redeem" Vader not only refuses to perpetuate violence through a retributive sensibility, but dislocates the sense of the need for an ultimately cathartic watching of a "just" violence against Vader. The tragic dimension demands that he becomes not an "other" whom our moral self-righteousness can exclude easily. In that way the Manichaean sensibilities dominating many Americans' approach to matters of evil is subverted. Moreover, the *tragic* direction of the subsequently screened Episodes I-III serves not to make this a cop out but rather provides something of a sense more of there being a tragic "too late" quality about the "conversion." For instance, while he finally sees Luke face to face as his "true" self (Anakin), as with Shakespeare's Lear and his youngest daughter Cordelia, their reconciling gaze is all too brief. Anakin's becoming one with "the Force," despite what Yoda argues with respect to not grieving but rather celebrating this event (*ROTS*), cannot "compensate" for the brevity of his pre-fallen life and for the fact that he never is able to embrace his daughter. The consequences of Vader's evil, in spite of his late personal repentance, remain and stain his legacy—Padmé remains dead; Luke and Leia have been raised apart for nineteen years; the Jedi Order is almost wholly obliterated, and all but two of its greatest Jedi have been massacred; the stores of thousands of years of recorded Jedi wisdom have been irretrievably destroyed or corrupted; and Anakin's own great potential in "the Force" has never been fully realised. *ROTS* enables the audience to feel the effect of these multiple loses.

Continuing to read *SW* as a dualistic set of filmic texts seems to have been one of the principal reasons (and therefore a more interesting one than the complaints leveled at young actor Jake Lloyd's screen performance) why many find it difficult to watch and take seriously the portrayal of Anakin in *TPM*. As a nine-year-old boy he is depicted in the brightest and least morally suspect of terms. He is innocent and immensely generous. So, for instance, his mother Shmi agrees categorically with Qui-Gon's positive assessment of the quite remarkable ethical virtue of the boy, that "he [always] gives without any thought of reward." Shmi recognizes that "he knows nothing of greed." Of course, when this movie was released in 1999 the audience was well aware of the fact that he was going to become the evil Darth Vader.[81] However, many in that audience, especially (but not only), are apparently distinctly troubled by the morally unambiguous characterization of the boy. That, perhaps, says more about American, perhaps even Western, culture's ideological horizons of expectation than the quality of Lucas' storytelling.

The tragic characterization of Anakin is explicated in such a way as to deny the Manichaean reading of "evil" in *SW*, and particularly of the nature of Vader as tragic hero. Evil is not something entirely other and substantial, and in this way Kaveney and others are simply mistaken in regarding the Sith as "evil because they are evil."[82] Anakin is, despite the prophecy associated with him and the suggestion of his birth from a virgin (*TPM*), an everyman kind of character. He faces the turmoil of learning, of teenage angst, of peer-pressure guidance, and so on. He is, in other words, human, and in his story wickedness appears as the misshapen desires he comes to develop. As Lucas claims, indicating the Faustian nature of the drama, "In this film [*ROTS*] you see he [viz. Anakin] is a human being—and you're going to understand him. I think you will come out of this film feeling sympathy for Darth Vader. ... He is a rather pathetic character, who's been locked in a suit, half-alive and half-dead—thanks to a pact he made with the devil."[83]

As a result particularly of the sensibility of Episodes I-III the saga becomes perceptibly less the heroic triumph of good over evil in and through the central character of Luke, and more the catastrophe, impoverishment, loss and tragedy of Anakin (even if there remains recognition and repentance in the end). The *SW* universe becomes since 1999 something considerably messier and more complex than Lawrence or Jewett suggest. In fact, the attempts of certain critics to perpetuate the notion of *SW*'s violent ideology, now comes to look distinctly simplistic as a result of the ethos of the prequel trilogy. In this context, Padmé's opposition to the progress into war and the resultant subversion of the democratic political system is instructive.

## *"I'll not leave you here. I've got to save you!" (Luke,* ROTJ*): A New Hope for the Fullness of Peace*

According to Wetmore, "The films visually and through narrative are lengthy ruminations on violence and power."[84] The question is what kind of ruminations? Critics have discovered in *SW* a glorification of a just violence, a constituting echo of the so-called "myth of redemptive violence." The question here, then, becomes one of asking about the appropriateness and the carefulness of their readings.

Steven Sanders makes several complaints about the majority of critical readings of science fiction genre so that "Unfortunately, good science fiction film criticism remains in perilously short supply."[85] Particularly, he continues, "Some bad science fiction film criticism is simply attributable to sheer incompetence, and some is due to the perverse influence of various disfiguring intellectual tendencies in academic circles that are estranged from what were once the humanizing methods of the humanities. This should concern everyone who cares about science fiction film because good criticism of it—by which I mean criticism that is clear, consistent, carefully researched, cogently argued, and unclouded by dogma— is essential to the integrity of the genre."

It may well be important to note that Lawrence and Jewett's assessment of *SW* was formed largely in advance of both *AOTC* and *ROTS* (thus not helping with providing a judicious reading of the saga). The point I have been making, however, is that there were enough significant hints in the "classic trilogy" of *Episodes IV-VI* and in *Episode I* to complicate their perspective on these movies. To begin with, one needs to bear in mind certain contextualizing features, such as Lucas' response to Vietnam expressed particularly through the dystopian *THX 1138*, and his claims that in the light of Vietnam and the Watergate scandal America embodies oppressive empire as much as rebellion for freedom. In fact, an important reading suggestion is to be found in the fact that Lucas had been significantly involved in conceiving of the politically subversive *Apocalypse Now*, and although Coppola's version differed considerably from Lucas' earlier scripting the themes remained broadly overlapping.[86] Lucas admitted, "It's the kind of film the government will probably run me out of the country for making. It's not about massacres or anything like that. It's about Americans. ... It's the same argument as *The Wild Bunch*: an anti-violence film. Francis [Coppola] says the way to make an anti-violence film is to have no violence in it, but I feel there should be so much violence in it you're disgusted."[87]

This claim about making "an anti-violence film" is suggestive. Stephen McVeigh, then, is right to acknowledge that *"Star Wars ... is a film that demands on several grounds to be seen in the light of the war in Vietnam"*[88] Lucas may have himself come from a politically conservative home, but too much cannot be made of that by critics[89] since he broke with his father's wishes, headed off to what his father George Lucas, Sr., considered to be the "sin city" of Los Angeles and the University of Southern California, became engaged in avant-garde filmmaking, and opposed the Vietnam War.[90]

Consequently, it makes sense to understand Lucas' claims in a different way—that *SW* enables Americans to have a *new hope*, and not to wallow in self-pity or pacifying introspection, but to learn to be responsible for one another. According to Lucas, "After the 1960s it was the end of the protest movement and the whole phenomenon. The drugs were really getting bad, kids were dying, and there was nothing left to protest."[91] In this context, Coppola had challenged his friend Lucas to make "a happier kind of film."[92] *American Graffiti* was the result, and with the positive fan mail expressing how it helped transform the lives of many young people Lucas claimed to have "found something they were missing." For Lucas, this meant that a more upbeat movie could be more valuable in certain ways: "I realized after making *THX* that those problems are so real that most of us have to face those things every day, so we're in a constant state of frustration. That just makes us more depressed than we were before."[93] In response, he introduced more humor in the third draft of *The Star Wars* script (1 August 1975) in order to lighten the more serious tone of the previous version.

While a number of his comments suggest that he hoped the movie, like *American Graffiti*, would lighten the mood of the youth in a culture in depression, many other comments suggest that he did not merely conceive of this as simple escapism, a momentary distraction from the ills of life. Lucas, it would seem, had an eye on social critique and thus on a form of moral *education*. He explicitly made the connection between the psyche and social change as early as 1974: "all ... [*THX 1138*] did was to make people more pessimistic, more depressed, and less willing to get involved in trying to make the world better. So I decided that this time I would make a more optimistic film that makes people feel positive about their fellow human beings. ... Maybe kids will walk out of the film and for a second they'll feel, 'We could really make something out of this country, or we could really make something out of our lives.' It's all that hokey stuff about being a good neighbor, and the American spirit and all that crap. There *is* something in it."[94] In 1977 he reflected on the making of *SW*, "Rather than do some angry, socially relevant film I realized that there was another relevance that is even more important—dreams and fantasies, getting children to believe there is more to life than garbage and killing and all that real stuff like stealing hubcaps."[95]

The post–Vietnam context is a significant moment. "A lot of my interest in *Apocalypse Now* was carried over into *Star Wars*. I figured out that I couldn't make that film because it was about the Vietnam War, so I would essentially deal with some of the same interesting concepts that I was going to use and convert them into space fantasy, so you'd have essentially a large technological empire going after a small group of freedom fighters or human beings."[96] (The first *The Star Wars* summary treatment was completed in May 1973, four months after the cessation of American military hostilities in Vietnam and the announcement of withdrawal. The last American troops departed in 1975.) Lucas claims that his intention was to generate a popular mythology that would not merely have a therapeutic effect on the mood of the culture but also have a positive *educational* effect, and reintroduce a fantasy life to ten-to-twelve year olds.[97] Lucas suggested that America itself was as much like the "evil empire" of *Star Wars* as the Rebel Alliance. So in notebooks of 1974, in developing *Star Wars* he reflected that "the empire is like America ten years from now, after gangsters assassinated the Emperor and were elected to power in a rigged election. ... We are at a turning point: fascism or revolution."[98] For Lucas, then, the movie was based around post-colonial worries about "a conflict between freedom and conformity," themes so starkly exhibited earlier in *THX 1138*.[99] The rise of the Emperor, part of the story of which was contained in the novelization, was inspired by the then recent Watergate scandal.[100] Andrew Gordon, like many others, is therefore mistaken when claiming that *SW* responds to the need for Americans to renew faith in themselves as the "good guys" on the world scene.[101] As Rinzler observes, in contrast, "the 'lost boys of *Peter Pan* have become, given the political sway of the writer's mind, jungle rebels with just a hint of the Vietcong."[102] While the reception of the movie suggested that many understood the Rebellion in the way Gordon did, *Star Wars Episode VI: The Return of the Jedi*[103] brought this subtext closer to the surface—on the forest Moon of Endor the technologically inferior Ewoks helped defeat the Empire in a guerrilla action.[104] In the draft notes of 1973 Lucas even referred to Aquilae as a small independent country "like Vietnam," threatened by a powerful neighbor.[105] Lawrence misses all this when he claims that only after Campbell's death in 1987 did the American President become the Empire.[106]

President Ronald Reagan, then, was exhibiting a distinctly limited ability to comprehend the critical post-heroic direction of the *SW* saga when he gave his significant "Evil Empire" speech in 1983, noticeably drawing on images from *ANH*, and subsequently named the planned missile defense system the "Star Wars Defense Initiative."[107] From Reagan's claims, it is clear that he associated the United States with the Rebel Alliance in defensive action against the "evil other," the wicked imperial regime (the Soviet Union). While there have been several readings of the classic trilogy in this vein it is worth complicating the picture by recalling that Lucas' *THX 1138* holds a critical mirror to American society and political self-understanding, and that the trilogy, particularly *ROTS*, consciously echoes this—as mentioned earlier.[108] If this is correct, then the victory celebration scene concluding *ANH*, with its conscious visual echoes of Riefenstahl's *The Triumph of the Will*, would come to look quite different—the Rebel Alliance, with its violent performance of a defensive reactive justice is no less implicated in wickedness, and is thus little different in significant ways from the Empire it violently resists (the Empire's Grand Moffs and fleet commanders, of course, visually echo the uniforms of Nazi officers, and the troops being referred to as "stormtroopers").

Of course, it is predominantly in the light of the "tragic drama" of I-III that such a claim can be made. Reading *SW* in its cultural and political context, and in the light of Lucas' hopes and plans for his *ANH* is insufficient. It needs to be understood in its particularity in the light of the movies in the saga that succeed it. This crucially indicates that the various features of *SW* that make its violence look like a politics of revenge against the "evil them" are subtly transformed through each succeeding movie in the saga. *ESB* is an entertaining movie, but it supplies deeper character development than its predecessor. While the Emperor is introduced and no explanation of his wickedness is offered (in fact, none is at any point in Lucas' saga, making the Emperor an archetypally wicked character), Vader significantly becomes more psychologically layered. That, as much as anything else, subverts the Manichaean understanding that many of the audience had gathered from *SW* three years previously, and the development of the Jedi through the introduction of Yoda equally complicates the notion of a "good violence." While there is still something of a "good violence" on display at this point it is markedly different in mood and matter from that of *ANH*. Moreover, and crucially, this transvaluation of the cultural values supposed in evidence in *ANH* is intensified by the considerably more complex prequel trilogy, in which the story of arc moves in a different direction from that of "the adventures of Luke Skywalker"—"the tragedy of Anakin Skywalker." Taking these detailed steps enables a deeper reading of *SW* than ones often heard, even in the scholarship.

## *Conclusion*

While *ANH*'s mood and style were quite different from both the avant-garde movies Lucas had planned and his earlier *THX 1138* project, the riskiness of a sci-fi project at the time is an indication that the director was not capitulating to a simple ploy for market-appeal. Even the title of *The Star Wars*, eventually being shortened to *SW*, was felt by the Twentieth Century–Fox studio to be unmarketable: "they thought science fiction was a very bad genre, that women didn't like it, although they did no market research on that until after the film was finished."[109] Lucas felt the project would be a disaster, with it at most appealing to the "$8 million worth of science fiction freaks in the U.S.A.," and he braced himself for the fallout.[110] As Biskind admits, "George made plans to be out of town, in Hawaii with Marcia and the Huycks for the opening of *Star Wars*, the way he was when *Graffiti* premiered. He was still afraid the movie was going to be a huge embarrassment."[111] After all, the pre-release screenings had not been entirely successful. As it transpired, Lucas even forgot the opening night, and spent the evening with his wife in a restaurant near Los Angeles' Chinese Theatre.

Crucially, while the *SW* saga, and particularly *ANH* within it, has frequently been read as, in some sense, glorifying violence, there are extensive grounds for distinguishing two versions of this "good war." Yet more significant than that is the move to radicalize or deconstruct the very monomyth that troubles Lawrence and Jewett. The Jedi philosophy, several broad lines of which are presented in *ESB*, ultimately subverts the very sources of violent conflict and reconnects with matters of the formation of characters of virtue. Violence comes from somewhere, and it is that "somewhere" that the Jedi are trained to resist in themselves, and self-givingly negotiate justly in the failure of other Republic-citizens to do the same. The parallels developed through the prequel trilogy between Anakin and his son Luke are striking,[112] especially in the form of an inversion where Anakin in *ROTS* chooses the other-violating and narcissistic (because self-aggrandizing) Sith way of peace as domination and control, in contrast to Luke who has moved from celebrating heroism (*ANH*), to deconstructing the very notion of heroism under the interrogatory guidance of Yoda (*ESB*), and finally to the self-sacrificial non-violence (*ROTJ*).[113] Seen in this redemptive light, talk of *fighting for peace* in the *SW* mythos comes to look radically and life-affirmingly different from that which is commonly supposed in the suggestions that a myth of redemptive violence corrupts its textual body. It, this chapter argues, possesses something of the quality of the peace affirmed by Augustine as the "respect for and development of human life ... [through] the assiduous practice of fraternity ... [and] 'the tranquility of order.'" This "Peace is the work of justice and the effect of charity."[114] That indeed is the Jedi way, the way that the aged and diminutive Jedi Master Yoda discloses in a Dagobah swamp during his first encounter with Luke (*ESB*): "Wars not make one great." Wars may not, but the non-competitive non-narcissistic construal of relations in a just life of self-giving service or charity will.

Lucas' work asks deep questions, questions about character, about morality, about what instincts drive us away from even the best in our moral reasoning. That is why watching Anakin's emotional collapse into the Dark Side is so morally interesting. He is the narrative answer to the question "What if the immense power of the Force was available to someone whose emotional instincts and psychological condition was less than virtuous and well self-controlled?" This forms something of a parallel to the disturbing movie *Chronicle*. The prequels, then, move closer to stripping away the mask of moral distance by graphically brutalizing the body of Anakin as a visual representation of the moral disrepair that has overcome him. Anakin is not to be idolized as a hero, but he is rather to serve as a mirror to our own moral disrepair. In this regard, the tragedy of Anakin Skywalker can function to interrogate the process of idolization in which heroes are chosen, without interrogating us and thus leaving us morally in a state of blithe spectatorial existence unencumbered by the depth of mutual commitment. As tragic text, *The Revenge of the Sith* can offer not a pedagogy conceived in terms of the didacticism of instruction, but rather a dramatic set of conditions for reimagining critical insight. Thereafter it can enable the generation of "critical pedagogy as a form of cultural practice," in the words of Henry Giroux.[115] In this vein, then, *ROTS* can provide "the conditions for a set of ideological and social relations which engender diverse possibilities for students ... to be self-critical about both the positions they describe and the locations from which they speak, and to make explicit the values that inform their relations with others as part of a broader attempt to produce the conditions necessary for either the existing society or a new and more democratic social order."

And yet we cannot end there. Judging from the highly popular reception of the *SW* movies as texts violently encoding the "culture of death," the movies' signs are as evidently ambiguous. As O'Shaughnessy claims, "Responses—how people choose to interpret material—may diverge from what the producers intended or what logic would anticipate."[116] Equally, the sensibility generated by the myriad of militaristic merchandise may provide a further signifying layer of it being a glorious violent adventure. Darth Vader *and* Luke Skywalker are culturally celebrated by a number of fans precisely because of their *power*, their Force-technical prowess, than for their moral exemplarism. And here is the irony of merchandising a Luke who becomes an important figure in child's role-playing *because* he comes complete with both a laser-pistol and a lightsaber.

Despite the trajectory of this deeper reading and the cautionary message about violence, then, there still remains a concern to be heard: the violence of *SW* is not horrifying. It does not create terror to prevent terrorising, or at least not until *Star Wars Episode III: The Revenge of the Sith*. Unlike *Gandhi*, for instance, the violence and the response to violence are not emotionally involving. The form of the violence in this space action-adventure still looks too much like good fun, and children will be encouraged, not put off, exhilaratingly engaging their "enemies" with a lightsaber or a blaster pistol in conscious mimicking of their swashbuckling heroes—Luke Skywalker, Han Solo, and Princess Leia Organa. Briefly put, the movies establish an emotional affinity between particularly younger viewers and the characters engaged in the conflicts within largely an adventure-serial violent drama.[117] Consequently, the saga can effectively function to curtail liberating potential for cultural resistance to the dominant codes of power, the heroic warrior cult, and the relating of persons to the "other" through a "politics of purity." And it can do this both because of the heroic violence it displays for many viewers, and by its tapping into the privatized ego of consumerist spectatorial satisfaction through its supposedly entertaining aestheticization of violence. In this regard, then, the type of cultural analysis found in Neil Postman's *Amusing Ourselves to Death* remains apt. The spectacle of modern forms of media, he suggests, transforms violent action into entertainment (what one might call a *belligertainment*). Thereby there is a loss of sense of the catastrophic nature of the violent inflicting of suffering.[118] This is made the more significant by *SW*'s high-culture connections. As Postman urges, "we do not measure a culture by its output of undistinguished trivialities but by what it claims as significant."[119]

Yet, to read the movies in this way is to reductively marginalize considerable signs of something different, and thereby fail to generate readings of it as a series of texts that display several sets of values deeply resistant to the naturalizing of violence in American culture. This is not to claim that the differences lie entirely with the reader, as a comment made by Lucas might otherwise suggest: *SW* was "designed for a youthful audience, ... [and] ultimately what happens is that most people need the reassurances that seem to come with the movie, so it ends up that everybody gets something out of it."[120] *SW*, as an extended moment of pop culture, may be intellectually thin in comparison with the literature of Philip K. Dick for instance, but it is far from having no philosophical value in contrast to Carl Freedman's problematic reading.[121] As Winkler entertains, "Just like westerns, the *Star Wars* films are modern morality plays, although less sophisticated than their cinematic precursors."[122] At its best it possesses potential to provoke a question when it holds up a witness to a radically different set of non-violent values from those celebrated by Western societies founded in the unconstrained promotion of freedom as primarily the atomizing freedom for individuality.

Cicero once claimed that the purpose of (formal) education is to free the student from the tyranny of the present. The potential for less formal sources of educative material is important to considering the formative role of cinematic products. According to J.P. Telotte, Lucas' *THX 1138*, for instance, "lays bare some of the more disturbing elements of American cultural ideology—particularly an inherent racism, a deadening disjunction between the individual and his or her work, and a capitalist reduction of everything and everyone to bottom-line budgetary numbers."[123] In its own way the later epic continues to investigate some of these themes and explores the kinds of self-understandings that generate and sustain them. This chapter has focused not so much on these as on the issue of its presentation of violent conflict. *SW*, conceived as the grand six-part space opera and not the isolated singular movie of *ANH*, is perhaps reasonably well placed to encourage a different form of sociality—one in which terms like "peace" and "freedom" have positive or non-reactive meaningfulness, and "love" does not have little practical significance for the publicly determinative relations we call "politics" and "economics." Only that kind of society and the people who form it will find it easier to relate to others in ways that do not resort to armed conflict and the violence that disrupts the making of inter-personal responsibility. This in itself would considerably contest the very conditions that make wars possible (dare I say "necessary"?) than those who watch the saga through the type of sentiment advertised on Midwestern billboards in 1975: "God, guns, and guts: that's what made America great!"[124] Telotte's assessment of *THX 1138* is equally appropriate of *SW*, or at least a certain radical way of reading it: it "challenges us to be less naïve in the face of a mediated world, to be more wary about the sorts of images [and ideologies] we consume."

# 3

# "There'll be no escape for the Princess this time"
## *Re-Gendering the Patriarchal Star Wars Texts*

According to Claudia Card, "Feminist ethics is born in women's refusals to endure with grace the arrogance, indifference, hostility, and damage of oppressively sexist environments."[1] As such, it is constituted, firstly, by the critical task of identifying restrictive and damaging practices, so as to expose the ethical problems with the conditions of what Elizabeth Kamarck Minnich calls the forcing of an "extraordinarily diverse people … into the singularity of the Woman who is Man's Other."[2] As Margaret Miles and Brent Plate argue, "how we see the other affects the way we treat the other. Film, as a medium of mass reception, promotes, negates, and generally alters our perception of identities, especially with regard to gender, race, ethnicity, and religion."[3] Secondly, it resistantly offers possibilities for imagining and constructing better environments and systems of representation that work to overcome the damage that has been, and is still being, done through existing power arrangements. In many recent works, the otherwise male dominated genre of science fiction has provided resources for what Melzer describes as "the imaginative testing grounds for feminist critical thought."[4]

This mention of "women … as Other" raises a set of concerns with Lucas' depiction of alterity, and such a concern animates a range of critiques of the role and function of women in *SW*.[5] It is from Leia at the Yavin IV medal ceremony that the male heroes receive their awards for valor, someone identified as a Princess in a narrative that opens with a distinctive reference to a fairy tale setting with "a long time ago," and a narrative that closes in the "happily ever after" mood. Soon after the theatrical release of *ANH* Dan Rubey claimed *SW* was a socio-politically conservative text that emphasizes a natural and hereditary social privilege that shapes a set of racist and sexist relationships between Luke and the other characters who are merely instrumental foils for the expression of his privileged and personally attained individualism.[6] That perspective has been echoed and developed at greater length in a plethora of studies since then, despite the substantial screen time given to Leia Organa and Padmé Naberrie Amidala in the two sets of trilogies. A variety of responses reach an extreme form in the claim by Anne Cranny-Francis, that "in the film *Star Wars* ... the characters Luke Skywalker, Han Solo and Princess Leia enact a patriarchal, bourgeois (liberal humanist), white supremacist narrative in a setting uncannily similar to today's USA."[7] Even if this is demonstrated to be an exaggerated criticism, there remains a significant issue to be asked concerning Lucas' space opera over the gendering of alterity so that women become *alien*ated, made alien, and thereby disempowered in the hegemony of a deeply culturally encoded identity politics. A point made more generally by Robert Stam and Louise Spence is useful to cite at this stage in the proceedings: an "insistence on 'positive images' ... obscures the fact that 'nice' images might at times be as pernicious as overtly degrading ones, providing a bourgeois façade for paternalism, a more pervasive racism."[8] The point is that the cinematic product of Lucas' imagination, whether intentionally or not, reflects deep hegemonic currents in modern American culture by defining the women in the narratives from the male perspective. In many ways, this reading should hardly be surprising given the prevalence of the perception of the *SW* saga as a politically conservative set of texts. Unsurprising perhaps, but morally troubling all the same, especially since *SW* remains culturally pervasive. Again, any claim to *SW* being "pure entertainment" will not provide any mechanism for defending these texts. As Henry Giroux astutely observes, "it is precisely when we have escaped, when we feel we are in the realm of pure entertainment, that the ideological world of the cinema becomes most seductive, lulling us into a dream state."[9]

Several substantive issues raised by critical viewers have centered on the main two female protagonists of the saga, Leia and Padmé, and the issues raised for the ideological formation of identity through viewing these movies is therefore of deep seated moral significance. The critique then, to use the words of Minnich, is to operate as "an expression of a commitment to a resistant, respectful, reflexive, critical approach that asks us to look behind, or below, received knowledge and dominant traditions [and their artifacts] in an effort to locate whether, when, where, how modes and methods of thought, deriving from old [patriarchal] exclusions and devaluations, may continue to skew our ability to think on all levels."[10]

## *"What do you think of her?" (Luke,* ANH*): Deconstructing the Princess*

According to Jeanne Cavelos, "George Lucas blazed a trail with Leia that many writers have followed, and all viewers who like seeing independent, self-reliant female characters owe him a debt of gratitude."[11] Not all commentators agree, however. The first criticism worth analyzing takes its shape from the observation that Leia's role is a marginal one in terms of the trajectory of the narrative. True, she occupies an exalted professional position as a representative of her home planet of Alderaan in the Galactic Senate. However, as Davies and Smith have admitted with reference to issues to race, "the post-civil rights demand to see 'a black face in a high place' now fails to get to the heart of racial politics or the politics of racial representations."[12] In fact, women in general play little part in what must be regarded as a "boy's own" adventure story. This is no minor matter since, according to Grace Jantzen, "women have been underrepresented in situations of power and esteem in western history, while men have been overwhelmingly overrepresented not only in situations of power but also in aggression and violence."[13] On the other hand, one must be careful not to claim too much from this. It is true that the socio-political invisibility of women as publically participative persons would indeed generate a morally discomforting sense as to the nature of representation in the narrative. So Cavelos argues that "the problem is not that women are supporting characters, though they are. Even a supporting character can be striking and compelling. Han Solo is such a powerful, heroic figure, [and] he nearly eclipses Luke."[14] On saying that, invisibility does not necessarily announce the status of non- or sub-persons since much depends on the particularity of the moment. It is equally not insignificant that the leader of the Rebel Alliance is Mon Mothma, and that the youthful Leia comes herself to occupy a significant position of authority in the Rebellion against the Empire. At an even more tender age Padmé is deemed sufficiently wise to be elected as Queen of Naboo, and there is a reference by Anakin in *AOTC* to having heard that Padmé's people had been so impressed by her performance that they had attempted to amend the constitution in order to prolong her leadership at the end of her second term of governance. Failing that she becomes, of course, the elected senatorial representative for Naboo. These are not simple concessionary moments to an otherwise absence of women from the *SW* screen. In fact, by their relative absence the moments of presence of such women become particularly striking. They are made more intensively epiphanic by virtue of their prominent positioning that is set in stark relief by the narrative's female scarcity. Consequently, Hanson and Kay appropriately observe (albeit with sole reference to Mon Mothma in *ROTJ*) that "sex is not a consideration with regard to leadership or station in life."[15] As in *Alien* in the late 1970s viewers are entreated to a visual suggestion that it is not unnatural for women to lead and for men to work with, and serve, them. *Alien*'s hierarchy appears to be more class related, and the conflictual relations between the crew is notable. Peter Lev is accordingly quite mistaken to claim that "white male humans are 'naturally' in positions of authority," and like Wilson who argues that "human males are fully in charge and other sorts of beings are unimportant or expendable," simply does not seem to have been watching carefully.[16] If anything, the problem of scarce screen-time and dramatic role is most pronounced with regard to non-white female human characters, so that Wetmore is entitled to ask "where are the women of color in the *Star Wars* universe?"[17] The important positions of Adi Gallia and Depa Billaba on the Jedi Council, in fact the only two female human or humanesque councilors (along with Yaddle in *TPM*, and in *AOTC* Shaak Ti from the Togruta species), is suggestive of the kind of egalitarian racial and gender politics that the movies assume and attempt to sustain within a modest dramatic labor. However, it is the ability of *SW* to maintain and sustain this at more than a subtextual level that has been questioned with regard to their performance of a politics of gender and ethnic difference for audiences requiring an emancipatory vision.

With regard to Leia more specifically, critics do recognize her relative marginality in the narrative, and this is what Rubey singles out for criticism, as she comes to take a secondary position behind the development of the main male protagonist into a hero, Luke (and to an extent even Han as well), in a Campbellian formatting of the narrative in terms of the (male) hero's journey. She may be the "token female" but her general importance may be a reflection of Joseph Campbell's archetypal figure of the "goddess/muse" who helps the hero fulfill his destiny.[18] Diana Dominguez lends weight to this notion when arguing that "although it has been the recipient of much ridicule, parody, and criticism, it should be noticed that her hairstyle (the so-called cinnamon buns) is modelled on the traditional hairstyle of the Hopi Indian Corn Maiden, who symbolizes both fertility and wisdom and which was worn by Pancho Villa's soldaderas (female warriors) during the Mexican Revolution of the early 1990s, as Lucas himself commented in a 2002 *Time* magazine interview."[19]

Lev complains that "the Rebel Alliance itself seems to be hierarchical and perhaps even authoritarian."[20] Nonetheless, anticipating the study in chapter 4 of this book, it can be suggested that he weakens his point with misinterpreted textual evidence when further claiming that *SW* "in no way challenges gender, race, or class relations. White male humans are 'naturally' in positions of authority. ... [M]ost of the aliens are relegated to the 'freak show' of the spacefarers' bar." The force of this criticism in relation to race and species is somewhat further alleviated by the introduction of Lando Calrissian and Yoda, and even in the introduction of Admiral Ackbar of the Mon Calamari species in *ROTJ* (continued in *TPM* with the military importance of the Gungans and the mixed species of the Jedi Order whose Council sits in a non-hierarchical circle).[21] This stands in obvious contrast to the purely human, wholly male makeup of the imperial navy, the purity of the white male. There are no females to be seen in the Imperial order (or, for that matter, among the Sith in their "Rule of Two"),[22] and it has even displaced the role of maternality with the bio-engineering of its infantry and pilots. The Rebellion, one can confidently maintain, represents something of the diversity of the pre–Imperial rule over against the oppressive homogeneity of the Empire. On the other hand, as will be argued later, the real difficulty may well be located in the fact that by making her the *sole* female voice, Lucas inadvertently constructs the Princess in the form of a product of Western gendered essentialization, and this process is consequently no less "metaphysical" than patriarchy is.

A second and related strand of criticism operates from the portrayal of Leia, according to Kathleen Ellis and Peter Lev, as the damsel in distress. This is a considerably more politically interesting critical reading than that which pins the difficulty on simple matters of screen time and narrative prominence. So Ellis claims that the characterization of Leia "reveals the patriarchal ideology Lucas unconsciously adopted." "She is thereafter the traditional damsel in distress and it would appear that her 'femaleness' is what prevents her from saving herself."[23]

While Leia's title of "princess" and her rather medieval garb are nods back to the fairy-story genre, the reference is to the feisty royal figure in Akira Kurosawa's *Hidden Fortress* of 1958. Initially, when searching for a story to tie a few visual ideas together (principally, the cantina scene and the space battle), Lucas shaped the story around Kurosawa's sixteenth-century adventure. The influence of this remains in several places in the final version: in the perspective on the story of the two squabbling peasants, Tahei and Matashichi (in *SW*, C-3PO and R2-D2); and in General Rokurota Makabe's (in *SW*, General Obi-Wan Kenobi) rescue of the young Princess Yuki (in *SW*, Princess Leia Organa) to return her to her own people (in *SW*, Leia's family on Alderaan, and then the Rebel Alliance on Yavin IV). What is significant is the fact that the design of the character clearly resists the stereotypical and Disneyesque damsel-in-distress, something picked up to good effect by Princess Fiona in *Shrek*, in a moment of Disney's self-mocking in *Tangled*, with Snow in the television series *Once Upon a Time*, and with fantasy fairytale movies such as *Maleficent*, *The Brothers Grimm*, *Mirror Mirror*, and *Snow White and the Huntsman*. Certainly the audience would have very little reason to contest this when Luke discovers the holographic teaser and finds himself fetishizing an off-worlder whom he refers to as "beautiful." The scene quite deliberately, and ironically given the regal figure the youth encounters later on, enacts a culturally conservative gender-nostalgia. Yet, Leia's self-assured response to Vader and to Grand Moff Tarkin suggests something different, dropping her feistiness only when her home planet of Alderaan is threatened with destruction. It is true that the young senator needs to be rescued from the Imperials' detention block on the first Death Star in *ANH* when facing termination, and yet the gender coding is soon complicated. It is so in part by her characteristic sassiness so that she can belittle the saving character before her with the memorable rhetorical power-deflation "Aren't you a little short for a stormtrooper?" The sarcastic remark is telling in breaking the silence of Luke's desirous gaze. Leia's voice, even in the midst of hostility, functions to resist the imposition of identity on her, and to chastise the male for his fetishizing gaze at her. A little surprised at first, Luke composes himself, removes the helmet from his white armored attire (a reference to the white knight?) and announces, as any great fairy tale hero would in his situation, "I'm Luke Skywalker. I'm here to rescue you." But, as if to emphasize that she is no typical damsel in distress, a puzzled Leia asks, "You're who?" This is no 1930s princess in the tower awaiting the shining white knight who ever gazes lovingly with wide eyes set on her liberator. As Diana Dominguez observes, here "Lucas instantly shatters the familiar fairy tale trope of the fair unknown knight or prince in shining armor who comes to save the silent but eternally grateful damsel in distress and whisk her off to safety and a life of happily ever after."[24] Leia's is no minor and unimportant character construal, and therefore there is good sense in Merlock and Jackson's claim that "after Leia, no longer would princesses be passive and salvaged simply with a kiss."[25] Lucas is quoted by Pollock as revealing that Leia herself is a bit of a pain: "She's sort of a drag and she's a nuisance."[26] For someone so "beautiful" in distress in Luke's eyes, she ends up subverting his heroic presence on screen. In fact, according to Carrie Fisher, Lucas directed her to regard the character to be "proud and frightening. ... I was not a damsel in distress. I was a distressing damsel."[27] *SW* spends considerable time de-objectifying its female protagonist, preventing her from being portrayed with culturally distinctive and identifiable managed "feminine" traits. The point is not lost on Cavelos for whom there is significance in the fact that the young woman "stood up to the men. ... Leia clearly believes she knows best and isn't afraid to let everyone know it."[28] At this point, to emphasize what is at stake, it is worth noting a comment made by Sherrie Inness. According to her, a woman exhibiting strength of character and physicality subverts the notion of the natural or stable gender coding, and this "throws into question the whole foundation upon which our culture is based. If masculine attributes, such as toughness, and feminine attributes too, are conceived as free-floating signifiers that refer to either a male or a female body, our whole culture is destabilized because it is based on what are perceived as the essential differences between men and women."[29]

The gender coding of the fairytale "princess" reference is further complicated by Leia's frustrations with the very ineptitude of the rescuing heroes that forces her to take her liberation into her own hands at key points. The implications are pronounced not merely for the portrayal of this female character but also for the culturally dominant sense of heroic masculinity. In the detention block corridor, for instance, she grabs the blaster off Luke and sarcastically announces, "This is some rescue," before blasting a hole in a grate with the words "somebody has to save our skins." Of course, the escape takes them from the proverbial "frying pan into the fire" for dramatic purposes, but this is not the point at issue and worth reflecting on. Dominguez argues, then, that "from the 'rescue' scene onward. ... Leia becomes a full-out rebel: outspoken, unapologetic, sarcastic, even bossy, and, shooting and killing without hesitation with the same skill as all the tough guys around her."[30] So much so that by the time of *ROTJ* the actress, Carrie Fisher, was bored of portraying such a tomboy even though she did equally ask for more action scenes.[31] Of course, it is also worth highlighting the subversive potential for this re-reading of *SW* by Leia's kiss of Luke immediately prior to grabbing onto him in order to swing across a platformless compartment in the Death Star—the moment becomes a heroic one for the male character. It will take a further movie in the series, *ESB*, to come closer to deconstructing the image of the hero, for instance, as warrior.

In the third place, flowing from the comment made here by Dominguez, some critics are bothered by the fact that Leia is all too rarely depicted with blaster in hand, but constantly has to depend on the saving violence and self-sacrifice of the male characters. However, this is simply not the case until late on in *ANH* and is certainly not true of her performance in *ROTJ*. Cavlos recognizes the radical import of the aggressive action in question: "Leia marked a major breakthrough for women heroes in film. George Lucas's creation was amazing and groundbreaking. Before 1977, few women in film fired a gun—the symbol of male power—and those who did generally fired once, missed, dropped the gun and started sobbing. ... Even more striking, she stood up to the men. ... Leia clearly believes she knows best and isn't afraid to let everyone know it."[32] The first part of this remark and the criticism it responds to, far from being supportive of a form of subjectivity usable for feminist theorizing, betrays it by assuming a more fundamental moral dislocation, what Jantzen names the necrophiliac obsession that she adjudges pervades the patriarchal West. In this regard, the deconstruction of violence that somewhat occurs in the saga, and the stress of Padmé on the continued need for democracy and diplomacy, witness to a set of values more conducive to Jantzen's feminist philosophy of natality. Speaking of Disney's *Mulan*, Giroux regards the titular heroine as being conveyed in terms that are distinctly morally problematic. "By embracing a masculine view of war, Mulan cancels out any rupturing of traditional gender roles. She simply becomes one of the boys."[33] It would be particularly problematic to announce that Leia is a role-model for young girls when she postures aggressively with blaster in hand. Of course this does not let Lucas off the hook, morally speaking at least. What is it that is being claimed by him when Luke Skywalker is seen a similar pose as well?

A more interesting form of critique occurs in the work of Rubey. This commentator rightly observes that the senator from the Royal House of Alderaan decreases in active significance in inverse proportion to Luke's importance in *ANH*, so as to be left a mere observer of the Battle of Yavin with General Jan Dodonna and C-3PO at the base as the pilots take the fight to the Imperials. On saying that, however, a case can be made from the narrative for Leia's lack of involvement in the assault on the Death Star—she is, after all, a politician and not a fighter pilot. So Lucas admits that as a principal commander in the Rebel Alliance and as a member of the Royal House of Alderaan she would not have flown in a fighter battle anyway. Nonetheless, the audience is entreated to a militarized airborne defense force composed solely composed of men (and humans at that). In terms of the make-up of the military personnel, little changes with the next two sequels. While Lucas rectifies that in the Naboo air defense units in *TPM* this change only serves to retroactively highlight what is missing from *ANH* even with the release of the edited special editions in 1997, a fact that is important to Rubey's case, for instance. Perhaps it can be advanced that Lucas' materials reflect standard military practice, but if so then it certainly does not offer a challenge to them. Something more promising occurs, however, when *SW* is read more expansively and properly over the course of the movies that succeed *ANH*. Leia herself does become useful when called upon to handle a blaster, retains a visible position of authority in the Rebel Alliance (and notably, the supreme commander is Mon Mothma in *ROTJ*), and exhibits her characteristic spiritedness, self-assurance and bold assertiveness. So at the opening of *ROTJ* she puts herself in danger when disguised as the bounty hunter Boussh in order to liberate Han from Jabba, and mercilessly slays her hedonistic enslaver. Whereas in *ANH* she is reduced to being a helpless bystander of the fatefully important final conflict, in *ROTJ* she volunteers to participate in the important assault on the shield bunker; she commandeers an Imperial speeder bike and chases an Imperial scout through the forests of Endor; and in the climactic triple battle she fights until the end, even incurring a wound to the shoulder in the process, to ensure the success of her part in the three pronged assault on the second Death Star. In fact, piloting a military craft is the only skill she does not appear to have among her vast repertoire, or at least does not exhibit if she does (although she is seen piloting the Falcon towards the end of *ESB* and is cardinal in saving Luke). This might all be even more significant by virtue of the fact that "Campbell denies the existence of female heroes—all of his heroes are male."[34] The image of Leia garbed in camouflage military outfit with blaster in hand in *ROTJ* is intensified by the reversal of Han Solo's quip in *ESB* to the claim "I love you" with "I know." And yet, Rubey, whose account was composed in the aftermath of *ANH* without the perspective of Episodes V-VI, continues by observing that as "Luke grows up into possession of power and the Force. ... Princess Leia retreats into the background. This happens because power in *Star Wars* is male power, the patriarchal power of fathers and sons."[35] Given that in *ESB* she is an authoritative presence in the Rebel base on Hoth, and in *ROTJ* is answerable in the Rebel Alliance only to Mon Mothma, another former senator, Rubey's particular critical claim about patriarchal power has to be assessed as being conspicuously overstated and now distinctly obsolete, at least in the form that it takes. Even then, Leia never gets to train as a Jedi despite the admission in *ROTJ* of her Force-conscious ancestry.[36]

### 3. "There'll be no escape for the Princess this time" 87

For Rubey, "by having no thought-out, consistent position on any of the issues he touches on, Lucas dooms *Star Wars* to repeat all the dominant ideological clichés of our society. That distant galaxy turns out to be not so far away after all."[37] It is worth noticing here that this analysis does not claim that Lucas or his product are sexist as such, but only that they do not do anything to confront the sexist ideology in his culture, and that this lack dominates the presentation of gender relations. This is a provocative and challenging thesis. Given the construal of Leia's character the critical point, then, is the more modest one that Lucas had not, it seems, sufficiently stretched out his imagination to explicitly visually challenge the traditionally constructed gender roles and therefore subvert the subjugation of women, or even the roles of ethnic order, at that point.

Leia, of course, becomes a lover in *ESB* and *ROTJ*, and this is a crucial source of critical concern. Philip Simpson regards Leia's feistiness as a form of *frigidity* that the movies then begin to break down, thereby constraining the impact that her character might otherwise have had. "It is ironic [and revealing], then, that a narrative that features two such strong female characters then works so hard to contain and even break down their power, first by coding their exercise of autonomy as *frigidity* and then placing both women in relationships that demand not just a *thawing* but melting of their icy feminine royalty."[38] Despite the politically authoritative positions that both Padmé and Leia occupy in the saga's narrative, and the depiction of them as self-assured and assertive, Simpson complains that "it is ironic, then, that a narrative that features two such strong female characters then works so hard to contain and even break down their power, first by coding their exercise of autonomy as *frigidity* and then placing both women in relationships that demand not just *thawing* but melting of their key feminine royalty. These women must suffer sexual abjection to an extent that subverts whatever power they otherwise manifest."[39] It has often been argued that the characterization of Leia (and Padmé by extension as a Leia-echo) reflects some of Lucas' own struggles with his wife Marcia at the time. Leaving that speculation aside, and without wanting to undermine the difficulties that critics detect, Simpson's remains an unconvincing thesis for a number of reasons.

The main difficulty with this reading is that the melting of her relational aloofness (by developing the love-story arc with Han) does not, in fact, mitigate the other character traits the movies have done much to explicate. In *ANH* while Leia is an object of the gaze of the competitive Luke and (to a lesser degree) Han she does not return their gaze or reveal desires other than those of political care for the well-being of the Alliance.

As mentioned above, her development in *ESB* equally takes the route of her becoming more significant as an authoritative character and leader, and also warrior. For instance, at the end of this movie released in 1980 she is involved in blasting her way toward an escape from Imperial overrun Bespin, barks at Chewbacca to turn the Falcon towards the pursuing Imperial Tie-Fighters in order to rescue a physically injured and psychologically traumatized Luke. It would take some superior interpretive gymnastics to maintain that Leia diminishes in stature *because* of her relationship with Han, as if only oppressed women are involved in heterosexual relations. There is simply no evidence for this in the texts. Even her attire remains utilitarian, and she is never (apart from the highly particular dancing girl outfit in Jabba's palace and on the sail barge) reduced to titillating "eye-candy" for the male gape. In other words, she is not reduced without reserve to the status of lover, or domesticatedly positioned woman, or even to the male gaze as a sexually charged character (although the fourth point below will later have to pick this point up again in the context of a controversial scene in *ROTJ*). This is significant, particularly as, according to Seyla Benhabib, "women's sphere of activity has traditionally been and still today is so concentrated in the private sphere in which children are raised, human relationships maintained and traditions handed down and continued."[40]

A further concern with Simpson's reading is that it does not take account of what it is that Leia importantly contributes to the development of Han's character. His "bad boy" persona is not stable and unchanging, but is bound up over the series by a telling de-*Solo*ing and a gradual multi-layering that involves the transformation of his self-enclosed subjectivity into one who is more responsibly engaged with others than himself. In fact, the significance of this is intensified in the context of the time, especially in the early 1980s. As Robin Wood observes, films during the Reagan era tend to be characterizable as "capitalist myths of freedom of choice and equality of opportunity, [involving] the individual hero whose achievements somehow 'make everything all right,' even for the millions who never make it to individual heroism."[41] Leia's role in this process of enabling Han to surmount, to borrow Davies and Smith's language, "the oppressive and atomising effects of capitalism" is vital.[42] Merlock and Jackson, for instance, make the point that Leia's relationship "converts Han (and later saves both him and Luke) where no other forces could have done so."[43] In other words, Han's character itself undergoes something of a "thawing," to use Simpson's language for Leia, as he moves from self-interested smuggler to becoming a responsible Rebel leader, and from cocky cowboy figure

### 3. "There'll be no escape for the Princess this time" 89

to friend and lover. The relationship moves well beyond the loss of self in the male other, and thus to the identifiability of Leia simply as "lover," or ever to the domesticity of narratively intensified maternality, as if it subsumes and subordinates the plethora of roles that identify her as agent. To adopt Elizabeth Stuart's terms from another context, borrowing from the work of Judith Butler and Sarah Coakley, "gender and sexual identity are not of ultimate concern, thus opening the possibility for love."[44] The relation could better be characterized in the terms used in Luce Irigaray's reading of Emmanuel Levinas: "The caress is an awakening to intersubjectivity," and this is a theme explored briefly but poignantly in *THX 1138*.[45] "Rather than violating or penetrating the mystery of the other, rather than reducing his or her consciousness or freedom to passivity, objectuality, animality or infancy, the caress makes a gesture which gives the other to himself, to herself, thanks to an attentive witness, thanks to a guardian of incarnate subjectivity."[46] Arguably, the flow of the narrative displays an improvement occurring not only in Han's character but in Leia's as well.

Given that neither of the options of domesticity or reduction to the male gaze is particularly prominent in Lucas' portrayal of Leia, one has to wonder how far the reading of Simpson is grounded in an unreflective Kantian subjectivity. In other words, Simpson's criticism sounds too close to being directed by an essentialist construal of subjectivity, of what Irigaray criticizes as the "Ego-in-itself."[47] The significance of this mutuality should not be lost, and a claim made by Simone de Beauvoir about a sexually construed binarism can be set in sharp relief to it: "She [the woman] is defined and differentiated with reference to man and not he with reference to her; she is the incidental, the inessential as opposed to the essential. He is the Subject, he is the Absolute—she is the Other."[48] This suggests that there is a real need to question forms of feminist reading that desocialize male or female, that set them over against each other as competitive, even if this is done in the name of a therapeutic response to the negation of women's subjectivity in patriarchal (or "kyriarchal") domination. Such a move, in retaining the modern binary construction of male and female becomes an act of skepticism that only subverts domination by evading it rather than transforming it, and thereby becomes morally debilitating. The "heroism" of the characters is not that of the self-aggrandizement of the pure self-construction of the moral subject, deflected from the web of responsibility in what Benhabib calls the immersion "in a network of relationships."[49] Accordingly, Lucas' Leia is not "othered" as an autonomous subject among other autonomous characters. The pull of her consensual intersubjectivity is too strong to permit such a disastrous post–Enlightenment construal of her identity, or rather identifiability. Or as Jantzen maintains, the pressure in such an account is towards various forms of violent competition. So she argues that "hierarchical binary oppositions ... [characterizes a way of thinking] that legitimates and reinforces competitive thinking and an us-and-them mentality."[50] "Now such a style of philosophical thinking," she judges, "corresponds to many other aspects of late modernity, reflecting and reinforcing them. ... It is ingrained in the entrepreneurs of a free-market economy, and thus in the interests of the competitive masculinist structures of power of late capitalism."[51]

Fourthly, much is made of the moment of the fetishization of Leia in *ROTJ*. In support of his reading of her as a sexualized character, Simpson, for instance, declares that "Leia's status as abject sexualized body on display as a nearly nude prisoner of the gangster Jabba—a stark contrast to her first white-veiled appearance in the series as a feisty but repressed freedom fighter."[52] Likewise, Wetmore claims that "She might be considered a strong female character, but the image of her in the slave girl costume on Jabba's barge, being grabbed by Luke ... and carried by him as he swings himself and her over to the rescue ship summarizes her position in the trilogy: she is an object to be rescued."[53] The sight of Leia grabbing hold of Luke in order to escape is a troubling one, an echo of a similar moment on the Death Star in *ANH*. Yet, this is a lazy reading. The force of it as a text indicating female weakness is distinctly mitigated by virtue of the audience watching her both dispose of her enslaver with powerful determination, and then direct the sail barge's gun onto its deck to end the hostilities. In fact, in this image of escape there may well be a point concerning interdependency and mutuality, so that Leia is both rescuer (of Luke in *ESB* and Han in *ROTJ*) and rescued (by Luke in *ANH* and *ROTJ*), just as Luke and Han are likewise both rescuers and rescued, and thus the activism/passivism that plagues some older feminist constructivist writing as much as patriarchal ideology is practically subverted by a more substantive sense of intersubjectivity or being-with-the-other. As Benhabib observes with reference to claims made by Hannah Arendt, "we are immersed in a 'web of narratives,' of which we are both the author and the object."[54] There is real danger in a critique that takes the form of an anti-relational or autonomy-shaped feminism, one that is reducible to the essentialized individuation that has been so pronounced in the post–Cartesian conception of modern subjectivity.

Moreover, Simpson's and Wetmore's criticism of the enslaved Leia utterly fails to engage appropriately with the context of the situation and its ideological framing with the characterization of Leia and Jabba. The camera, after all, does not gaze at her in the way Jessica Simpson, Megan Fox, Jessica Alba, Julia Roberts, Jane Fonda, or Raquel Welch become the objects of suggestively prolonged and seductive attention in *The Dukes of Hazzard, Transformers, Sin City, Pretty Woman, Barbarella*, or *1 Million Years B.C.* respectively. Leia's appearance as scantily clad dancer is a condition of abject subjugation that has been imposed on her rather than a position that has been chosen by her. In other words, it is the outcome of Jabba's abusive action that enslaves her in order to satisfy his own fetishizing desires. The otherwise confident and self-determinative character, whose dress has been generally relatively asexual, has now been reduced to a position of passivity, reduced to the dominating grip of her jailor who demands the titillation of his meagerly attired female performers. (The audience is, interestingly, denied the opportunity of gazing on a sexually charged dance performance by Leia). It is quite astonishing and damaging to a healthy perspective on the material that the ideological suspicion of certain readers is displaced from the festishizing and victimizing male gaze onto criticism of the abused victim as sexualized object of the abusive gaze.

Dominguez responds well to this type of claim by insightfully arguing several notable things. According to her particular account, it is suggestive that the sexualized victim uses her status in a moment of empowerment to punish her oppressor. Further, she recognizes that the enforced sexualization of Leia "may simply be a reflection of the fact that women are particularly vulnerable to such victimization as a means for torture and humiliation."[55] As mentioned already, Jabba enacts a relation of pure domination over those selected to be the instruments of his pleasure. After all, the contrast between this enforced sexualization and the gradual flourishing of Leia's consensual relationship with Han is marked. Moreover, the latter's carbonite immobilizing imprisoning serves a similar function of imposing a torturing, humiliating, and objectified body-as-trophy position on the protagonist, albeit without the sexualization of the character as occurs in the case of Leia. The normally financially driven gangster makes just such an admission when the young Jedi Luke Skywalker attempts to bargain for the former smuggler's life.

Something similar corrupts numerous readings of the moment of Ellen Ripley's undressing in *Alien* as a reduction to the objectifying gaze, when the scene's visual display would seem to have a different signifying reference from the voyeuristic fetishization of her female form. As Cornea observes, "At the time of the film's release, the imposing figure of Ripley defied traditional gender roles and her very physical appearance suggested a disregard for the markers of sexual difference, as more normally encoded within mainstream cinema (she is 5'11" tall and her body type could well be described as androgynous)."[56] For Cornea, "Ripley's 'reassuringly' female form is exposed as she removes her clothes to don a spacesuit. Although she is voyeuristically presented in her near naked state, this is immediately offset by the appearance of the alien and the violence of the actions that follow. The viewer is surely punished for the voyeuristic gaze here." It is this visual contrast that is significant. According to Barbara Creed, the contrast is particularly marked between Ripley with the cat and the monstrous and armored alien (and, for Creed, the movie actually subverts its feminist potential).[57] However, it is difficult to read this as a psychosexual suggestion without too much self-projection. Creed's reading oversteps the material by depicting *Alien* through Julia Kristeva's theory of abjection: "We can see its ideological project as an attempt to shore up the symbolic order by constructing the feminine as an imaginary 'other' which must be repressed and controlled in order to secure and protect the social order ... [as it thereby] stages and re-stages a constant repudiation of the maternal figure." Perhaps the scene is actually not one referencing the act of voyeurism at all, but is providing a reference that lies elsewhere. This is the moment of her vulnerability, her moment of preparing for the passivity and docile dependency that comes with mechanically induced and supported sleep during deep space transit which is viciously interrupted by the stow-away as it aims to invade her body. The image of vulnerability is one of intensive embodiment, contrasted in *Aliens* by her donning the physically enhancing machine in order to "power up" against the alien queen. As Roz Kaveney observes, it is important to recall the image of fellow crew member Kane awaking earlier in the film from his cryogenic stasis semi-naked, rubbing the sleep from his eyes, especially when compared with what hatches from the eggs, is an image of vulnerability.[58] Moreover, the construal of Ripley as the saving figure, destroying the alien to protect not only herself but the planet the craft is bound for, who is competently able to handle weaponry, enables her character to perform a substitutionary role. She is the action hero, in other words, who now displaces the sole male of power for the audience's catharsis. (On the other hand, despite the way the movie develops a woman-savior motif, Ripley is unable to save others, or at least any human other.) Accordingly she transcends the boundaries that had been determined for female characters in the Hollywood movies, especially that of the passive object of saving male rescue. According to Anna Dawson, "the 'action women' title was coined" from Ripley's performance in *Alien*.[59] In this regard, there is

### 3. "There'll be no escape for the Princess this time" 93

something odd in Ridley Scott's portrayal of her in the end as a sleeping beauty, and of Gerard Loughlin's comment on this: "a princess awaiting her prince, sincerely sleeping in her glass coffin."[60]

Ripley is "one of the few science fiction characters who has truly expanded women's roles."[61] This moment sets the stage for the likes of Sarah Connor in *Terminator 2*, although she is something of an ambiguous hero whose instinctively conceived *ressentiment* is morally deconstructed both by the moral conscience of her adolescent son John and the paternal role adopted by, and the salvific heroic self-sacrifice of, the reprogrammed T-1000 Terminator. "Her function as protector to her son is consistently undercut by the 'good' Terminator's superior tactical knowledge and even his superior parenting skills."[62] Cornea, for instance, regards the very physicality of the brawny Sarah Connor as itself manifesting an ambivalence towards female heroes: "the authority of the female hero that emerged in science fiction films in the 1990s was, initially at least, marked upon her body in ways that have more traditionally been associated with masculine prowess; creating an arguably more ambivalent characterization than her nonetheless dynamic predecessors. ... [A] Sarah who has acquired aggressive 'masculine' traits and a pumped-up, muscular body to match."[63] Arguably, this critique of Sarah's built-physique as parody can carelessly enact and naturalize an untransgressive bodied gender stereotyping—that "hard bodies" are for men and "soft bodies" are for women. As Kristeva argues more sensitively, the very concept of gender itself is "metaphysical," by which she means a violent stabilizing of the sheer precariousness and ambiguity of sexual identity into some self-identical essence.[64] More appropriate is the fact that Cornea observes that this protagonist remains both visually and narratively caught in the grip of a gendered hierarchy. On the one hand, "it is ... evident that her newly acquired physique is placed within a hierarchy of muscularity in which the Terminator's more bulky appearance signals his superior strength and importance. In other words, she is 'out-performed' by the Terminator throughout the film and instead of emerging victorious against him, the ending of the first film is rewritten as it becomes the Terminator's altruistic choice to sacrifice himself at the close of *Terminator 2*." On the other hand, "according to the narrative of the first film, Sarah's main purpose was as the vessel for the birth of a future male savior. Given the appearance of her son in the sequel, her warrior status is written into a narrative in which, like the comic-book female superheroes, she is predominantly characterized as fighting *for* patriarchy. Sarah is relocated to an outside world where she fights in defense of a patriarchal future. So, the threat that the female hero may offer to the stability of traditional gender hierarchies in *Terminator 2* is ensnared within a narrative that strongly upholds patriarchal values. At best, the attempts to recuperate and confine the image of the female hero in *Terminator 2* may signal her potential agency as a disruptive and threatening figure."

Nonetheless, there then emerges a stream of heroic female leads: G.I. Jane as a female Rambo figure; and Trinity in *The Matrix*, although she does come to take second stage in narrative prominence to Neo; Xena in *Xena: The Warrior Princess* (1995–2001); Buffy in *Buffy the Vampire Slayer* (1997–2003); and even Arwen in *The Return of the King*, even though the Elven Princess is less dramatically important in the narrative than Aragorn; and Neytiri of the Na'vi in *Avatar*, who nonetheless gives way to Jake Sully in the hierarchy of the movie's heroes and who remains the main point of narrative identification. Cornea astutely observes that "the female hero that emerged in the 1990s was more closely sutured to the [masculine] codes and conventions of the modern action genre. Consequently, their heroic status was written upon their bodies, in terms of their pumped-up musculature and/or their physical fighting skills."[65] While this does offer a striking contrast with the "serial queens" of 1930s cinema, "depicted as evil and seductive and they were frequently pitted against a male adversary who eventually brought them under control," they remain caught within the hegemony of the male action genre.

The importance of Leia in *SW* can be seen in contrast to the role of women in Hollywood cinema, perhaps especially in science fiction cinema. As Doherty argues, "In classical Hollywood cinema perhaps only the western outdid science fiction in its relegation of women to a peripheral and predictable status."[66] So, Doherty continues, "barred from full admission to the upper echelons of the space crew, women entered as novelty and decoration, sometimes even filling the role of scientific expert in an erotically charged white-coated and horn-rimmed-glasses way. Like Raquel Welch in the biological exploration film *Fantastic Voyage* (1966), the space bimbo filled out a tight-fitting uniform to distract and entice. Though a woman of science, she was destined to lose her composure and succumb to a sheltering masculine shoulder at a crucial moment."[67] In Lucas' narration, in stark contrast, "Leia's contributions," Merlock and Jackson proclaim, "not just to the destruction of the Empire but also to the establishment of a new kind of female role model and to the possibility of feminine potential cinema and popular culture—merit a degree of appreciation."[68] Her "boyishness" unsettles speculations as to the borders that "separate" male and female, and positions her apart from the gender construction involved in the fetishizing gaze.

### 3. "There'll be no escape for the Princess this time" 95

The characterization of Leia is not far away from that of Ellen Ripley, in several instances, however. As Doherty indicates, Ridley Scott's portrayal of Ripley is "the generic reversal of the space bimbo motif," and this "was the most audacious narrative twist in *Alien*: in this future world, the natural order of things really was upside down. Against all science fiction expectations, the prettiest babe on board is also the shrewdest operator."[69] Loughlin argues that "all four *Alien* films make a woman—warrant officer Ripley—their central character; and there is little doubt that her success lies in being more resolute, resilient and courageous than any of the other, largely male, characters. In short, one could argue that Ripley survives because she is more of a man than are the men."[70] This last claim, however, can re-inscribe and perpetuate the construction of gender stereotypes, even as it seeks to transgress the boundaries. In a moment of intensification, James Cameron's sequel, *Aliens*, offers an "aggressive self-sufficiency and ruthless logic" that stands in even "more of a contrast to the [otherwise macho] men around her [like the incompetent lieutenant Gorman] who freak out or freeze in the face of danger."[71] For Cornea, "where *Alien* destabilized both sex and gender norms, *Aliens* reinstated differences based upon sex, even as the boundaries of traditional gendered roles were extended."[72] An important scene in her argument occurs early on in the movie. When working-out Private Vasquez is verbally accosted by another marine who insults with the rhetorical question "Hey, Vasquez, have you ever been mistaken for a man?" Vasquez's witty reply is "No ... have you?" The exchange reveals not only conflictual military banter, but the fact that gender roles in this futural environment, particularly in the military, are not so interchangeable for there not to remain gender stereotypes. According to Cornea, then, "the sight of the female undertaking a role associated with the male becomes a source of humour and the comment works to assure the viewer that sexual difference still operates in this world."

Moreover, it needs to be emphasized that Leia's is not the kind of female figure who pervades the voyeuristic scenes of movies of the time, not the Jane Fonda *Barbarella* representation of female sensuality for instance, or the representation of the femme fatale in *Blade Runner* who is reduced to a fetishized object as a hollow and rather passive agent.[73] (Very oddly, Cavelos speaks of *Barbarella* as reflecting "the independent, sexually liberated woman of the 1960s"—the voyeuristically titillating opening would suggest instead the kind of "independence" and "liberation" that encourages some girls to dream of being glamour models while no longer naming it male "exploitation.")[74] Nor is it the unfeasibly formed figures of the adolescent fetish for the physically enhanced female figures of superheroes like Wonder Woman, Batgirl, Powergirl or Catwoman, or for Lara Croft, or Colonel Wilma Dearing and Princess Ardala in the *Buck Rogers* series in the early 1980s. In many ways, given Ripley's androgynous dress throughout the movie, and her lack of make-up to catch the eye, there is little to specifically distinguish her from the other female crew members or indeed even from the male ones (other than the length of her hair, and this moment of modest undress). The sexually defining moment is the metaphorical rape scene which displays the android Ash in what might be understood as a "paranoia about male violence."[75]

By reducing Leia to "sexual being" it would appear that Simpson has, in fact, improperly read into the saga the Expanded Universe stories, and subsequently distorted the text.[76] Unfortunately, and I will have to leave this as an assertion for now, too many of the types of gaze at, or readings of, *SW*'s sexuality that one finds in the likes of Andrew Gordon, Martin Miller and Robert Sprich, and Roger Kaufman could arguably be characterized as textually loose and speculative moments of eisegesis that as much reflect the interests of the observers as the particularity of these texts.[77]

The character of Leia Organa in the "classic trilogy" in fact enables Lucas' creation to go some way toward mitigating the cultural pressures toward providing an easy masculinizing reading of the gender-politics of *SW*, and thus leave potential for disrupting the stability of modern gender binary systems and symbolics. Lucas once commented that Leia "is extremely bright and well educated and used to taking charge of situations. ... She is a natural-born leader."[78] In terms of Campbell's summary of the classic themes of mythology Leia occupies more the role of the goddess. Interestingly, then, and largely in a counter-intuitive perspective given the dominant readings of the material, Dominguez regards Lucas as having "so ably and consistently (and I firmly believe, deliberately) subverted and questioned in five of the *Star Wars* films" "traditional tropes and stereotypes." In particular, she claims that Leia "stands out as a strong feminist role model. ... Leia presented (and still presents) an alternative femininity to the one I had most often been exposed to in my life."[79] With this character Lucas' *SW* offers a protagonist with plenty of potential, with rich possibilities for development in ways that contest and overcome the dominant gender hierarchies, and with the ability to displace the control of female identifiability by male projective symbolics. Therefore, Merlock and Jackson make a fair point when they claim that "unlike Luke, however, Leia inherits far more strength and strategy from her mother than the naïve, hapless Luke has, especially in the earliest movies."[80] The iconicity of the gender relations are rendered incidental and thus both maleness and femaleness become symbolically liminal and slippery or floating signifiers.

That the movie did not provide a satisfactory exploratory study of gender relations and adequately challenge the binary oppositions of stereotypical gender constructions, some might argue, has to do with those ideological structures that constrain the *male* author's imagination of the hero as something of an idealized echo of himself, Luke (Lucas!) Skywalker. But this too is an insufficient reading. In fact, the reasons for the paucity that critics identify but labor to explain may lie elsewhere. Mention has already been made on two occasions above of the narrative *idealization* of the character of Leia in the classical *SW* trilogy. What is at stake here requires to be contextualized. Western feminist discourse on matters of identity until well into the 1980s was caught in attempts to essentialize women's experiences, to identify women's identity as a common pre-given that has to be defined in binary terms over against a singularity identified as patriarchy. However, as Amartya Sen argues regarding what he calls our "diverse diversities" in his critical response to Samuel Huntingdon's difference-flattening talk of a clash of civilizations, "the people of the world can be classified according to many other systems of partitioning, each of which has some—often far-reaching—relevance in our lives: such as nationalities, locations, classes, occupations, social status, languages, politics, and many others."[81] Accordingly, he continues, "The incitement to ignore all affiliation and loyalties other than those emanating from one restrictive identity can be deeply delusive and also contribute to social tension and violence."[82] Sen's argument is that there are complex networks of identity-forming conditions operative in the construction of any particular person or group of persons. One such complication has to do with the way that numerous critics have boldly suggested that the essentializing of "woman" and "women's experience" has been a problematic venture that has actually, and unwittingly, served to contribute to the marginalization of the voices of many women, pre-eminently non-white and non-middle class women. "'Experience' is a notoriously slippery notion."[83] Whose experience is being referred to? If the response is "women's experience" then a further difficulty emerges with construing matters in such a singularly categorizable manner. In 1851 no less, a freed slave named Sojourner Truth complained that "that man over there says that women needs to be helped into carriages, and lifted over ditches, and to have the best place everywhere. Nobody ever helps me into carriages, or over mud-puddles, or gives me any best place! And ain't I a woman? Look at me!

Look at my arm! I have ploughed and planted, and gathered into barns, and no man could head me! And ain't I a woman? I could work as much and eat as much as a man—when I could get it—and bear the lash as well! And ain't I a woman?"[84] Feminist studies have, in more recent years, become more properly attentive to multiple forms of difference, to the different forms of constructed positioning that have occurred in relation to the flow of, and access to, power that comes with the performance within differences of race, ethnicity, class, sexual preference, nationality, age, and so on. So Benhabib claims that "our identities as concrete others are what distinguish us from each other according to gender, race, class, cultural differentials," and so on.[85] Beatrice Hanssen, for example, asks rhetorically from materialist feminism, "might not the category of 'Woman' in feminine writing refer to a problematic myth, rather than to a historical materialist practice, implying that 'women do not belong to history, and that writing is not a material production'?"[86] It may well be, then, not so much that Leia takes shape in the context of women historically having "been forced through the features of a male socialization process," in the words of Hanssen, but rather from a Cartesian-inspired decontextualizing binary essentialism.[87] The difficulty is that this too, according to numerous theorists, is bound to forms of masculinizing discursive strategies that are conducive of structures that violate gendered particularities, and thereby disembody or de-gender women and deny what Teresa de Luretis calls the "historical fact of gender."[88] The need remains to interrogate the determinative "epistemic violence,"[89] or as Hanssen puts it, "the exclusionary presuppositions and foundations that shore up discursive practices insofar as these foreclose the heterogeneity, gender, class or race of the subject."[90] According to Melzer, "Considering that race and gender are inseparable categories of identity formation, attempts to assert a female subjectivity denied by traditional Western philosophy need to integrate the theoretical deconstruction of 'woman' as a stable gender identity."[91] Therefore, to put the matter in Margaret Kamitsuka's terms, there is the need "for complicating the notion of women's experience and decentering privileges of whiteness and heterosexuality in feminist" reflections.[92] Abstractions such as "woman" and "women's experience" require appropriate refusing since such categories lend themselves to hegemonic Western, bourgeois models of binary representation, thereby doubly disempowering non-white women. They are categories that essentialize gender without reference to a multiplicity of discursive practices and determinative conditions that affect experiences in substantive ways.

## 3. "There'll be no escape for the Princess this time" 99

In this regard, the real danger of *SW*'s material is that the depiction of Leia (and arguably of Padmé in the prequel trilogy) involves constructing her in terms of an essentializing symbolic. The refusal to sexualize Leia remains a refusal to adequately particularize her, as in the kind of liberal Cartesianism such as that animating the writings of Mary Wollstonecraft.[93] She represents woman, and this status thus opens the Leia-woman-device up to womanist critiques more attentive to historical and material considerations. Leia, then, may well be a part of "the figment of the 'generalized other' that dominates substantialist versions of universalism."[94] Such an interpretation suggests that there is a problematic other-blindness being enacted through George Lucas' universalizing move that makes Leia into a "woman-type," and this issue of race will need to be explored at more length in the following chapter.

## *"I think the Republic needs you" (Anakin,* AOTC*): Padmé, the Tragic Heroine*

While in Episodes IV-VI there remains a noticeable paucity of females among the heroic group of warriors, despite any virtues that may be evident in the characterization of Leia herself, this changes in *TPM*. Padmé's decoy attacks the Trade Federation in occupied Naboo Council chambers, a female pilot appears with a speaking part in the scene depicting the Naboo air force, and in *AOTC* and *ROTS* there are important female Jedi warriors.[95] While there is a real sense in which Leia is somewhat less than central to the main father-son story of the classic trilogy, Padmé Amidala is more integral to the prequels.

In "The Beginning: The Making of Episode I" Lucas specifically notifies his design staff: "Anakin [is] kind of duplicating ... [of] the Luke Skywalker role, but you see the echo of where it's all gonna go. Instead of destroying the Death Star he destroys the ship that controls the robots [viz., the Trade Federation battle droids]. Again it's like poetry, they rhyme. Every stanza rhymes with the last one."[96] The parallelism is not limited to Anakin and Luke, however. The prequels work hard to demonstrate the character likeness of Leia to her mother. So Padmé is portrayed as a self-confident character possessing real conviction, a political activist determinedly committed to justice, someone who possesses significant insight and practical political wisdom beyond her tender years, and one who exhibits a deep integrity and courage even when that involves risking her own life in the service of her task as in *TPM* and becoming the target of assassination attempts as in *AOTC*. When her life is in immediate jeopardy on Geonosis she responds to Count Dooku's demand that Naboo join the alliance of rebellious Separatist factions by displaying both personal valor and the stubborn courage of her convictions. Padmé counters with an uncompromising refusal: "I will not forsake all I have honored and worked for and betray the Republic." It is she who moves for swift action to solve the Naboo blockade crisis in *TPM*, and for the sake of the just representation and well-being of her sovereign people she refuses to follow the self-aggrandizing heel-dragging compromises of the senatorial politicians around her. "I will not watch my people suffer and die," she doggedly announces, "while you discuss this invasion in a committee."

There is something else that is significant in the depiction of her strength of personality. There has been something of a trend towards the muscular, *an echo of the male*, in certain Hollywood offerings—*Terminator 2*, *GI Jane*, even the *Alien* quadrilogy. The female body becomes not the figure of the power of human flourishing or the empowerment of the woman but her masculinization and thus the very erasure of the female body. Noticeably Lucas offers *self-confident female characters* with Leia and Padmé, and the former was a key leader in the Rebel Alliance considerably earlier (1977) than these other femuscular texts. Nonetheless, the boyishness of Leia (Lucas insisted the actress Carrie Fisher had her breasts taped down since there is "no sex in *Star Wars*") perhaps is an indication of the death-dealing violence she is involved in effecting. Likewise, when Padmé wields a weapon in *AOTC* she similarly appears in boyish attire (a moment in *TPM* might be an exception). There is, then, something of a gender destabilization occurring here, one that does not slip into romanticizing essentialist gender coding but, in fact, challenges the naturalization of this coding in such a fashion as to reveal its historicity, its emergence from a social and historical process of the contingent construction and discursive performance of gender differences and roles.[97] Moreover, another consequence may well be to echo a claim of Jantzen to the effect that "the incidence of *violence* is heavily showed to be male."[98] This observation would indeed make sense of Padmé's contestation of the naturalness of violence. As Jantzen suggests, "If women are very much less aggressive than men, then aggression cannot be a natural human instinct or innate to human nature. At most it could be argued that aggression is instinctive to *male* human nature." At her least visually masculine, Padmé is the voice of diplomacy, democratic conversation and reasonable nonviolence.

There are a number of features of Padmé's political work that are important to mention here. She serves as something of an inverted image of the self-interested ambition of Palpatine, the emerging power of the Republic, and she continually demonstrates the virtue of compassion in contradistinction to new Chancellor's philosophy which is gradually revealed to Anakin from the scene in the Coruscant Opera House onwards. Politically, she executes a Greek chorus-like commentary on the direction the Republic is taking while actively opposing the loss of democratic liberty when and where she can, including risking her own career in opposing the Chancellor during an intense time of galactic civil war. Padmé alone, without even the support of the Jedi Order which appears to be oblivious to the dark realities of contemporary political events, seems to be well-equipped to remain astutely suspicious of the swift drive to war, even when the Jedi fail to be sufficiently critically interrogative. In the complex political life of the last days of the Republic, we see Padmé's diplomatic sensibilities preventing her from rushing in with others to commend the growing militarism in *AOTC* and worries about the conduct of the war in *ROTS*—"This war," she insightfully announces to Anakin, "represents a failure to listen." In contrast, hers is the voice of reason, the voice of diplomacy, and the revelations in *ROTS* eventually suggest that her perspective is not only the most insightful over what has been occurring but is also perhaps the most morally astute.[99] And so we hear her urge the Republic's Senators, in a deleted scene from *AOTC*, to "wake up. ... If you offer the Separatists violence they can only show violence in return. Many will lose their lives, all will lose their freedom. I pray that you do not let fear push you into disaster. Vote down the security measure which is nothing less than a declaration of war." As Mary Wollstonecraft observes, women do not *by nature* "act as creatures of sensation and feeling rather than as rational beings," but only do so as a result of the social conditioning provided by a faulty education that results in women being reduced to "plumed and feathered birds" rather than as morally virtuous agents.[100] The young senator puts her own life on the line for the cause of a truthful and justly democratic peace, enduring several assassination attempts in *AOTC*. The feeling that she brings to the movies may provide something of the sensibility that Pollock discovers through interviewing Randall Kleiser, an actor in Lucas' early student film *Freiheit*: "Lucas disliked USC students who felt it necessary to die for one's country to defend democracy."[101] Arguably, she may even be, in many ways, the most compelling character in these movies as a result.

Nonetheless, Dominguez regards Lucas' treatment of women as having regressed from his subversion of the fairytale damsel to the Padmé of *ROTS*, the final chronological installment of Lucas' movie canon of the

*SW* franchise, terming it "an eerie parallel to ... [an] adolescent loss of self."[102] The issue for this particular commentator is that Padmé's feisty outspokenness meant that "the unravelling and disintegration of her spirited character in *Episode III* was not only a disappointment, but smacked of betrayal as well." She is reduced to a weepy stereotype of a woman coming undone. As Veronica Wilson argues, "the Padmé of *Revenge of the Sith* seems to have lost her forceful personality and much of her independent intelligence ... [as she] becomes passive and ineffectual."[103] "I felt catapulted back into the world of traditional fairy tales and medieval romances where damsels wasted away and died of broken hearts, pale and weepy, unable to live for themselves if their knights abandoned them. The tracking shot of Padmé's funeral procession and casket brings to mind Sir Thomas Malory's and Alfred, Lord Tennyson's tale of Elaine of Astolat/Lady of Shallot, the beautiful maiden who dies of a broken heart after being rejected by Sir Lancelot and floats down the river to Camelot in a flower-strewn boat."[104]

This, Dominguez, continues, means that "she can thus be read as an alarming reflection of the complex, confusing, and contradictory messages today's young women receive from society and the media."[105]

There are three main concerns commentators admit to in this regard. Firstly, there is the fact of the erosion of a powerful female character. The difficulty is that this is, while the drama is emotionally difficult to watch, as it should be given the prequels' narration in the form of tragic drama. Her disintegration is precisely the point—it is tragic, and that is to be expected given the narrative trajectory of the prequels.[106] Reading the classic trilogy as tragic drama indicates why it is that young Anakin on whom so many hopes rest, who displays immense potential and even generosity of character, so slips into the violence of a situation controlled by the political puppet-master. Given the close relationships of passion and trust between Anakin and Padmé, the latter is drawn unforgivingly and fatally into the unfolding disaster. The profoundly talented and virtuous young woman becomes more sinned against than sinning, to cite Lear's self-referential words, a victim of circumstances largely beyond her control. Padmé becomes a victim of the tragedy, and her independent strength is sapped as she slips from determination into the moral emaciation of despair once she observes everything she has fought for crashing down around her, including her relationship with Anakin. To lament this feature of the narrative is to capitulate to the voluntarist naïveté that pervades earlier constructivist forms of feminist subjectivity founded on the modern liberal subject as agential free and spontaneous. Such a perspective has to be problematized, de-situated and transgressed by something more attentive to the more complex interplay of agency and the framing determination of agency. The unraveling of Padmé under the overwhelming pressure of neo-totalitarian violence may well provide a critical politico-cultural comment on the rise of trenchant and highly visible forms of patriarchal muscle-flexing masculinity in the contemporary Western world.

Secondly, the role of Padmé's complicity in Anakin's growing compulsiveness troubles Wilson. According to this particular commentator, for example, Padmé is actually to be blamed for Anakin's "excesses insofar as she makes virtually no attempt to counter them."[107] What does this mean? After all, Padmé criticizes Anakin's articulations of his ambitions in her quarters on Coruscant, and she listens to his grief stricken rage at the death of his mother on Tatooine. In the earlier scene Anakin begins to express his pain about his desires: "Something's happening. I'm not the Jedi I should be. I want more, and I know I shouldn't." His wife attempts to console him: "You expect too much of yourself." Immediately following the destruction of the Jedi Temple, and realizing that something terrible has just occurred, in fearful and personally helpless concern she asks Anakin at her senatorial home what had been happening. The story he tells that she finds difficult to believe is that the Jedi had attempted a political *coup d'état*. Yet she has no substantial reason to doubt her husband's interpretation of what he had seen concerning Master Windu's attempted assassination of the Chancellor, and of his expressions of threefold loyalty to the Republic, the Chancellor, and her. It is quite difficult to see what else Padmé could or should do, especially given both the young Jedi's occasional privacy (so his wife appears unaware of the unhealthy hold Palpatine is coming to have over him) and her own business as a senator. The viewer must be very careful of imposing on the characters a "god's eye" form of spectatorial perspective that is privileged to her gaze.

In the fateful scene on Mustafar Padmé confronts her husband about the stories Obi-Wan has been telling about Anakin's slaughter of Jedi Younglings and his turn to the Dark Side. She refuses to succumb to his assertions about power as the way to protect her. "I don't believe what I'm hearing. Obi-Wan was right. You've changed. ... I don't know you anymore. Anakin, you've breaking my heart. You're going down a path I can't follow ... because of what you've done, what you plan to do. Stop, stop now. Come back." Wilson, however, finds this final speech to Anakin in *ROTS* a particularly problematic one: "This speech is so out of character for the once-strong-willed senator Amidala that the audience almost invariably titters or winces in dismay."[108] In shock the young woman pleads with the emotionally disturbed young Jedi Knight. This is a man she loves deeply, and she offers him a moral mirror in order to curb his burgeoning destructive desires.

Until this point we have seen little of Padmé private life and so we simply do not know how she relates to the people she genuinely and intimately loves. There is a danger not only of speculative overextension of the material but of projectionism in the commentator's criticism of her relationship to Anakin. Certainly the ability of Lucas to portray young people in love in a realistic fashion, and to write meaningful romantic dialogue, has been legitimately questioned. Yet it is quite another matter to complain that the self-confident woman becomes vulnerable in her most intimate and personally determinative relationship. To begin with, there is a strange and quite disturbing understanding of any relationship if it does not involve real *vulnerability* of one to another, or a *mutuality* of self-givingness that displaces and transforms autonomy (even if Anakin, for his part, does become abusive in *ROTS*, a all too realistic story). The *SW* saga's portrayal of persons-in-relation and of flourishing as occurring then in fruitful mutual dependence (in contrast with the representation of the destructive instrumentalization of life among the colonializing Sith and Empire) resists the anthropological reduction of subjectivity to the modern post–Enlightenment mode of the ontologically atomized and pre-social self. As with Leia's impact on the reformation of Han, Padmé's relation to Anakin contests the isolationist essentialism of any pre-relational construal of selfhood by being bound up in responsibility to "the other." Moreover, we have, in fact, seen nothing of Padmé's psychology, and there is always the slim possibility that her frosty exterior is a psychological projection that masks real need. If this is a possible psychological route, then the issue would be less of Lucas' failures with *AOTC* than with his failure to provide a significantly developed insight into Padmé's psychology in Episodes I-II.

Having little sense of how tragic drama works Wilson laments that Padmé "seems unwilling or unable to resist becoming a victim of Anakin's growing obsessive madness and gradual fall to the dark side."[109] It is difficult to know what to do with such a criticism. In what way is Cordelia morally responsible for King Lear's madness and her victimization at the hands of her unscrupulous sisters? Can Othelia be held accountable in any straightforward way for the impending collapse of Hamlet? One of Wilson's particularly alarming arguments sees her criticizing Lucas for *blaming* Shmi and Padmé for Anakin's problematic emotional health, akin to blaming Cordelia for Lear's eruption, for instance. The first stage of the accusation refers to Shmi Skywalker: "Lucas posits this loving mother-son relationship, strangely enough, as a primary cause or source of events that will gradually transform Anakin Skywalker into the terrifying Sith Lord Darth Vader."[110] Anakin has been separated from his mother, at an age that Yoda and Mace Windu worry is beyond an age that will not cause psychological damage. Naturally, the child in *TPM* feels understandable separation anxiety, a fear over loss which intensifies as he grows without being able to fulfill his promise to return and free his mother from slavery. He had been unable to keep this pledge, and the resultant heavy feeling of culpability was intensified further by the fact that his mother had even put the burden of responsibility on his very young shoulders: "Anakin, this path has been placed before you. The choice is yours alone." Also, rightly or wrongly, he comes over the next few years to blame and gradually resent the Jedi Order itself for this preventing him from rescuing her. This is the reason why he turns his rage against Obi-Wan and the Order in the aftermath of his mother's death. The dreams of his mother suffering and dying have made matters worse. How can this not psychologically not deeply scar and torture an adolescent, and leave him susceptible to the direction of a seemingly benevolent Palpatine? What any recognition of these features cannot do, therefore, is lead to the kind of simple blame game that lays causal responsibility at the feet of the Anakin-Shmi relationship in any straightforward fashion. Wilson's is unfortunately an idiosyncratic reading that Procrusteanly reduces a complex set of conditions down to one, a simplistic one.

In fact, while this is a crucial element in shaping Anakin's emotional development, it is nonetheless only one factor leading towards his tragic *hamartia* and *metabole*. By the time of *AOTC* Anakin has become a more complex figure than the boy of ten years earlier, although he was crucially the neurotically intensified product of the loves and desires of that child. The flaws lie deep within his person-forming soul. Thus while Anakin's fall into the dark side (his "Sithing," so to speak) may seem abrupt to many viewers of *ROTS* it has been a long time in the making. Significantly, he is now even rather ominously wearing darker colored robes than his Jedi kin. Speaking of the nineteen-year-old Anakin Lucas summarizes: "In this film, you begin to see that he has a fear of losing things, a fear of losing his mother, and as a result, he wants to begin to control things, he wants to become powerful, and these are not Jedi traits. And part of these are because he was starting to be trained so late in life, that he'd already formed these attachments. And for a Jedi, attachment is forbidden."[111] Yoda portentously warns Anakin of this in *ROTS*. Elsewhere, Lucas reveals that an unhealthy form of "attachment" "makes you greedy. And when you're greedy, you are on the path to the dark side, because you fear you're going to lose things, that you're not going to have the power you need."[112] In other words, the problems lie in Anakin's own emotional formation, and there are multiple contributors to it. It is imprudent to claim, as Wilson does, that *AOTC* "takes a dramatically misogynist turn, blaming both Padmé and Shmi for Anakin's violent possessive emotions and his subsequent blatant betrayal of Jedi rules and values."[113] It is precisely the possessive love of Anakin that is unable to truly requite Padmé's eventual care for him that has such catastrophic consequences, a possessiveness that is revealed in a scene on the transport cruiser in *AOTC*.

What we are treated to in the grief scene on Tatooine in *AOTC* is the way Anakin's anger, guilt, resentment and sorrow, all growing out of his attachment to his mother, take on a new form. In his anguish he claims to desire the power over life and death, the power to be able to "fix" life in the same way that he can exercise technical expertise over machinery. He simply refuses to listen to Padmé's caution. Here is an early indication that Anakin can mechanistically reduce others' lives to the status of *things*, notably echoing the instrumentalizing disregard for the independent lives of others that is characteristic of the way of the Sith.

Anakin painfully verbalizes that he "should be" all-powerful, and he then threateningly expresses a new-found determination "that some day I will be. I will be the most powerful Jedi ever. I promise you. I will even learn to stop people from dying." This is not merely his "grief talking" since a little later, when in a calmer frame of mind, he promises at his mother's graveside: "I wasn't strong enough to save you, mom. I wasn't strong enough. But I promise I won't fail again." He imagines that the solution is one of sheer power and brute force as well as technical skill. The spirit of the Sith-way is already directing Anakin's consciousness, and is dramatically fulfilled later when—after dreaming of Padmé dying in childbirth—he moves to secure the *power* he thinks is necessary for her safety from the scheming Palpatine/Sidious [*ROTS*]. He proclaims to Padmé that "love won't save you Padmé, only my new powers can do that." His wife despairingly asks, "But at what cost?" That Anakin has not given much consideration to. Instead, his response is to possessively assert his power: "I won't lose you the way I lost my mother. I am becoming more powerful than any Jedi has ever dreamed of, and I'm doing it for you, to protect you." The themes of vicious rage fuelled by guilt and grief, and arrogant adolescent resentment of his mentor literally combine melodiously. An inconsolable Anakin spits out his fury-filled diatribe two musical motifs are detectable—those associated with both Darth Sidious and Darth Vader.

Wilson, however, supports her claim through reference to a scene in which Padmé deflects Anakin's romantic attentions with reference to their vocations, but nonetheless being suggestively attired in an arousing skin-tight, strapless, and cleavage bearing dress in the style of a *femme fatale*. Clearly Padmé, despite her ideals, is attracted to Anakin, and somewhat emotionally torn between pure political duty and erotic desire, just as the Jedi Padawan is torn between his monastic oath and his desire for the senator from Naboo. Again, however, while this could, at most, encourage the flowering of Anakin desires for the young woman it certainly does not *cause* his destructive neuroses, determine his catastrophic choices under the guidance of the self-aggrandizing plotting of the tempter, or force him to lose control of his Jedi instincts in eruptive bursts of violent fury. Wilson's description sounds perilously close to the blaming of the victim for the victimizer's action, and that would be a disturbing turn for a feminist reading. She makes at least a more sensible sounding point when announcing that "it seems as if much of Anakin's rage stems from his resentment over the 'control' Padmé exerts over him without even intending to—to problematic and potentially 'castrating' force of his emotional dependence upon her. Thus he tends to blame her, in the long run, for his own turn to darkness."[114] Yet there simply does not appear to be any evidence for this. Anakin's rage at his wife in the texts derives more from his fear of losing her—not only through death in childbirth, but through some deep-seated insecurity that imagines in *ROTS* Obi-Wan to be a love threat.

Wilson is indeed right that "Anakin's fraught relationships with these two women lie at the heart of his growing darkness and willful, knowing betrayal of Jedi precepts and values."[115] However, she draws problematic conclusions from the textual materials. It is not Anakin's appropriate desires *for the females* that cause his fall but the utterly *inappropriate form* of his desires for the females—his possessive, grasping, and ultimately self-absorbed desires which reflect an emotional immaturity and a distortion of the proper desire for the other as other. As Irigaray warns, "The will to possess you corresponds to a solitary and solipsistic dream which forgets that your consciousness and mine do not obey the same necessities."[116] Therefore, she continues, "in a conception of sexuality centered upon instinct, drives, affect, the partners ... come to be defined as either haves or have-nots of corporeal 'objects' capable of producing and experiencing *jouissance*. They are no longer considered subjects. Interpreted in such an instrumental manner, sexuality is left uncultivated, or rather, assimilated to a *technē* which does not take intersubjectivity into account."[117] In the monastic context Anakin's desires cannot mature, and it is this that has led to Lucas' indication that the post–*ROTJ* New Jedi Order changes the form of rule of Jedi nonattachment—so that Jedi Younglings can remain at home for longer, and that they are permitted to marry (for instance, in some versions of the New Jedi Order stories Luke marries Mara Jade).[118] If the scholarly value of Lucas' hints and suggestions that have subsequently been developed in the Expanded Universe materials does not convince Wilson, then two simple textual elements should give pause for thought: firstly, the fruit of Anakin's desires, his progeny, are "the new hopes"; and secondly, the prequels indicate that many of the Jedi's practices lead to their complacency and contribute to their fall.

Fatefully, Wilson's critical commentary inadequately neglects the importance to the impending tragic fall of three particular sets of relationships. Firstly, the developing father-sonlike bonding between Palpatine and the young Jedi. Ian McDiarmid interestingly comments that "if you wanted a subtitle for these movies it could be 'Fathers and Sons.' And while Palpatine isn't, we must assume, Anakin's natural father in this film [viz. *ROTS*] he is certainly a father-figure for him."[119] Secondly, Anakin's lurking suspicions of the Jedi High Council. Thirdly, the youth's intense resentment of his Jedi tutor: "It's all Obi-Wan's fault! ... He's holding me back!" Not only does Anakin's tragic turn to the Dark Side not emerge from a vacuum, there are a host of complex causal factors involved that cannot be summed up in any simple way, as Wilson has done, and certainly not in terms of blaming the two women in Anakin's life. With hindsight we can say that the processes and activities involved in Anakin's training by his trainers, just as much as in the boy's being trained, contribute to the looming tragedy and the emotional mess that Anakin ends up in. Anakin's is, as Jeffrey Overstreet sympathetically remarks, something of an understandable fall into wickedness: "We can't help but sympathize with Anakin as he surrenders to the Dark Side. Lo and behold, Darth Vader did not strive to be a heartless villain. He became one by trying to protect the one he loved, going blind to the greater good in the process. The stakes are finally high enough to earn gasps, and the ensuing tragedy is almost Shakespearean. ... Anakin isn't just arrogant; he's reacting to a seeming lack of trust, care, and compassion from the Jedi Council."[120]

To the suggestion that Padmé was not privy to her young husband's troubles Wilson complains that "she also seems completely unaware of how thoroughly Anakin is being seduced by the blandishment of Supreme Chancellor Palpatine."[121] So Wilson asserts that "never ... does Padmé warn Anakin about Palpatine's possible hidden agenda or suggest that the Chancellor may be using the Jedi Knight for his own sinister purposes."[122] This is another textually unjustifiable claim, however. Certainly the young senator opposes Palpatine's growing power, but there is little indication of the Chancellor's political machinations until a startling revelation to Anakin in his chambers. Padmé herself had been unwittingly manipulated by him in *TPM*, and it was she who aided in his election to the position of Chancellor by virtue of calling for a vote of no confidence in Valorum. When the most insightful and prescient of the all characters, Jedi Master Yoda, finally confronts the self-proclaimed Emperor he enters the room saying, "I hear a new apprentice you have, Emperor, or should I call you Darth Sidious?" It is for this reason that Obi-Wan explains the terrible recent events and Anakin's succumbing to the Dark Side by admitting that "he was deceived by a lie. We all were. It appears that the Chancellor is behind everything, including the war." The revelation climaxes with Obi-Wan's taking a couple of steps towards Padmé and sincerely elucidating that "Palpatine is the Sith Lord we've been looking for. After the death of Count Dooku Anakin became his new apprentice." The fallen Jedi's wife turns away with words of disbelief, but her body language suggests that she is not going to protest too much—after all, Obi-Wan is a trusted figure—and she admits "I can't" believe you.

On the other hand, a third complaint centers on Padmé's death as a result of the injured woman giving up life. Given the subject matter it is dealing with (the material that predates *ANH*) Lucas has to find some way of disposing of Padmé (just as, at time of writing, the *Clone Wars* animation series has finished without finding a way of removing Asajj Ventress and Ashoka Tano, possibly even Captain Rex of the Legion of the 501st). Of course, the question remains as to whether the movie did this dramatically well, and this is indeed a good question. It is distinctly arguable that there is something dramatically very flat about the directorial decisions concerning the way in which Padmé dies, something rather unrealistic, especially when one considers her assertion to Obi-Wan that "there is still good in him" which, if it is to be something more than a vain counterfactual whistling in the wind, sounds like it is the kind of thing that should give her hope. Padmé's death is largely, then, a plot device in the tragic drama. The form that it takes is chiefly a symbolic gesture that cleverly and quite beautifully (in a stylistic, rather than a narrative, sense) enables death (and one which has just given life) to be juxtaposed with the scene of "life" (in which Vader's "life" is constructed and imprisoned, a sort of living death). Saying that, of course, is still quite different from claiming that Padmé's death itself is beautiful or romantic. Dominguez, however, astutely recognizes the moral difficulties involved in the depiction of her succumbing to despair and then death. "Throughout *Episode III*, she is focused mostly on Anakin's needs, almost to the exclusion of the problems of the Republic and completely to the exclusion of her own compromised career and status."[123] This way of putting matters is not quite appropriate, however, since there are several occasions when she appears in her political role, albeit one interesting scene that witnesses the birth of the Rebel Alliance had been cut from the theatrical release of the movie. Lucas has certainly not helped his case by deleting this scene which indicates Padmé's and Mon Mothma's leading roles in giving birth, along with Bail Organa, to the Rebel Alliance. But the writing and filming of these, at least, subvert Wilson's claim that Lucas "has created a patriarchal political system in which human males are fully in charge and other sorts of beings unimportant or expendable."[124] However, for the sake of pacing the director deemed it unnecessary, and such pacing considerations *only make sense if the material has been considered unnecessary to the flow of the movie, and that is particularly the case if the material has been covered elsewhere.* In contrast, it remains important to retain scenes depicting Padmé's anguish in order to indicate how far she succumbs to despair, to indicate her humanity, and to suggest the intensity of the passionate commitment of the lovers to each other. Furthermore, while Padmé is indeed domesticated she is not *purely* domesticated. She remains a recognizable political figure whose significance is mitigated by the rising power of Palpatine. Wilson's reading also takes a particularly eccentric turn at this point, bizarrely equating Sidious with witchcraft, and logically leaping further to note that that has predominantly been associated with women. This leap, therefore, enables her to regard the Jedi-Sith conflict as one between Christianity and paganism (this might be broadly arguable if for no other reason than some Christians boycott *SW* for involving a conflict between black and white magic). Sidious at the moment of Vader's rebuilding appears to this critic like "an aged, withered crone" rather than, more appropriately, an image of a cowl-wearing Death who is styled on Ingmar Bergman's *Seventh Seal*.[125]

The moral trouble that Dominguez has with the form Padmé's death takes has to do with its apparent irresponsibility. "Her death is both a supreme form of martyrdom ... and a supreme form of selfishness."[126] With this Wilson agrees: "Padmé chooses her personal pain over her political duty, placing self-centered emotional distress above all other considerations. ... Lucas chooses to have her embrace a selfish and needless martyrdom and perish."[127] In a sense it is a manifestly worrying criticism since it does not sense the collapse of Padmé's world around her—the Republic has fallen, the Jedi have been slaughtered and their Order lies in ruins, the responsibility for this falls heavily on the shoulders of the man she is lovingly devoted to, and she too has become a victim of his murderously violent rage. The events are traumatic. Is it any wonder that she despairs? Where the issue of irresponsibility may well stick, however, is in the fact that two infant lives are now going to be left motherless.

## *Conclusion*

Vivian Sobchack claims that "despite all their 'futuristic' gadgetry and special effects ... the *Star Trek* films [of the 1970s and 80s] are conservative and nostalgic, imagining the future by looking backward to the imagination of a textual past."[128] Science fiction in general has been a male dominated genre, and the ways it constructs and represents gender can express a nostalgia for gender coding and gendered flows of power in favor of male domination. Yet, according to Patricia Melzer, "significantly, it is within science-fiction film and literature—a genre usually understood to be predominantly male, that we seem to reimagine gender relations most radically."[129] With the space operas of George Lucas, however, the issue of gender has been particularly noticed by, and remained controversial among, numerous commentators. There had, of course, been a disagreement over the planned ending of Lucas' 1973 movie *American Graffiti*, with the male-only conclusion leading him to be accused of male chauvinism by influential film critic Pauline Kael.[130] Lucas vehemently disputed this on the grounds of cinematic pragmatism: "It's a movie about the four guys." According to Pollock, for instance, "Lucas vehemently rejects the chauvinist label—it upsets and hurts him. He does not go around saying that the female of the species is inferior, and he has given women more management positions than most Hollywood studios."[131] In an interview in September of 1977 the director of *SW* revealed something very significant concerning how the redirecting of his vision of the heroine was forced upon him by the criticisms of others: "The first version [of the script] talked about a princess and an old general. The second version involved a father, his son, and his daughter; the daughter was the heroine of the film. Now the daughter has become Luke, Mark Hamill's character. There was also the story of two brothers where I transformed one of them into a sister. The older brother was imprisoned, and the young sister had to rescue him and bring him back to their dad. But this posed some horrible problems. Nobody would believe it, it wasn't realistic at all."[132]

SW's intertextual references to the likes of the *Flash Gordon* serial adventures and to the swashbuckling and Arthurian legends certainly display a nostalgic cinematic appeal. However, in this context, the envisioning of Leia is a move with no little radical possibility, contesting, among other things, the power-relations and ideological constructions of specifiable gender differences common to pulp science fiction. Here is an act of what Darko Suvin has famously called the operation of cognitive estrangement that provides a critical reflection on contemporary sociopolitical orders.

Nevertheless, by no stretch of the imagination can Lucas' subsequent *SW* saga be called a "feminist text" or a racially emancipatory text, or to adapt Edith Wyschogrod's term a "saintly" text.[133] For good or ill, its energies clearly are too focused elsewhere. "Ultimately," Cavelos stridently maintains, "Leia is unconvincing both as an action hero nor as a passive victim. The coherence of her character has been sacrificed to the story and the male characters."[134] However, that rather intellectually uninteresting observation does not necessarily entail that it can be easily read as an inscription of patriarchalism (Dominguez), and even more disturbingly "misogyny" (Wilson), or at least not in the straightforward terms characteristic of the criticism that has been leveled at it. So Merlock and Jackson argue in contrast that while "*Star Wars* can obviously be classified as updated, boy-oriented space opera ... the well-executed presence of Leia meant the inclusion of a strong female character in the midst of the blossoming feminist movement."[135] As a result, *SW* may well be considerably more ambiguous in its moral depiction, both reflecting and simultaneously displacing and challenging the filmic conventions and values dominating the ideological landscape and reforming the ideological gaze of audience expectation, than these critics care to observe. Of course, this is not to necessarily disagree on a narrative level with Cavelos' criticism that the female characters are distinctly underdeveloped, and that particular character flaws "increase until eventually they drain all strength, coherence and believability out of her [viz., Leia]."[136]

Nonetheless, the time has come for commentators to resist the seemingly self-perpetuating textbook mistake that the saga has no "moral ambiguity" but presents "straightforward, innocent and fresh-faced heroics," to refuse the oversimplifying and generalizing readings of the text as straightforwardly culturally and politically conservative in their nostalgia, and to attend more concretely to the subtleties and nuances of the texts in order to identify more specifically what is ideologically problematic about them.[137] There is real danger in investing Leia and Padmé's characterizations with burdensome symbolic significance, a move that can imperil any attempt to de-essentialize the separationism involved in gender opposition. In other words, too much weight is placed on the shoulders of the two leading female characters, and this is the result of an imagination that construes them too neatly in terms of being representations, of being types of "woman" in a move that some consequently compresses multiple forms of engendered performance into a singularly essentialist depiction.

On the other hand, there is potential for providing a more progressive reading in observing the way alienating forms of alterity work in these cinematic texts. Booker, for instance, recognizes the way in which the *SW* movies' binarism functions, not in terms of race or gender in any essentialist moment of opposition. "To a large extent, the opposition in [the classic trilogy of] Star Wars is couched not in terms of East vs. West [or, male vs. female, white vs. non-white, or human vs. non-human], but of human (the rebels) vs. inhuman (the Empire)."[138] The movies trade on unmasking unhealthy forms of social organization and of the determinative desires in ways disturbing of the politics of "self-interest." It is Palpatine who is, and who remains, an unredeemed character, most closely slipping into a modified form of binary coding between Jedi and Sith, culturally negotiated as perversely self-interested and self-aggrandizing (even to the point of assassinating his former Sith master, Darth Plagueis the Wise, and demonstrating the expendability of his own apprentices Darth Maul, Darth Tyrannus and Darth Vader). With the depiction of the Trade Federation, *TPM*, moreover, expresses something of the contemporary concern with the objectives and undemocratic means used by large corporations in reordering political relations and conditions in the absence of old-fashioned military colonialism.[139] In Booker's account there is an admission of the metaphoricity of the imagery used for the "evil" in the trilogy: "Emperor Palpatine, looking somewhat like the grim reaper with his darkhoodedly cadaverous visage, seems anything but human. Darth Vader, the most prominent villain in the original three Star Wars films, has literally lost his humanity: as announced by the signature whooshing of his mechanical respirator, he is in fact mostly machine, the majority of his body replaced by mechanical parts. Even all those legions of imperial storm troopers, who are presumably human, seem inhuman because of the armor they wear, making it more acceptable to have them serve in the film largely as cannon fodder."

Booker, however, draws the wrong ontological conclusion from this, claiming that "this human vs. inhuman structure represents an us vs. them mentality that reinforces the good vs. evil polarity of the film. However, it also makes the seemingly clear moral message of the film somewhat problematic in that it tends to send an almost subliminal suggestion that those who are like us are good, while those who are unlike us are evil."[140] Despite being composed in the aftermath of the release of the prequels, and certainly with a number of years of hindsight available after Episodes V-VI—even, in fact, in the form of their Special Editions of 1997—Booker's derivative analysis conservatively perpetuates the stereotypical "Manichaean" reading of the saga. His analysis fails to account for the tragic thematic in the Vader character, and therefore the fact that "evil" does not come from nowhere or have substantive form beyond the distorted desires formed by habituated action and ignorance. As a result *SW* does not support and maintain exclusionary forms of identifiable Othering, configurations of power through subjectivities formed by biological essentialisms, although *ANH* does come the closest to so doing. Reading *SW* in this way as a utopian attempt to envisage patterns of equitable relations, friendships and sociality as culturally positioned as transgressively liberated from, and reconfiguring of, exclusionary relations based on racial, gender and economic arrangements generates interesting possibilities.

In a haste borne from, among other things, an alacrity to attending to certain complicating elements within the saga, overdetermined readings are insufficiently sensitive to the deep ideological investments that pressure the "natural" and its subversion. Given the weight of reader concern with the ideological constraints of the *SW* movies and the layered ideologically transformative contention provided by the progress of the narrative itself, particularly in relation to the projections of alterity onto non-human (especially mechanical) characters, makes the texts sites of ideological contention and produces contradictory effects, including overdetermined ideological projectionisms on the part of the reader. Peter Krämer observes that in a poll conducted by Michael Ryan and Douglas Kellner in 1986 about half of the respondents understood *SW*'s Empire in general terms "as an embodiment of evil," as opposed to 24 percent who viewed it as representing right-wing dictators, and 12 percent who read it as representing communism. Krämer comments, "This poll suggests, then, that audiences were not only willing to attach political meanings to this science-fiction fairy tale but did so according to their own political beliefs, drawing on both historical precedents and current events."[141] To claim that *SW* is racist and/or sexist or not is to say as much, then, about the politics of the reader's gaze. And the multiplication of critical commentary from any given perspective is frequently a sign of the cultural conditioning of viewing as well as the typical cloning of perspectives and arguments that then become reinforcing by repetition. What it does not do, fortunately, is to evacuate the texts of their potential not only to exhilarate but fascinate.

# 4

# "We don't serve *their* kind here!"
## Star Wars *and the Politics of Difference*

In Kenneth Branagh's Shakespearian-like foray into the superhero genre with *Thor* (2011) one scene offers a conversation between the New Mexico based scientists which draws a contrast between "science fiction" and "science fact." The underlying assumption can be utilized to suggest that the genre of science-fiction is largely an imaginatively predictive genre, a narrativist use of a form of futurology.[1] In contrast, H.G. Wells once articulated the relation between science-fiction literature and the future in a quite different way. He claimed that "the fantastic, the strange property or strange world, is only used to throw up and intensify our natural reactions of wonder, fear or perplexity. ... The thing that makes such imaginations interesting is their translation into commonplace terms."[2] In this case, it is observable that science-fiction has often functioned as thought-experiment, a "revealing cognitive disjunction" from contemporaneity. In so doing it offers a different version of reality (even a different universe, or time) from that which we know and experience as everyday. But it does this as a way of asking socio-political questions about our sense of experienceable reality. So Keith Booker concludes his study by claiming that "SF films have provided the popular imagination with some of its most compelling visions of both the possibilities and the dangers of a future increasingly dominated by advanced technologies." This might enable the genre to operate as a thought-experiment related, for instance, to the consequences of certain technological developments, offering cautionary tales about their abuse much in the manner of Mary Shelley's highly lauded work *Frankenstein*. In this regard the technoscepticism of James Cameron's *The Terminator* provides a recent instance. It trades on a problematization of technology at several points, although arguably the disaster it designs is not so much a result of technology in and of itself as of the decisions taken concerning it, and what it makes of persons. According to Constance Penley, "in one of the film's most pointed gestures toward the unintentionally harmful effects of technology, the police psychiatrist fails to see the Terminator entering the station when his beeper goes off and distracts him just as their paths cross."[3] This ambiguity of hybridization is indicated by Forest Pyle who claims that Sarah Connor's act of crushing the Terminator means "she gets to make good on what the film has constructed as our collective desire to crush the threatening technological other. ... *The Terminator* is in this sense about the reassertion of sheer and absolute human agency, 'the triumph of the will.'"[4] The point is not so much that the movie exhibits a Luddite sensibility as much as it longs for a limiting of that which accentuates the sense of a runaway world, a world out of control and enhancing the prospects of the annihilation of human life.

That construal of technology, of course, is far from all that science-fiction is involved in doing, and its frequent political implications are pronounced. In fact, a study of the post-human, of the notion of the fluidity of identity in non-essentialistic anthropologies, for instance, would pay particular attention to the construal of "Otherness" in these texts. On saying that, however, the genre has frequently been overlooked as a source of socio-political critique, offering instead the awe of gazing on the visual astonishment of the spectacular dimension of human self-imagining. According to numerous critics, American cinema, particularly that produced and controlled by the Hollywood entertainment industry, exudes a politically conservative temperament. The shadow of Theodor Adorno and Max Horkheimer looms large over the political reception of the culture of the cinema.

To read science fiction in a politically interrogative mode, then (and not merely as expressions of dominant cultural trends), is to offer something of a form of reading resistance. Booker, for instance, provides a useful allusion to the important work of Darko Suvin: "Perhaps more importantly, such films, despite being widely regarded as mere entertainments, have often provided serious and thoughtful explorations of important contemporary social and political issues. ... While the estrangement from reality provided by the projected worlds of science fiction might make the political messages of SF film seem less threatening to some, that very estrangement also helps to provide new perspectives from which audiences can look at the world in which they live, potentially bringing into focus aspects of that world that might otherwise be less clear."[5]

The suggestions here are that science-fiction products, despite their commercial form, can be resistant or politically radicalizing texts. In this regard, the constrictions provided by the commodified massification of culture so important to Adorno's critique of the culture industry, or the predictability of the science-fiction genre announced by Susan Sontag, are subtly transcended.[6] To cite Scott Bukatman, "Science fiction ... has ... served as a vehicle for satire, social criticism and aesthetic estrangement. ... By positing a world that behaves differently—whether physically or socially—from this one, our world is denaturalised. ... What science fiction offers, in [Frederic] Jameson's words, is 'the estrangement and renewal of our own reading present.'"[7]

Elsewhere I have already had reason to contest the claim to liberation in *The Matrix*, for instance, although I provided a rather underdeveloped hint that something quite different emerges from Ridley Scott's *Blade Runner* and even from George Lucas' *THX 1138*.[8] Continuing the considerations of ideology and violence, indeed of violence-sustaining ideologies, that were at issue in the opening two chapters of this book, critical reflection cannot escape from a set of claims that identify crucial difficulties with the representation of otherness in Lucas' *SW*. The political importance of the issues hardly needs to be stated, since as Kevin Wetmore argues, "in the innocence of childhood are the seeds for a dark future of Othering, oppression, appropriation and imperialism ... because of stereotypes and models of oppression built into popular culture."[9] After all, outlooks and perspectives are not inbuilt but received, learned, and negotiated. As Kenneth Surin avers, "There is ... no such thing as a 'pure' politics existing only in and for itself. Every kind of politics is a politics motivated and driven by some regnant ideological notion of the nature and scope of the political."[10] In particular, it is driven by some notion of who one is in relation to others.

Recent years have seen a proliferation of the figure and presence of the alien in cinema, from *Contact*, the *Men in Black* trilogy, the redesigned *The Day the Earth Stood Still*, the *Transformers* series, *John Carter on Mars*, *Monsters*, *Skyline*, *Battlefield Los Angeles*, *The Darkest Hour*, and *Robot Overlords*, to the comedies *Paul*, *The World's End* or *Alien Autopsy*, and the horror of *Area 51*, *Apollo 13* and *Alien Abduction*, to name but a few. So Heidi Kaye and I.Q. Hunter observe that "the alien, in the very sense of the word, has become central to popular culture."[11] What has been noticeable has been the shift towards a reactive politics of fear and subsequent exclusion with the image of the alien as threatening Other in or in movies such as *Cowboys Versus Aliens*, with the *Alien* franchise's crossover with the *Predator* series and with its prequel *Prometheus*; and the appeal of the proliferation of alien invasion narratives such as in the parody of 1950s alien movies in *Mars Attacks!*, *Independence Day*, the revamped classic *War of the Worlds*, even the *Avengers*; as well as a substantial presence in television series like *Invasion*, and the more recent *Falling Skies* and *The Whispers*; and so on. Kaye and Hunter observe about the shift from alien visitation to invasion motifs, "When a gung-ho Will Smith announced in *Independence Day* ... that he couldn't wait to 'whup E.T.'s ass,' he cheekily dispelled any lingering affection for our friends from outer space." It is just such a motif that is parodied by *Mars Attacks!* For Kaye and Hunter, this shift in narrative depiction of the alien serves as a sign of a shifting political culture, of "popular culture's hardening of attitudes towards 'aliens' of all descriptions." They continue by observing that "sci-fi has returned with anarchic glee to the 1950s' paranoid injunction to 'keep watching the skies.'"[12] In fact, *Falling Skies* and *The Whispers* come at a time when the paranoia of the *X-Files*, or even Spielberg's *Taken* or *The 4400*, has been played out in considerably less subtle ways in conflictually xenophobic settings for science-fiction dramas like *Fringe* and the colonistically themed *V*. While it is certainly an overstatement given those depicted as co-operating with the humans in these dramas, and of the reappearance of the benign alien in movies like *Earth to Echo*, what emerges, to some degree at least, is the sensibility that "the only good alien is a dead alien."[13] Nonetheless, at least in one sense these cultural critics observe a marked difference from the 1950s. Without mentioning the Othering of the Middle East and the paranoia over the-terrorist-within that has become a staple of many a political drama (such as television's *Homeland* and *Spooks*, or the movie *The Siege*), they notice the post–Cold War desire for an enemy: "their aliens no longer seem to stand for anything. Instead of metaphors for invading Communists and the dangers of conformism, they are simply and conveniently 'other'—all purpose outsiders against which the warring chaos of American identities can muster and unite." As mentioned earlier in this book, Paul Verhoeven, the director of *Starship Troopers*, asserts that "the US is desperate for a new enemy. ... The Communists were the enemy, and the Nazis before them, but now that wonderful enemy everyone can fight has been lost. Alien sci-fi gives us a terrifying enemy that's politically correct. They're bad. They're evil. And they're not even human."[14] Verhoeven's lack of irony in using the phrase "politically correct" with regard to such an use of terms for the alien such as "enemy" and "evil" is revealing of a powerful strand in American political culture.

It is in this context that politically subaltern consideration of George Lucas' *SW* saga would illuminate the struggles and strains suffusing the

American political consciousness over the past three decades—struggles with identification of self and other. According to Aubrey Malone, D.W. Griffith's 1915 epic *"The Birth of a Nation* portrayed blacks so negatively that it all but ratified the demonic deeds of the Klan. Its propaganda effect relegated blacks to the back of the bus—both physically and metaphorically—for decades afterwards."[15] Commenting on this, Davies and Smith argue that *"The Birth of a Nation* has been seen as articulating a biological discourse of racial inferiority, whereby blacks are represented as happiest when dancing or working, and unable to cope with the responsibilities of citizenship. The work of exposing and critiquing these images, and the production and dissemination of positive images of African Americans, is very necessary due to the iconic status of *The Birth of a Nation* in Film Studies and American Studies courses, popularly, and for other filmmakers."[16] While moving in a markedly different direction from Griffith's movie, racial difference is, critics aver, nonetheless handled by the *SW* saga in a distinctly troubling way. The saga reduces, this reading argues, any politically progressive impact Lucas' movies may otherwise have. For Wetmore and others, *SW*, then, becomes a distinctly ideologically problematic text most specifically in regard to its treatment of the alien as the "Other." In particular, according to Matthew Kapell for instance, *SW* uses categories of "race" in order "to reinforce ideas of difference and to reinforce discriminatory practices."[17] Keith Booker, moreover, links this up with what he perceives to be an us-versus-them scheme, or a pronounced Manichaeism, pervading the movies.

> This human vs. inhuman structure represents an us vs. them mentality that reinforces the good vs. evil polarity of the film. However, it also makes the seemingly clear moral message of the film somewhat problematic in that it tends to send an almost subliminal suggestion that those who are like us are good, while those who are unlike us are evil. For example, the imperial storm troopers (who are slaughtered en masse in the film) seem to be human, but the film intentionally dehumanizes them in ways that seem to invite us to ignore the humanity of those whom we have identified as enemies. This same kind of thinking can also be seen in the representation of aliens in the film. As the famous cantina scene makes clear, the faraway galaxy in which Star Wars is set is populated by a number of intelligent alien species. However, these aliens appear to play a very marginal role in galactic politics, where humans (or former humans) remain the only major players. The very fact that the film's most memorable portrayal of aliens occurs in the cantina scene (where most of the alien patrons seem to be criminals or outcasts of one kind or another) may be very telling. Other aliens depicted in the film and its sequels (Jabba the Hut, the Sand People, the Jawas) tend to be criminals or outlaws as well. Whenever aliens are portrayed sympathetically (Chew-

bacca or the Ewoks of Return of the Jedi) it is with a substantial amount of condescension (they tend to resemble cuddly pets or perhaps stuffed animals) that clearly marks them as subsidiary to humans.[18]

This chapter analyses the arguments commonly advanced to justify such a reading with Steven Sanders' warning firmly in mind: "Virtually all bad writing about science fiction film reflects poor thinking about it, not only cheapening science fiction film criticism but also trivializing science fiction film itself."[19] It will be maintained, however, that properly educative and argumentatively valid ideology criticism still has some considerable way to go in relation to this set of movies. According to Christopher Deis, when commenting on the rebooted *Battlestar Galactica* television series, "audiences have difficulty with critically interrogating science fiction because race is in many ways erased. ... In this genre, racial intolerance and humanity's triumph over racial prejudice are used as thematic devices, but the existence of fully realized, racially Othered characters is relatively uncommon."[20] Accordingly, the contention is that although "otherness" is not often construed explicitly in racial terms, especially as a marker of difference among the human characters, the *SW* narrative is indeed shaped by considerations of difference and its problematic erasure in such a way that the most important feature of the eradication of difference in a colonialist mode occurs in the depiction of the Empire, and that is presented as an oppressive force. Of course, it is this political narrative and the use of the alien as other that intensifies the noticeable lack of non-significant non-white human characters in the saga, in not insignificant ways.

## *"Where are you taking this ... thing?" (A Death Star Commander,* ANH*): The Politics of Representation*

Returning to the closing scene of *ANH* which was the launch pad for critical reflection on the readings considered in chapter 3, the issue of racial difference can be raised through asking questions concerning the fact that Chewbacca does not receive a medal. What troubles commentators is the fact that his life had been put on the line as much as Han's in the decision to enter the fray in the Millennium Falcon. The difficulty, it would seem, lies in what numerous critics perceive to be the tactical decisions of the writer/director which exhibit an inability to portray alterity well. After all, for the audience's mirth Lucas had Leia earlier in this movie utter the memorable line "will somebody get this big walking carpet out of my way" at the Wookie's expense. This is hardly the behavior of a senator who comes from a galactically democratic family supportive of the Republic and the egalitarian sensibility that is characteristic of democratic politics. In fact, it distinctly echoes the reference to Chewbacca by a Death Star commander in the disgusted utterance of the term "this thing." The character from Kashyyk certainly has plenty to do that is noteworthy in the drama of the piece, but his configuration almost seems to function as a pet to Han Solo. Of course, it is well-known and perhaps significant that Lucas developed this co-piloting character from having his dog Indiana in his car's passenger seat, and while that may explain some of the role that the Wookie plays it raises for critics significant issues regarding the master-slave dialectic in terms of the Solo-Chewbacca relationship.

Kevin Wetmore's study is a case in point. He makes a number of critical claims that result in the assessment that *SW* problematically perpetuates stereotypes, although the appropriateness of his examples and the arguments he develops from them varies considerably. A substantial part of his account has to do with indicating that in these movies non-white human characters are distinctly under-represented. For instance, apart from a few exceptions, in the original or classic trilogy the humans tend almost wholly to be white and male, and only white human characters occupy key roles (Vader's arguable non-whiteness has to be very carefully handled, as will be explained below). Lucas, Wetmore admits, had played around with the idea of casting a black actor in the role of Han Solo, and, of course, in early designs the character was a green non-human. However, "as a result of his desire to make a socially relevant, if not socially active film, Lucas ended up making a film without a single actor of color in a speaking role."[21] One should recognize that this observation does not determine the text to be racist as such, but it does at least suggest that it is insufficiently attuned to culturally liberating motifs and thereby the egalitarian potential, if such a thing could be legitimately identified in Lucas' *SW* work, is distinctly curtailed. The complicity, then, would at the least be one of omission, and this "having the human characters almost exclusively white is," Andrew Howe declares, certainly "disturbing."[22]

More significant, however, is Wetmore's argument that the non-Caucasian human characters that do appear are depicted in a less than positive light. Three particular examples are used to justify this claim from the classic trilogy. The first example is that James Earl Jones is the only black presence in *ANH*, and he plays the unseen role of the *voice* of the archetypal screen villain attired from head to foot in black. So, Wetmore asserts, "in *A New Hope*, evil is black and good is white."[23] In this form Wetmore's claim is distinctly careless, however, even in the context of *ANH*, and Wetmore himself is compelled to recognize the fact that the stormtroopers are garbed in white armor, and the Imperial officers' uniforms are green-grey (a metaphorically suggestive Nazi grey). Furthermore, one would add, the light pastel color used for the Tusken Raiders in *ANH* and later in *TPM* and *AOTC*, and also the draping of the Imperial bodyguard in red in *ROTJ*, equally destabilize any *simple and straightforward* case made on the basis of color palette. Wetmore's evaluation is consequently refigured to claim that "black and white are intermixed on the evil side. The problem is that no such commingling of black and white occurs on the heroic side. Not all bad guys are black, but no good guys are."[24] The use of the black waistcoat over a white shirt for the morally ambiguous Solo in *ANH* would further support this argument. However, with regard to the moral matter of identifying the human characters' ethnicity a claim made on the basis of visual metaphors concerning the movie's metaphysics is a somewhat difficult one to sustain without stretching the material beyond what it is capable of doing. The contrast in the movie is instead largely between the starkly sterile mechanized environments of the Empire and the naturalized tones of the Rebels' location, and equally between the communal solidarity of both the Rebel Alliance (better articulated through the introduction of more non-human characters in the sequels) and the Jedi Order (in the prequels), and the distinctly evident species homogeneity of the Imperials. In fact, a little later, this chapter will develop the counter-claim that Lucas addresses issues of racial prejudice and exclusion precisely through the use of non-human species and droids. For now it is worth indicating how the use of color is accentuated in the prequels, through citing an observation made by Christopher Deis: "The bright and earthy colors that are closely associated with the *Star Wars* prequels correlate with the diversity of peoples that populate the Republic. As the narrative progresses, and the democratic institutions of the Republic decay and eventually collapse, we see the beginnings of an increasingly homogeneous universe. Here, as the color literally disappears from the film, the diversity of peoples and aliens literally disappears as well."[25]

Wetmore's critique references a reading made in 1979 by Michael Pye and Linda Miles. This earlier study likewise fails to develop the deeper connection of the visual stylization of the Vader character with the medieval tradition of the black knight. As Andrew Howe notices, "the association of whiteness with purity and good, and blackness with taint or evil, cuts across religions and cultures. In so marking Vader visually, George Lucas was doing little more than partaking in a symbolic form of cinematic narrative extending back through the black and white cowboy hats of *Shane* and other Westerns to the very roots of Western expression."[26] Howe's point is that the special pleading of the heavily stylized use of coloration for archetypal characterization purposes is inattentive to the ethnic projections of a late twentieth century and early twenty-first audience. Of course, this is far from the end of the matter, since the question remains here whether the movies' creator and design teams were themselves not sufficiently sensitive to shifts in cultural sensitivities. That is no minor matter, of course, and it stretches far beyond the issue of whether those involved are *consciously* projecting pedagogically problematic imagery that emerge from, and inadvertently or not support, morally questionable forms of ethnic representation. There can be nothing "innocent" in what audiences learn from gender stereotyping that "naturalize" racial hierarchies and anti-democratic forms of social relationality that locate power in ethnic differences. Such representational coding regulates perception and judgment, what Stuart Hall describes as how we "come to know how we are constituted and who we are."[27]

Pye and Miles compare the iconographic blackness of Vader with the black depiction of the warlike gorillas in the 1968 movie *Planet of the Apes*, based on Pierre Boulle's 1963 novel *La planéte des singes*, and this association results in the kind of problematic judgments made on loose uses of textual material that is occasionally the case with some film critics. The film relies on allegory to explore and expose issues of race-relations and conflictual power-politics (the reference in *Rise of the Planet of the Apes* is, on the whole, one of the maltreatment of non-human species by instrumentalizing behavior).[28] Cornea, for instance, argues that "given the long history of racist discourse that likens the ape and monkey to peoples of African origin, it is hard to imagine that audiences at the time would really have missed the racial implications in these films."[29] Likewise, a few years earlier, Eric Greene identified the racial allegories, such as the reference to the slave trade that brought Africans to the Americas in the scene depicting the capture of the humans, and the constructed binary opposition between apes and humans: "the makers of the Apes films created fictional spaces whose social tensions resembled those then dominating the United States. They inserted characters into those spaces whose ideologies, passions, and fears duplicated the ideologies, passions, and fears of generations of Americans. And they laced those characters in conflicts that replicated crucial conflicts from the United States; past and present."[30] It is significant in the 1968 movie that the apes have evolved well beyond (white) human beings, the latter being portrayed as uncivilized and pre-linguistic, and this is an undoubtedly radical move in the context of white supremacist arguments concerning black people's intellectual capacities at the time. Moreover, even if one wanted to make a case that blackness is associated with violence in this movie, it is crucial to notice not only that the political oppressors are not the gorillas or the chimpanzees but the primary apes in the racially ordered political hierarchy, the orangutans, and it is notable how the film's conclusion puts radical questions of interspecies co-operation or egalitarian politics to the ruling establishment. In fact, it is worth mentioning with more detail the hierarchical nature of the ape kingdom. As Cornea recognizes, "Much darker in complexion, it is the guards who blithely mete out punishment and who act as the enforcers of orang-utan law. In contrast, the orang-utans have blond hair, are paler in complexion than the chimpanzees, and dictate the law of the land. Complexion therefore dictates certain behavioural characteristics: the dark chimpanzees represent an extreme unthinking, animalistic violence and the pale orang-utans represent a cold and controlling rationality."[31] Accordingly, she concludes

> on the one hand, the species war that ensues in the film obviously draws upon racist myths and can be read as playing out the fears of white Americans concerning the civil rights movement and the violent, racial confrontations of the period. On the other hand, the films can be understood as working to expose the essentialist myths at the core of interracial antagonism and inequality. Unlike patently liberal films of the time that also approached race relations, like *Guess Who's Coming to Dinner* (dir. Stanley Kramer, 1967), the *Planet of the Apes* series does not present audiences with ready-made solutions to racial conflict. For example, by the end of the first film inter-species conflict is not resolved through peaceful understanding and a conclusion is only brought about upon the geographical separation of ape and man. Distinct from the *Star Trek* series of this period, the *Apes* series of films did not present audiences with a futuristic vision of a peaceful society in which harmony is restored or difference subsumed by an all-encompassing Federation. Instead, they presented audiences with a future/present world in which racial difference equalled inequality, violent discord, division and conflict.[32]

The contrast between this political vision and that of Griffith's 1915 *Birth of a Nation* is marked, given that the latter depicts the Ku Klux Klan's *liberationist* function as being one of *saving* the United States *from* Americans of Afro-Caribbean descent. As Davies and Smith observe, this movie, "through its representation of the fictional excesses of black-dominated legislatures, the film represents the granting of civil rights to blacks as catastrophic."[33] Griffith utilizes the narrative to make a claim about the ability of the North and the South to become united against a common foe, an alien other, in order to enable American flourishing. Lincoln Geraghty recognizes the countercultural challenge to racist supremacism and violence: "Films of this period [the late 1960s] stood out as bleak warnings from the counterculture that continuing down the path of nuclear proliferation [*Dr. Strangelove*] and social injustice [*Planet of the Apes*] would ultimately lead to America's and humanity's destruction."[34] In fact, in many ways this earlier movie can help the commentator make the opposite case from that of Wetmore. It can provide a context for Lucas' *SW* to address issues of racial discrimination, prejudice and violence in subtle ways using non-human characters to depict otherness. As Darko Suvin argues with respect to science fiction literature, the genre is notably marked by a form of perspective-distancing, what he calls "cognitive estrangement."[35] Accordingly, the genre defamiliarizes reality and encourages the contemplation of the known world from perspective that is distanced from it. "SF," he continues, "is distinguished by the narrative dominance or hegemony of a fictional 'novum' (novelty, innovation) validated by cognitive logic." Lucas' *SW* saga offers a perspective on issues of race that are distinctly distanced, by portraying certain power-relations between the human and the non-human. Such an approach is problematic in the view of several commentators, and serves to defer the problems of the text. In this regard, it is worth citing an observation about *Battlestar Galactica* made by Deis: "While the show is anchored in many ways by encounters with and considerations of the Other, *BSG* does not overtly engage questions of racial difference among the human survivors. This is significant because race has historically worked to order societies, structure power-relationships, and to determine which groups have access to resources and privilege. This omission is especially problematic given how deftly *BSG* has introduced and considered other questions of difference throughout its narrative."[36]

The issue for Deis has to do with the "choice to move the lens away from the humans and onto the Cylon Other [and this] represents a lost opportunity for explicitly exploring human nature and human society in a time of crisis."[37] The reason for this, he claims with reference to an observation made by Gregory E. Rutledge, is that the imagined future has eliminated "the inconveniences created by such problems as racism and prejudice ... [among humans] with the category of the Other transplanted onto aliens, cyborgs or robots."[38] This, he argues, occurs in two main ways: "by an appeal to human progress (as in *Star Trek*) where humankind has outgrown such ostensibly petty differences, but in other instances, racism and racial inequality are corrected by removing people of color from the narrative." The danger is that this absence can, unwittingly, "give rise to a white that reinscribes existing racial divisions."[39] Deis makes a valuable point, but how far it can be pressed is not clear. After all, the alienizing of depictions of prejudice can indeed serve to bring otherness, ethnicizing hegemonies of power and of racial exclusion in a politics of purity into view. So the significance of just such a procedure of projection of the other is recognized as a valuable one by Cornea. She argues that "the alien, monster or robot of science fiction may provide an example of Otherness, against which a representation of 'proper' human subjectivity is established, interrogated and, on occasion, problematised. Images of Otherness in science fiction can be understood as a metaphor for forms of Otherness within society or between societies and in this way the genre can engage with the fears and anxiety surrounding a given society's Others."[40] Here she echoes a claim made by Tzvetan Todorov: "The best science fiction texts are organized analogously. The initial data are supernatural: robots, extraterrestrial beings, the whole interplanetary context. The narrative movement consists in obliging us to see how close these apparently marvellous elements are to us, to what degree they are present in our life."[41] In fact, in her post-colonialist study of science fiction literature Patricia Kerslake declares that rather than mask issues of difference the alien releases it to view: "While the presence of the Other is essential to a human self-perception, it is equally important that the Other is distinctly non-human, so that we may more easily see our differences."[42]

Moreover, the link between Vader and James Earl Jones should be much more carefully handled than Wetmore's evaluation allows, since as the cultural commentator himself admits Jones was only introduced to provide vocal gravitas to the character in postproduction, and the actor was even originally uncredited in the end. In other words, there is no *necessary* racial coding in the depiction of Vader, and claims to the contrary tend to overstrain the material. Moreover, in this context, the way Lucas develops Vader over the coming sequels is particularly suggestive of the need to be distinctly hesitant with respect to this protagonist. Wetmore comments that "when Vader is no longer bad he is no longer black. His voice changes."[43] Daniel Bernardi likewise asserts that "once Vader returns to the Force, to the side of good, he literally turns white."[44] These critics, however, put substantial strain on the material in order to make it perform a function it not equipped to undertake, since if race was integral to characterizing Vader *ESB* had already determined him to be white by virtue of the later revelation of his identity as Anakin Skywalker, something which would fit well with the racial and species homogeneity of the "racial and totalitarian imperial state."[45] In that regard, Vader does not *turn* white but the audience instead comes to see what it already knows when Anakin and Luke are face-to-face. After the self-revelation to Luke in Bespin the audience is able to watch a considerable number of minutes of Vader's monstrous menacing onscreen time in the awareness that he is Luke's father. On the forest moon of Endor Anakin takes his place alongside Obi-Wan and a non-white and non-human Yoda. Nevertheless, what is certainly required by *ANH* is a form of racial coding that mitigates the problematic associations of non-whiteness and wickedness.

In many ways Lucas would seem to have provided that with the introduction of Lando Calrissian in *ESB*. It is undoubtedly suggestive that the imagination behind the saga introduces a black character and sets him up to occupy an important function in the unfolding drama in *ROTJ*. Elvis Mitchell, for instance, feels that "[Billy Dee] Williams' addition to the cast of [*The*] *Empire* [*Strikes Back*] showed an admirable sensitivity on Lucas's part, an empathy that few filmmakers would've displayed."[46] Yet, the characterization is regarded as being deeply flawed so that "Lando is a kind of roué cliché," on some occasions a token and on others a stereotype.[47] Wetmore makes several important critical claims in this connection. Lando, he argues, is little more than a Chewbacca-like sidekick. "Vader leaves the dark side and becomes white, Lando joins the Rebellion and becomes ineffective."[48] For instance, in the rescue team he is apparently the least useful member who himself requires rescuing from the grip of the Sarlaac by a visually impaired blaster wielding Han Solo. On the other hand, the scene develops Lando in this fashion for dramatic effect while importantly demonstrating that he is not, in the end, a dispensable character (and therefore on par with the Skywalker twins, Han and Chewbacca). It is also worth presuming that his infiltration of Jabba the Hutt's palace guard has yielded significantly useful information for the development of Luke and Leia's rescue mission, although this is speculative and it is certainly not visually enacted for the audience's benefit. A second layer of this figure's dramatic ineffectiveness is identified in terms of the lessened importance of the climactic tri-pronged attack on the Empire in *ROTJ*. So Wetmore argues that "the destruction of the second Death Star is presented as secondary to the objectives of the other Rebels in *Jedi*."[49] This is a misleading way of couching the problem, however. The eradication of the Empire's second version of its weapon of mass destruction is, in fact, the ultimate aim of the Alliance's assault, and it explains Lando's confident rejoinder to the Admiral's commitment for the fighters to disengage and retreat on learning of the Death Star's weapons being fully operational: "We won't get another chance at this Admiral." Nonetheless, there still remains a question concerning the importance of this leg of the attack *for the dramatic narrative*, given the increasing centrality of the Luke-Vader story arc in particular. This is seemingly what Wetmore has in mind in his otherwise loose criticism given that he traces the limitations placed on the screen-time devoted to, and the ease involved in, Lando's efforts in the Millennium Falcon. This underdevelopment of Lando's character owes much to the fact that the saga is not only most concerned with "the adventures of Luke Skywalker," but that the Luke-Vader relationship comes to occupy more and more of the focus of the drama's interest. While that focus certainly does not undermine complaints about the health of presentations of ethnicity in the movie, and thereby deflect the sense that he largely remains a token figure, it does at least suggest that the critical questions need to be framed in a way different from those readings that too neatly and simply assume and assert that the *SW* movies' depict a form of racist politics.

Wetmore's argument is far from finished, however. He regards the depiction of Lando's days prior to assuming the role of Cloud City administrator as a scoundrel as constituting a problem when, as the sole African-American in Episodes IV-VI, there is no "positive African-American counterpart" to balance out his character flaws.[50] These concerns are intensified with regard to the character's initial role in the saga as "betrayer," and as "a sexual presence." Again, however, the critical reading here is distinctly exaggerated. To begin with, it is not insignificant that these vices are not displayed again in the narrative. So Howe admits that "although there is much to criticize in Lando's entry into the narrative, the character never again displays this facet of his personality."[51] In fact, with regard to the latter, it is vital to the development of the character that he quickly (considerably more quickly than Han, in fact) exercises moral responsibility, including risking his own life to undo the duplicity that delivered a carbon-frozen Han into the clutches of Jabba. If anything, he initially appears not as one attempting to secure his own position, as Wetmore believes, but rather as someone placed in a tragic dilemma involving conflicting duties to his responsible relations. Revealed as a kind of Han Solo character initially, this former gambling scoundrel and rogue had already become the responsible administrative leader of the Bespin mining colony. After all, Han plays the role of sexual tempter in *ESB*, and prior to that one half of the love rival with Luke for Leia's interests in *ANH*. According to Richard

Dees, then, Lando has been given no choice but to become the betrayer: he is responsible to the Bespin mining colony and accordingly acts against his "friend" in order to resist tyrannical Imperial control over the business and its people. Lando's choice is seemingly the utilitarian one of the "greatest good for the greatest number." "To his credit," Dees observes, "when he realizes that his goals are hopeless, he does what he can both to evacuate as much of the colony as possible and to save Leia, Chewie, and Threepio from Vader. After losing his colony he doesn't think of himself at all."[52] He compassionately gives himself for others, and later actively attempts to right the wrong of his earlier Faustian pact with Vader (which he could hardly be accused of being morally culpable for, according to Dees). Dees continues by claiming that "far from being a narrow egoist, Lando is in fact one of the most morally courageous figures in the *Star Wars* saga."[53] This, however, is not quite the stamp Lucas puts on the situation. Lando is "a foil for Han," a type of Han from *ANH*.[54] The important issue for Rees is whether Lando truly feels himself to have no moral choice, or, and this is more likely, merely willing to give up the life of his old friend Solo (and the lives of his friends) for simple quantifiable economic considerations. In this second possibility he is not too far removed from those who speak of human casualties in military calculations as "collateral damage," evaluating people's worth in dehumanized terms. Lando's actions suggest that his so-called friend's well-being is less valuable than his business enterprise—Han's life consequently becomes a commodifiable product, part of a tragic business transaction. The Luke who rushes to save his friends even if he dies trying and the Han who is carbon frozen are the important moral foils here, and this instrumentalizing utilitarian ethic is itself one that Lando soon dispenses with in the moral development of his character. What the drama does not do in the way it does with Solo is provide sufficient time to display the moral formation—that occurs quite swiftly in the narrative of *ESB*.

The third test case is Jedi Master Mace Windu. Following on from the introduction of Lando as an important and heroic character, the use of Samuel L. Jackson to depict a leading member of the Jedi Council, the ruling body of the Jedi Order, is telling. According to Wetmore, however, "Mace Windu is the underling of a puppet who is slowly losing his ability to use the Force."[55] Yet Mace is the second-most authority on the Jedi Council (meaning that neither of the two most significant Jedi were white!). It is he who executes the highly skilled bounty hunter Jango Fett in the Geonosian arena (who had earlier defeated Obi-Wan on Kamino). It is he who is also proven correct with regard to his intense suspicions of Anakin that are voiced throughout the prequel trilogy. If anything, therefore, the race-case against Lucas' characterization here has to be the weak one of criticizing an instance of character underdevelopment, and anything more than an attempt at substantive criticism of the movies' positive ethnic sensibilities appears particularly feeble in this instance. Indeed, Wetmore's case is not that Mace is a stereotype, or at least not in the sense that Wetmore regards Lando as being on significant occasions. Howe's point is a good one: Samuel L. Jackson's "presence in the narrative constitutes one long, distracting cameo having little to do with race."[56] After all, it is well-known that he announced his interest in being involved in Lucas' project on a British Channel 4 talk-show *TFI Friday*. The criticism focuses on the Jedi being under-utilized and therefore as lacking the ability to be a positive black role model in the saga. In this regard, Mace would exist as another token gesture who is involved in the drama largely for terms of political correctness. He "is passive to the point of being inert for most of the second trilogy."[57]

The final set of examples derives from the trilogy of prequels. According to Howe, "Clearly, George Lucas learned a thing or two from the criticism he received for the initial trilogy. Indeed, the sixteen-year gap between *Return of the Jedi* and *The Phantom Menace* allowed him to rethink the manner in which he populated Naboo, Coruscant, and the other planets featured in the prequel trilogy. This narrative arc is populated with more minority characters than its predecessor."[58] Yet *TPM* in particular actually intensified the critical complaints concerning problematic depictions of otherness in racially stereotyped fashion. From the moment of its release a number of the movie's characters were roundly denounced as concrete instances of ethnic stereotyping. Wetmore follows a substantial body of critics in complaining that "the Other is represented not by Asian, or African, or Arab, but by the truly alien—monstrous beings from other planets. ... Lucas follows a long cultural tradition in the West of viewing the East as home of the monstrous and non-Westerners as non-human."[59] Critics suggest that there is a "Jewish-like" character depiction of the avaricious of junk-dealer Toydarian Watto; a "Caribbean"-styled servile Gungan people (see below); and a "Japanese" reference in the portrayal of the greedy Neimoidian businessmen of the Trade Federation.[60] Howe, however, suggestively dismisses these suggestions. With regard to the Neimoidians, he observes that even if Nute Gunray possesses what can be interpreted as an East Asian accent (and that by British actor Silas Carson) Tey How does not (to Howe's ears, in fact, he sounds more Hispanic). Moreover, the association of Asians with capitalist greed may say more about how these readers unwittingly understand Eastern people than about *TPM*'s characters. With regard to Watto, Howe's counter is to ridicule the vast array of readings of him as Jewish (because of his nose, which is actually a trunk, and business acumen), as Arabic (because of his thick guttural accent and unshaven look), and as Italian (given his gangster connections to the Hutt family). "Can this character really be all of these things? The answer is clearly no. Watto is another example of a character reflecting the racial tensions of the general society. ... Watto demonstrates the richness of signs in Western culture, whereby the active mind will find whatever it seeks in the cultural referents presented."[61]

These counter-claims of Howe suggest that it would not be inappropriate to ask whether Wetmore's case is one of substantial exaggeration so that *SW* becomes a Rorschach test reflecting the critic's own prejudices. As Howe asserts, "In some cases, accusations of racial typing were overstated with such strange and exotic creatures serving to reflect cultural anxieties, particularly among viewers weaned on preconceptions regarding race in the initial trilogy."[62]

The critical point concerning the depiction of race in Lucas' *SW* universe is an important one, depending of course on how far one attempts to press it. The strong thesis would be that the relative invisibility of non-white human characters renders the texts locked in a hegemonic politics of identity. However, a weaker and more subtle thesis observes the implicit political hegemony in operation. As Melzer claims, "It is important to destabilize claims of silence" over the presence and role of non-white persons in science fiction "for they themselves often have the effect of silencing."[63] After all, in a largely racist genre, she continues, "next to the racial politics of the science fiction community, the texts themselves often ... propagate a typical liberal color blindness."

There are, further, substantial hints of something quite different pervading the saga. These appear in two main ways. In the first place, the way in which Lucas construes the politics of representation and alterity takes a quite unexpected form. In *The Gospel According to Star Wars* I drew attention to the role and character of the aliens and robots as functioning to make (however subtly) a point about discrimination.[64] After all, on one occasion in *ANH* Luke's droids are barred from entering Mos Eisley's cantina with the bartender's snide remark being "we don't serve their kind here. Your droids, they'll have to wait outside. We don't want them here." The racist overtones are particularly noticeable in the novelization which records the bartender continuing as follows: "'I only carry stuff for organics, not,' he concluded with an expression of distaste, 'mechanicals.'"[65] On another occasion Luke has to tell his newly acquired protocol and translator droid C-3PO to address him as "Luke" rather than with the more deferential "Sir Luke" which is instinctive to the droid, and which carries overtones of the American pre-bellum slave-master. The fact remains that it is these somewhat less obviously dramatically heroic and socially important characters, modeled on Kurosawa's comic relief duo in *The Hidden Fortress*, who dominate the opening screen-time of *ANH*. The galaxy's fate even rests in large measure on the mission appointed to the astromech droid R2-D2, and the droid's claim at various points invites disbelief from his counterpart such as the assertion that the diminutive character is having "delusions of grandeur." Among other things, he saves Amidala's Royal Starship from destruction at the hands of the Trade Federation in *TPM*, is integral to Anakin and Obi-Wan's locating of the Chancellor aboard The Invisible Hand in *ROTS*, and so on.

Here Howe observes that "the bulk of minorities in this [classic] trilogy derive from aliens and droids, suggesting a post-human world whereby racial difference has ceased to become a marker of identity when there are other species against whom identity barriers can be formed."[66] So the exotic use of non-human species in politically equitable relations with the human characters offers a perspective on alterity that cannot be underestimated. This is the kind of approach that drives movies like Steven Spielberg's more sentimentally styled *Close Encounters of the Third Kind* and *E.T.* and the more recent *District 9* and *Earth to Echo*, among others. The second and last of these four involves the "alien as friend" motif, not merely displaying the alien as Other but as non-threatening Other and therefore as defined out of the positive projections of the desires of the human characters. According to Kerslake, "Regardless of worthy intent, any text that attempts to relegate the Other to the position of 'friend' is guilty of the very crime it strives to prevent. Whether the alien is portrayed as aggressive and troublesome or friendly and sociable is academic. The issue is not the approachability (or otherwise) of the Other, but that the myth of the alien as the noble savage has been perpetuated."[67] The aspiration here is "for the Other to become as they would have them be." Filmed in a documentary style, *District 9*, in contrast, is more complex in its depiction of the aliens, and refers to the aliens in a derogatory fashion as being "prawns," implying that they are "bottom feeders" and "scavengers" as well as making an observation regarding their physical appearance. There are numerous signs on the streets and on buildings of human/alien separation in Johannesburg that provides important political echoes of the conditions during the apartheid regime. For this reason, the aliens were interned in a temporary camp that subsequently became militarized and quickly afterwards "a slum" that is referred to by one new reporter as a "township."

Noting the significant departure from the "invasion" and "abduction" narrative devices for encounter with the alien, John Wright proclaims that "at its most basic level, *Close Encounters* reverses the negative fears of otherworldliness and presents the alien other as a being to be engaged merely for the sake of that engagement. ... The monstrosity of the alien other of previous cinematic images is thus changed, not only for the characters in the film but also for audiences of the late 1970s, mirroring a cultural period in which the simplistic othering of communism and non-American ideologies that occurred in the 1950s and 1960s was blurring."[68]

Keith Booker, however, offers an interesting challenge to the reading of the alien as Other in Lucas' *SW*. "As the famous cantina scene makes clear, the faraway galaxy in which Star Wars is set is populated by a number of intelligent alien species. However, these aliens appear to play a very marginal role in galactic politics, where humans (or former humans) remain the only major players. The very fact that the film's most memorable portrayal of aliens occurs in the cantina scene (where most of the alien patrons seem to be criminals or outcasts of one kind or another) may be very telling. Other aliens depicted in the film and its sequels (Jabba the Hut, the Sand People, the Jawas) tend to be criminals or outlaws as well."[69]

The claim about the cantina characters is rather weakened by recognizing that this is supposed to be frontier of the galaxy, an outlying system in which the Empire has little interest or presence, and therefore precisely an environment for the congregation of all manner of disreputable character. Moreover, the "low life" Obi-Wan selects for the task is a *human*—Han Solo. On the other hand, Booker's suggestion is that the alien tends to disappear from central positions of power. Again this way of couching the criticism also deteriorates somewhat under the pressure of recognizing that the racial homogeneity of the Imperials is precisely one of the problems at issue for Lucas in the narrative, that is, of course, until one observes that in *ANH* the Rebellion itself appears to be rather racially homogenous in its own way. But what about Chewbacca? "Whenever aliens are portrayed sympathetically (Chewbacca or the Ewoks of Return of the Jedi)," Booker continues, "it is with a substantial amount of condescension (they tend to resemble cuddly pets or perhaps stuffed animals) that clearly marks them as subsidiary to humans. ... Star Wars is, from this point of view, anything but an endorsement of otherness."[70] Nonetheless, while this set of observations is interesting as a reading of *ANH* it is less useful for explaining Yoda for whom the narratives reserve a particularly prominent and reverential place, and in which this ancient sage performs numerous crucial functions.

For instance, while the film does not develop its critical suggestions very far beyond the *symbolic* depiction of various issues, so that it understandably becomes more a vehicle for the spectacular rather than a re-education in value judgments and moral presuppositions, a revealing moment is the introduction of Yoda. As mentioned in chapter 2, Luke has the impression that power is to be met with greater power. The opening scene of *ANH*, then, is solved (if not by being bigger at least by being better, as with the use of the SOMF, the small one-man fighters, against the super-weapon in the climatic battle of this movie). Carl Silvio's economic reading misplaces the David-versus-Goliath motif of this scene: "The opening scene of *A New Hope* enthrals us, in part, because it invites us to invest it with both our fascination and fears of late capitalist techno culture."[71] Luke's training under the diminutive Jedi Master involves a deconstruction of a certain understanding of power, and the use of the non-human character for such an important task in guiding the redemptive journey of Luke is deeply significant. It, therefore, is simply not straightforward to argue, as Veronica Wilson problematically does, that Lucas "has created a patriarchal political system in which human males are fully in charge and other sorts of beings unimportant or expendable."[72] Wilson has had to exclude large and significant moments from consideration in order to provide such a forceful reading.

Yet, as if to underline the fact that depicting Otherness constructively well beyond being exclusionary is a significant issue that is at stake *within* the narrative itself, the Jedi Master is only one of several non-human and/or non-white figures seen to occupy significant positions of authority in the pre-imperial Jedi order. The Rebel fleet itself in *ROTJ* is commanded by a Mon Calamari, Admiral Ackbar. The important senator Bail Organa, husband to the Queen of Alderaan, and played by the Chicano actor Jimmy Smits, becomes the infant Leia Skywalker's adopted father. Perhaps the point could have been reinforced by configuring Chancellor Finis Valorum in non-human terms, although interestingly that might have suggested that the leading figures are not human, thereby re-raising the issue of specism in an inverted form. Actually, on saying that, the constituting of Valorum as non-human or as a non-white person could intensify an important moral function—the rise of Palpatine leads to the increasing homogenization of the Empire in terms of the power of white humans.

Howe makes the case that "given the perception of aliens as racialized others, Lucas may be attempting a multicultural statement about race and power in his portrayal of edges of empire."[73] In fact, the visionary behind the saga himself explicitly makes just such a claim according to the creator of *SW*'s biographer Dale Pollock: "'Chewbacca's nonhuman and nonwhite,' Lucas says. 'I realise it seems rather obscure and abstract, but it was intended to be a statement.' Lucas claims to be a fervent believer in equality. 'I get quite upset over injustice and inequality,' he says. The robots and Chewbacca were there to demonstrate that no matter how odd or different people seem, they can still be true and faithful friends."[74] The cantina scene in the Tatooine of *ANH* displays the exotic visual feast of a microcosm of a universe teeming with super-abundant life-forms, and does so not as something on which judgment concerning superiority is offered but as an alterity that is natural to daily interactions in parts of the universe that Tatooine is otherwise quite remote from. For this reason, it is significant that it is Chewbacca whom Obi-Wan converses with about the prospect of being chartered to Alderaan. Here, in this scene, the audience becomes directed towards a character in whom it will have significant emotional investment over the course of the series, and who, while humanoid in physical shape, remains alien. In fact, part of the backstory is that after the invasion of Kashyyk the Empire enslaved the Wookie race, traded by Trandoshan slavers—Han Solo rescues Chewbacca from these conditions of bondage, hence the life-debt faithfulness that is evident of their relation in the classic trilogy. The political import of this is noteworthy. According to Kearney, "Rather than acknowledge that we are deep down answerable to an alterity which unsettles us, we devise all kinds of evasion strategies."[75] One such strategy, he remarks, in fact the primary one, "is the attempt to simplify our existence by scapegoating others as 'aliens.'"

Added to this is the multiplication of non-white characters in the prequels. There are no white human characters on the Jedi Council itself, the human characters being the black Adi Gallia, the Chalactan character (with an ethnically Asian actress) Depa Billaba, in addition to another non-white actor playing the humanlike councilor Eeth Koth, the Iridonian Zabrak character. Again, while this appears to be an attempt to respond to critics' concerns over ethnicity and identity politics in the classic trilogy, the question remains as to whether this non-white presence is dramatically sufficient to be anything more than a token gesture. On the other hand, when the movies are watched in episodal order then something interesting emerges, as suggested above: the plethora of different human races and non-human species in the galaxy is muted through the growing power

## 4. "We don't serve their kind here!" 137

and control of the totalitarian governance of the Emperor and the racial hygiene of the Imperial state, so that difference is only really seen on the Empire's borders on place like Tatooine. The movies depict the rise of the instrumentalization of others' lives in the racial singularity of the Imperial system, as is symbolized well by the use of clones for the armored and ultimately expendable and endlessly replaceable infantry. Deis here makes an astute point: "As the narrative progresses, and the democratic institutions of the Republic decay and eventually collapse, we see the beginnings of an increasingly homogeneous universe. Here, as color literally disappears from the film, the diversity of peoples and aliens literally disappear as well."[76] That would mean that while Wetmore is right to recognize that *ESB* "still manages to promote the idea that while humans are everywhere in the galaxy, the vast majority of them are white" the evaluative point would be quite different from the one he and others are making with regard to the whiteness of the saga.[77] The screened sensibility does not provide an ethnic sense of problematic otherness, but rather of the destructiveness of certain forms of political agency and thus of moral performance. Lucas turns the issue away from that which is substantively locatable in differentiating strangers through race, gender, and economic class. The divisions rather have to do with issues of power, oppression, self-aggrandizing hegemonic moves.

Crucial in this regard is the prequel's highly controversial addition to the *SW* universe among even the saga's most hardened fans of Jar Jar Binks.[78] The Caribbean accent critics have found particularly disturbing. However, Howe believes that "the similarities to this culture end there."[79] As he explains in a puzzled tone, "The suggestion that Jar Jar's ears are representative of dreadlocks is strange, as they look very much like ears." The bewilderment echoes Lucas' own: "Those criticisms are made by people who've obviously never met a Jamaican. ... How in the world could you take an orange amphibian and say that he's a Jamaican?"[80] Howe's evaluation of the critical argument is certainly quite promising for an alternate perspective. "Creating a space alien with a recognizable accent is a bit thin when denoting Lucas a racist, however."[81]

Moreover, and substantially, critical readings must complicate their accounts in several further ways. For instance, it is evident that Jar Jar's accent is noticeably different from that of other Gungans, and the accents of Boss Nass or Captain Tarpals in particular are not as easy to geographically place. Secondly, Wetmore's citation from Brent Staples concerning the pidgin Gungan dialect of Galactic Basic as making them "the stupidest species in the film" sounds like the worst form of colonialist condescension towards pidgin English speakers.[82] Is it really a sign of lack of intelligence, or is it the way cultural way the language has evolved in this part of the galaxy among a quite isolated and private people? Thirdly, any claim about Jar Jar as stereotyped Caribbean involves an ample generalization in relation to the other Gungans—there can be no claim about any Gungan other than Jar Jar with regard to being lazy, incompetent, and even a "servant" and so on.[83] This is simply not what is displayed onscreen. After all, Jar Jar has been excluded even by his own people. Fourthly, Wetmore's claim that the Gungans are "primitive" appears more of a projection of his technophilia—i.e., that blasters, space ships, etc., are demonstrations of an advanced civilization—whereas the significantly sophisticated *defensive* weaponry (Fambaa transported shield generators, energy shielding, and light-explosive plasma energy balls), submariner Bongo transportation devices, and stylish underwater cities protected by powerful hydrostatic membrane fields are considered to be signs of techno-archaic cultures.[84] According to David West Reynolds, for instance, "The Grand Army employs both technological wizardry and traditional weaponry."[85] Fifthly, the important function to the saga of this bungling Gungan entails that he is not merely reducible to either comic relief or the sales of figurines to pre-adolescents. Not only is he, in his dim-wittedness, the senator who sounds the horn fatefully proposing absolute emergency powers for Chancellor Palpatine (*AOTC*), but his acceptance by Qui-Gon Jinn is morally significant (*TPM*). The Padawan Obi-Wan doubts his worth only to have his own lurking elitism, surfacing in comments of seeming disdain for the Gungan, exposed and challenged by his Jedi Master. The contrast between Qui-Gon's attitude and that of Vader when judging beings' worth solely on their ability and performance, and disposing of those who prove to be without worth, is evident. Whether Lucas could have played down the possibility of marking him as Caribbean certainly remains a live question, however, but not one that can have the effect of mitigating the important iconoclastic role he plays in relation to issues of power and exclusion. "A driving theme in Star Wars is appearance versus reality. This issue takes on new meaning with Jar Jar, as his value is hidden deep within him. So deep, in fact, that a Jedi such as Obi-Wan cannot see the value in him. Only Qui-Gon and Amidala find his worth."[86] Padmé's role here is made even more significant by the lurking humanocentrism that she has been born into and has imbibed the spirit of in her own ideological formation. So Reynolds reveals that "like all the Naboo, Queen Amidala was taught to think of Gungans as barbarians."[87] It is for this reason that when Padmé, while Queen of the Naboo, bows in humble submission before Boss Nass of the Gungans she is making an important symbolic statement about the symbiosis of all life-forms.

Wetmore is at least positive about *TPM*'s addition of Captain Panaka, played by a British actor of Ghanian descent, and the pilot known to viewers by his call sign, "Bravo Three." While the latter plays a role in the Naboo attack on the Trade Federation battleships, the former is worthy of note. Panaka is the head of Naboo's Royal Security Forces, acting as the military head answerable only to the Queen elect herself. His advice is considered seriously by the Queen, even if she does not necessarily follow it; he is of independent mind and on occasions expresses his disquiet with his political superior's plan of action, including the return to Naboo when in forced exile on Coruscant. He leads the military planning for the attack on the usurping Trade Federation forces, and displays courage and integrity throughout. In fact, Wetmore contends, "Captain Panaka is a sensible, forceful, thoughtful character who plays an active role in the narrative. ... The role is one of the smaller in the film, but it is a significant one in terms of positive characters of color."[88]

Nonetheless, the cultural commentator slips from this constrained critique into one that plays far too freely and loosely with the concrete particularities of the text when he grandly announces that in "the *Star Wars* films ... the good guys are almost all white males and the bad guys aliens who stand in for other Earth ethnicities."[89] So he asserts later, "Lucas casts European (Caucasian) actors in the heroic roles and reduces the evil characters to literally alien Others." Presumably, just to be pedantic for a moment, he means ethnically "European" actors, hence the reference to "Caucasian," since Han and Luke, among others, are played by nationally American actors. It is worth unpacking this in relation to the texts themselves in order to demonstrate its problematic exaggeration. In *ANH* the "good guys" (an oddly child-like phrase, but perhaps it works appropriately to describe the rather morally simplistic conditions of Episode IV) are Luke, Han, Obi-Wan, and the Rebel squadron (all white males). However, one cannot overlook the role of Leia, Chewbacca, and the two droids. Women are significantly underrepresented in Lucas' boys' adventure story which is focused on Luke Skywalker, and non-white humans are absent. However, even here in what is arguably the most morally problematic of the six *SW* movies (*ANH*) one cannot claim that "the good guys are almost all white"—of the main characters mentioned above, four of the seven are not males, and three are not even human never mind white. As for the simplistic and leading language of "the bad guys," Ponda Baba and the Tuskan Raiders are certainly alien, as Wetmore's critique allows, and with the special edition of 1997 we could add Jabba the Hutt to this group. Yet Dr. Evazan is human-like and, in fact, he is a *white male*. Indeed, the two distinctly racist comments made in the movie come from the white characters, the Mos Eisley cantina bartender and a Death star officer. Moreover, of the main group of movie "baddies," Darth Vader's ethnicity has not yet been revealed, Grand Moff Tarkin and the entire Death Star's entire commanding body are *white males*. In *ESB* again Luke, Han, Obi-Wan, the Rebel squadron, and the Rebel infantry are all white males; but to Leia, Chewbacca, and the two droids the movie adds Yoda and Lando. Again while women are underrepresented, and there are no non-white human women at all, now six of the nine heroic figures are not white males. Of the Imperials, again the officer class is composed entirely of white human males (in fact, they are all have English accents), the Emperor appears to be white, and the revelation of Vader's identity puts him into the same category. Of the group of bounty hunters that appears on the Star Destroyer Boba Fett's ethnicity is hidden from view, Dengar is a human white male, IG-88 and 4-Lom are both droids, while only Bossk and Zuckuss are non-human "alien" males. The same trend towards maximizing the non-white male presence occurs in *ROTJ*. To the groups mentioned above, the Rebel Alliance becomes more visibly complicated with the introduction of Mon Mothma (a white woman), Admiral Ackbar with his ship's bridge ethnically deriving from his Mon Calamari species, and Nien Nunb who co-pilots the Falcon in the assault on the Death Star. The non-human Ewoks are significant to the unfolding drama as well. Further, Jabba's entourage is predominantly composed of male non-humans, but not entirely, and his Twi'lek palace supervisor Bib Fortuna is white. Once again, the contrast with the personnel of the oppressive Imperial system is stark and significant.

The prequels intensify this complication of the racial and gender coding further. In *TPM* white males are in the majority of the body of the main characters the movie identifies with—Qui-Gon, Obi-wan and Anakin. However, while Padmé is white she is certainly not male, and while for his part Yoda is male he is not a white human being. Added to this is a Jedi high Council composed of *no white male Jedi*, and which has three females all of whom are non-white (albeit one is non-human). The Naboo are not racially or gender homogenous, and the Gungans are non-humans. Equally, the Senate representatives express the galaxy's species diversity. Certainly here the enemies of these groups are now all non-human but for Sidious/Palpatine. In *AOTC* the black male Jedi Master Mace Windu occupies a slightly more significant role than in Episode I.

It also adds the two non-white males Senator Bail Organa and Captain Typho as Senator Amidala's security officer, as well as the non-human male Dexter Jettster. The non-white male Jango Fett and his cloned "son" Boba are attached to the list of enemies of the Republic (they were played by Maori actors), but the white male Count Dooku/Darth Tyrannus is a Sith Lord seen to be configuring the anti–Republican rebellion by the newly formed Confederacy of Independent Systems ("the Separatists" for short). *ROTS*, for its part, introduces the non-human Wookies and the Pau'ans, as well as the non-human male General Grievous (a mechanically rebuilt a former Kaleesh warlord) on the Separatist side, while unleashing Anakin and the Clone troopers against the government of the Republic, the Jedi, and even the non-human Separatists.

The most one could say, then, from this lengthy and intellectually lightweight observation from statistics in response to Wetmore's claim that "the good guys are almost all white males and the bad guys aliens" is this: in the classic trilogy, the very small group of the movies' main heroic protagonists are white and two-thirds male (Luke, Han and Leia), while the commanders of the Imperial enemy are wholly white and male. In the prequel trilogy, the main protagonists are three-quarters male but only half are white human male (Anakin, Obi-Wan, Padmé, and Yoda), along with an increased racial and gender complicating among the important supporting characters; the commanding Sith are white human males (at least once Darth Maul is disposed of), and they use a variety of non-humans disgruntled with the Republic to seize power.

In the second place, Lucas' treatment of the "evil within" entails that wickedness is not racial, ethnic or gendered, but rather misformed character. Peter Lev admits that while "Lucas is not responsible for the uses politicians and governments make of his film ... the ease with which his ideas were put to political and military ends shows something about the Manichaean quality of the story."[90] Despite the propensity of certain critics like Lev to continue reading the movies in a dualistic vein, 1980's *ESB* comes to problematize just such a mood. Crucially, for instance, in the training of Luke Skywalker in Jedi wisdom there appears a considerably more complex dialectical interplay between the exteriorization of evil (so dominant in *ANH*) and the *interiorization* of evil. And yet, even given the powerfully simplistic aesthetic of good-evil's characterization in *ANH*, dualistic readings of the earlier Episode in the saga should already have been somewhat chastened by the double material thematics of a self-serving Han Solo and a Darth Vader (all-too) briefly revealed by Obi-Wan to have been "a young Jedi ... who was a pupil of mine before he *turned* to evil. ... Vader was seduced by the dark-side of the Force." Already with *ANH*'s back-story of Vader there is a highly significant inverted *metanoia*. It is this that the prequels develop as their narrative arc.[91] What emerges is the fact that particularly after *ANH* Otherness functions as a way of depicting arrangements of post-racial, post-species and post-gender cooperation and equity in a celebrated differentiability. The way that problematic Otherness is depicted is in terms of the *behavior* of those who are self-aggrandizing (whether of the Sith, the Empire, the capitalists, or the gangsters). Now we are in a better position to appreciate the significance of the fact that, in obvious contrast to the oppressive homogeneity of the wholly white male and human makeup of the Imperial navy, the Rebellion and the earlier Jedi Order represent something of interspecies and gendered diversity. Thus it would seem, then, that the saga does indeed exalt a "politics of difference," a relating of one to another that is not organized on the basis of exclusive forms of race (even species), gender, or economic relations. There is something more fundamental to the sense of identity and the organization of relations than these allow for in "politics of exclusion in indifference to difference." It is this imagination of a properly configured inclusion of all manner of difference that is integral to identifying the shape of the distortions of evil and suffering. Consequently, a reading such as Matthew Kapell's is idiosyncratic to the point of seriously distorting the material. He asserts that the racial stereotyping serves merely "to emphasize the larger underlying fact that *Star Wars* reduces the behavior of both aliens and humans to their biology."[92] Whatever one makes of the controversial reduction of Force-consciousness to biology (Kapell's notion of undemocratic hereditary rule is narratively bizarre given the fact that the Jedi are *not the galaxy's rulers, only its guardians*), especially when seen alongside J.K. Rowling's characterization of "muggle" wizards in the *Harry Potter* series, he entirely misses the importance of training and educative habituation in the saga (not only of the Jedi Padawans), of the nature of the Anakin story-arc as *tragic* drama, of the moral redemption of the Han and Lando characters, or simply the nature of complex relations and moral responsibility that undergird and direct the narrative. His reading of the clone troopers as personality-determined is confused precisely because he has missed the point that they are forms of instrumentalized life, bio-engineered killing machines—bio-droids, in fact. Kapell laments that "behavioural traits—independence and violent abilities—are not merely genetic but so biologically based that they can be modified."[93] Yet, this trades on a dualistic anthropology that suggests that psychology and physiology are not interdependent, a science fiction evasion of what is known from how personality can be substantially modified on occasions of physical trauma to the brain.

On the other hand, the fact that Lucas never allows for the performative moral redemption of the Tusken Raiders in *SW*'s political depiction of ethnic and cultural multiplicity is not an insignificant and disturbing flaw that morally marginalizes these "others" without critically inclusive reserve. Whether one attempts to ethnically code them as Arabs, given the desert location of this nomadic people on Tatooine, or a North American indigenous tribe, given their threat to the settlers on the outer rim, it is a difficult to respond to them as anything other than in terms of the pure binary construction of pure "other," a malignant "not-us/me." There can be no hospitable agency of conversation or negotiation with this monstrously violent other, and no compromise. All that can be expected as a consequence of this regulative ideological representation is property theft and death. The exploitative portrayal of the alien as pure bestial colonizer, therefore, secures rather than disrupts the politics of othering by alienating the species from "decent" or civilized life and agency. The alien as a *race* or *species* as a whole is ruled to be perilous, and therefore this particular one on the loose is not an exception. At no point are the Sand People depicted with any redeeming qualities, other than the strategically clever quality of masking their numbers of riding in single file, according to Obi-Wan in *ANH*. The elderly Jedi Master depicts them in terms of cowardice: "the Sand People are easily startled," and in *AOTC* Cliegg Lars describes them to Anakin with racist overtones as being sub-civilized, "vicious, mindless monsters" who only "walk like men." The fact that they are portrayed as communicating solely through unintelligible grunts, snarls and howls, adds to the bestiality of the representation of the species, and therein they are effectively silenced. Crucially, in this regard, when Jar Jar first meets the Jedi in the Naboo swamps and is rhetorically asked if he is "stupid" he responds with "I spake." Such a possibility is denied to the nomadic inhabitants of the desert planet of Tatooine. They remain throughout, then, solely as uncultivated, savage and threatening characters. Importantly the reference to the species as Tusken *Raiders* is a discursive strategy that defines them purely as problem, as threat, and therefore this reference linguistically offers already the parameters for making ethical judgments on their diminished character and moral worth. Admittedly, one of the backstories to *TPM* describes Jedi Master Eeth Koth as having trained Tusken Jedi Sharad Hett, a simple little detail that could have had a considerable transgressive effect on the Othering of the Tusken Raiders in the cinematic saga.[94] The only factors that can in any way mitigate the force of this Othering have to do with *SW*'s description of the violent conflict as a moral one, one of the character of human action and desire. In other words, its Other is not so much meant to be the Tuskens but the dispositions of the Sith, echoed somewhat with the saga's gangsters, Trade Federation and Jawas. On the other hand, there might be the slightest inclination of a refusal to simply type them as Other for the heroes' Other-destroying self-protection in *AOTC*. This undermines the bravado of pure Othering, of the celebratory violence enacted against the Other as threat. The reference to the "women and children" provokes moral critique from within the narrative itself, a realization by Anakin that his actions were deeply problematic. The guilt suffered over this action is returned audibly in Anakin's execution of Count Dooku, a Sith menace, in *ROTS*.

Formally, then, despite the way in which Lucas develops a colonial and post-colonial context for reconsidering the nature of subjectivity, with his transgressive aliens construed as subjects-in-relation, the Sand People continue to echo some of the elements used to depict Grendel in *Beowolf*, or the creatures in *Troll Hunter*, or the H.R. Giger designed creature in the *Alien* series, elements that suggest that all is not terribly well with Peter Lev's confident argument that "*Star Wars* creates an ideologically conservative future, whereas *Alien* and *Blade Runner* create future linked to liberal and socially critical ideas."[95]

It is worth spending a little time on Ridley Scott's 1979 movie *Alien* in order to set into relief the use of the "alien" in *SW*. It is noteworthy that the relations of the crew of the deep space vessel *Nostromo* operate seemingly beyond racial and gender distinction. The contrast takes a different form, between that of the vulnerable flesh of the humans, and the bodies of violence of the alien. The movie opens to audience view with the sight of the sleep *pods*. The reference, here, may well be to *Invasion of the Body Snatchers* in which the pods bore that which is monstrous, that which induces dread. If so, the allusion here is a subversive one—the pods in *Alien* are protective cocoon-like devices to hibernate the crew for the lengthy duration of the deep-space voyage. From this a dichotomy is produced between this protective image and the starkly contrastive pod image later in the movie that takes the form of the eggs. As Roz Kaveney observes, the image of crew member Kane awaking from his cryogenic stasis semi-naked, rubbing the sleep from his eyes, especially when compared with what hatches from the eggs, is an image of vulnerability.[96] "The egg is a Malign Sleeper, the thing you awaken at your peril."[97]

The titular "alien" in Scott's movie, then, becomes construed as an Other in the basest of senses—instinctual, destructive, self-preserving, and so on, a pure and deadly threat to the now fragile lives of the human crew (and indeed, the world that the crew is attempting to return to). Otherness, the unreasoning beyondness, is simply that which necessitates either destruction or one's being destroyed by it, at least once encounter with alien otherness becomes unavoidable. This constitutes an intergalactic echo of the terror-inducing mood of *Jaws*, or of other monster movies like the pair of American made *Godzilla* movies and of *Cloverfield*, movies which often accentuate the sense of threat and generate the mood of foreboding by the use of the confined space and the dark lighting.[98] "The Sulaco is like a great shark, or like a Swiss Army Knife—it is an image of brutal strength and ingenious efficiency. Horner's score, as we watch the ship move through space, is at the same time military and mournful, horn and trombone calls and drumbeats—there is a tremendous dignity here, but also a sense of foreboding."[99]

Nonetheless, very soon the crew descends into bickering. The relations between them are antagonistic, conflictual, driven by self-interest. Kaveney insightfully observes this theme from the *Nostromo* reference: "The Nostromo takes its name from a novel by Joseph Conrad and the June 1978 draft of the script has, as one of its epigraphs, Conrad's aphorism 'We live, as we dream—alone.'"[100] It is this that sets Ripley's character as female off from the others for Kaveney, always threatened by self-interested betrayal by the male characters.[101] Consequently, "one of the reasons why Ripley's relationship with the cat is so touching is that there is nothing in it for her—it is one of the few entirely selfless relationships in the film. The fact that she is capable of this, even if it is not her default mode, is the thing that makes her the creature's opposite."[102]

Likewise, James Cameron's *Aliens* portrays a moment of maternal care of Newt by Ripley, a moment that prevents her from being consumed by the machismo image of the hero. As Doherty argues well, this tempers any masculine reading of her "strength and assertiveness" through "maternal devotion."[103] In one celebrated scene she stands brandishing her weapon with the young girl protectively in her other arm, "at once the woman warrior and the solicitous mother."[104] In fact, Cameron's movie depicts the interrelationships in quite different ways, although the marines have an aggressive and offensive form of camaraderie-in-arms. Even natality is not sentimentalized, since the humans are brutalized by the Queen and the consequent birthing from them is a monstrously violent one. Here *Aliens* depicts the aliens' colonizing instincts with a further reference to *Invasion of the Body Snatchers*, as the bodies become incubators for the species' maturation.

The *Alien* of Ridley Scott and James Cameron, not to mentioned

David Fincher and Jean-Pierre Jeunet, then, characteristically enacts a deep cultural Manichaean move that is bound up politically with the scapegoating mechanism, as Richard Kearney recognizes. The monstrous, is the unintegratable "other," and it is to be excluded otherwise it will destroy human existence. According to Kearney, "various exchanges between the characters focus on the *monstration* of sacrificial scapegoating, thereby exposing the ways in which our most feared monsters can serve as uncanny doubles for our all-too-human selves."[105]

Kearney's is an analysis that moves with the psychoanalytic approach to these movies methodologically common to the important reading of one like Barbara Creed.[106] "Human space travellers actually find themselves playing 'host' to the hostile monster from outer space, thus discovering (to their horror) that the monster is not just 'out there' but 'in here.' The dragon-shaped alien, recalling portraits of the satanic beast of the apocalypse, is capable of invading our most intimate being. So that the thing these human astronauts consider most foreign is in fact the most familiar. What really terrifies them is the alien *within*, already inscribed in the homely but such that it cannot be integrated or named. The extraterrestrials in the series thus serve, I am suggesting, as imaginary personifications of our inner alienation, reminding us that we are not at home with ourselves, even at home. They are, we might say, postmodern replicas of the old religious demons: figures of chaos and disorientation within order and orientation."[107] In this regard, the "chest-burster" scene, in which the monstrous "other" is violently "born" out of Kane, takes on a particularly important resonance.

For Kaveney, "the film explores these areas of body horror so comprehensively that it is almost impossible to map any one interpretation of the creature as a single correct one—were it possible to accuse *Alien* simplistically of gynophobia, Ash would offer a useful balancing paranoia about male violence."[108] Nonetheless, it is significant that the gender and racial differences between the human crew are distinctly relativized by a conflictual other of pure monstrous proportions and qualitative difference. It is this radically always alien difference that drives Scott's first foray into science-fiction/horror genre fusion. Otherness, the unreasoning beyondness, is simply that which necessitates either destruction or one's being destroyed by it, at least once encounter with alien otherness becomes unavoidable. Here is an inter-galactic echo of the terror-inducing mood of *Jaws*, accentuated if anything by the use of the confined space and the dark lighting. These conditions intensify the sense that this movie involves a catastrophic encounter with the monstrous. There can be negotiation with this monstrously violent other, and no compromise (unless death is courted).

There may, however, actually be a quite different way of construing the characterization of the alien, and that might, then, lead to a politics less supportive of the simplistic "us-them" scheme. Given the conflictuality evident among the crew members, and the life-instrumentalization and self-interest of the corporation (the Company), the alien is an intensified version of the self-interested humans. In Scott's movie, Ash's lack of concern for Kane, in protection of the alien, represents the inhumanity of the corporate culture in its intensified culture of self-interest. "The novel *Nostromo*, after all, deals with the machinations of a mining company whose intentions to its workers are anything but good and with mined silver that brings death to all who have anything to do with it."[109] "Ash on the other hand is a menace precisely because he has been programmed, programmed to act as the perfect company man who will always do as he is told."[110] This critical perspective on big business is accentuated by Cameron's take on the material. In this contribution to the *Alien* franchise, the company is called Cyberdyne, a distinct intertextual reference to the technology company named in *The Terminator* franchise. This is the corporation responsible for the invention of the Skynet missile defense system, an A.I. that becomes sentient, and in that moment of self-awareness turn, like Adam and Eve, turn on its creator.

*Aliens'* Carter Burke, the company representative, is portrayed as entirely without redeemable qualities. Late on in the movie Ripley is forced to castigate him by announcing that the aliens do not betray each other for a percentage. Yet even Ripley's moral condemnation of Burke's profit-making desires cannot entirely mask the overlap of the predatory instinct of capitalism and the monstrousness of the alien. Interestingly Cameron depicts a number of aliens all co-operating with each other without individualistic self-aggrandizement and through this the contrast is drawn between two sets of predators—those belong to the corporation's determined military personnel and the collectivity of the alien species. After all, Cameron's is largely a combat movie. In fact, there is even a reference in *Aliens* to Vietnam. The high-tech corp. defeated by ill-armed Vietcong is reflected in the defeat of the technologically advanced troops by the survivalist mechanisms of the alien other. Thomas Doherty, for instance, observes that "the freak-outs, wild firefights, scrambled video, surly grunts, lower-class ethnicity, macho posturing, even the calculated appropriation of military vernacular, play like a Vietnam-period run-through-the-jungle."[111] If this is the case, then while *Aliens* does raise political questions concerning issues of colonialism in America's foreign relationships it nonetheless does not present the Viet Cong with the kind of sympathetic treatment that Lucas'

*ROTJ* does with its design of the dramatic role of the Ewoks in the narrative. In other words, Cameron's own admission that his depiction of the Marine mission to LV 426 is a replay of the Vietnam War accentuates the political effect of the "othering," with the alien as the monstrous threat that can only be engaged with through violence.[112] Consequently, Amy Taubin regards this movie as "the most politically conservative of the series."[113]

Such a scapegoating mechanism is exhibited in much superhero literature, even in Peter Jackson's cinematic depiction of Tolkien's *Lord of the Rings* and *The Hobbit*. While much has been rightly made of Tolkien's Augustinianism, the very way he works with archetypal characters tends to make evil something that Others possess a little too neatly, and these Others as *species/races* are thereby excluded from the sympathies of the viewer. Of course this is significantly offset by the notion of temptation and change, especially with the Smeagel/Gollum, Sauruman, and the Frodo characters. Even the possessive fetishizing of the ring of the Men, and the fracture of the relationships between Men, Dwarves and Elves, suggest something more interesting than the descriptions of irredeemable Orcs, Gobblins, Uruk-Hai, and especially Sauron might otherwise suggest. For its part, the thing that partially saves *Alien* is the Othering of the Company and its interests so that the way that otherness is depicted, then, is of class struggle and the implications that acquisitive desire has for the wellbeing of the multi-ethnic crew. Given the conflictuality evident among the crew members, and the self-interest of the corporation, the alien is an intensified version of the self-interested humans. According to Judith Newton, *Alien* "evokes, in rather explicit fashion, ... [an] uneasy recognition that now everyone is forced to be a company man or understood by them, and somebody who is finally expendable in the name of profit. The title of the ... ship, *Nostromo*, 'nostro homo,' our man, provides an allusion, of course, to Conrad's working-class hero, another company man, who dies understanding that he has been betrayed by 'material interests.'"[114] As mentioned above, even in the sequel *Aliens* Ellen Ripley's moral condemnation of Burke's profit-making desires cannot entirely mask the overlap of the predatory instinct of capitalism and the monstrousness of the alien.

## *Conclusion*

According to Andrew Howe, "Despite being set in a distant galaxy, the *SW* franchise has never been able to escape the gravitational pull of contemporary racial politics."[115] Lucas presents an environment of human and non-human, white human and colored human co-operation among those not associated with the enforced racial coding of the Imperial system. For the cosmopolitan Jedi Order, the old Republic, the Rebel Alliance, even Jabba's court racial difference does not appear to be an issue that marks out problematic forms of otherness. At least in narrative terms, there is no reference to the ethnicity of Lando, Mace Windu or Captain Panaka, in fact of any of the human figures. In that regard, racial difference has been denied its naturalizing biological essentialism, and this subverts the equation of any hegemonic performance with true subjectivity, implying that they are historically contingent constructions, manifestations of certain modern colonial arrangements that emerge from hegemonic situations of power and the exclusion of those denied power. In contrast, the movies portray otherness in terms of those determined by virtues of social responsibility and those who instrumentalize life for self-aggrandizing purposes. In the politically focused narrative it is the Empire and the Rebellion who are paradigmatically "other" to each other. Lucas simply refuses to invest skin color and ethnicity with moral significance, as if, as Lola Young observes in the early history of Hollywood, "to be black was to *be* evil, to *be* hypersexual, to *be* morally debased, to *be* inferior."[116] Both the socio-cultural utopianly designed Rebel Alliance and the Jedi Order subvert binaristically self-purifying categorizations of otherness in any racial differentiation among the human characters. Moreover, the alien is rarely depicted through the binary symbolic of "the monstrous." Otherness and difference are, therefore, simply not presented as in and of themselves sources of threat. The "other" is no Grendel who functions as the occasion for the flexing of human (and male) heroic muscle. The closest one comes to such a motif is in the threat to Luke posed by Ponda Baba and Dr Evazan in the cantina in *ANH*.

The danger, however, is that by marking out characters such as Lando, Captain Panaka, and Mace Windu positively and naively "innocently" as *representative* figurations of visibly black subjects Lucas' movies are nonetheless in danger of essentializing race, and thereby unwittingly assuming "classificatory models largely constructed in the nineteenth century [that assumes] the race in question is homogenous and that individuals belonging to various racial groupings are the vessels of essential racial characteristics," even as those characteristics are gesturally redefined by the saga's representations.[117] This would involve an attempt to offer "positive" images, but which would be rendered insufficient by a process directed by what Cornel West calls a "homogenizing impulse," assimilating black people into white-dominated discourse and rendering blacks all essentially the same (and therefore able to be represented by a singular character).[118] As Cornea admits, and this is a distinct difficulty with the history of the genre, "Science fiction writing has traditionally dealt with ideas; often subordinating characterization (or creating what are commonly called 'flat' characterizations) to a more overarching premise."[119] Moreover, there is equally a danger that real differences have been elided and displaced rather than explored and negotiated with, that as with *Star Trek* the use of the "alien" has to bear too much weight that simply has been "solved" in the system other than its most remote outer rim planets (some of the repair in the *Star Trek* franchise comes with *Star Trek Voyager* and the recognition that identity involves not merely being a part of the Federation). In this way, to use Melzer's claim regarding much of the science fiction genre, the texts continue to refuse "to deal with 'actual' racism, which results in an abstraction of the issue into metaphors and avoidance of any treatment of existing power structures."[120]

Race remains a defining occasion for socio-political identity, for inclusion and exclusion. Not to refrain from recognizing the radical import of its inclusiveness, the *SW* saga conceptually deflects racial issues onto the status and treatment of droids. The droid-signifier then serves to destabilize in some quite non-trivial ways forms of engaging with alterity. Peter Lev, consequently, is quite mistaken to argue that *SW* "in no way challenges gender, race, or class relations. ... [M]ost of the aliens are relegated to the 'freak show' of the spacefarers' bar."[121] In that regard Wetmore's approval of Tom Carson's assessment, equally lacks sufficient care and attention to the texts themselves: "in the *Star Wars* films white people are human beings and everybody else is Other, in what is an 'old fashioned racial schema.'"[122] It takes a quite spectacular contortionist effort to make the texts equate "non-human" (one cannot speak of "alien" since there is no geographic core to define the "Other" against) and "inhumane." It is simply not the case that *everybody else is Other*. Non-whites are not excluded Others in their racial differentiation, even if they do lack the representative presence one would expect from broadly politically liberal movies made since the late 1970s. Moreover, no persons are Other in an ethnic sense other than the droids who suffer a racist slur from the bartender, Chewbacca who is the object of two derogatory comments, and the Tusken Raiders who are never depicted as anything other than a threat to the frontier families. Finally, the phrase "white people are human beings" is very odd. Does this suggest that white people can be anything other than human beings? If that is the case then the non-humanness of the white High Council Jedi Masters Ki-Adi Mundi and Evan Piell contradict that.

Or does Wetmore mean that white actors play human beings in the saga? This version of Wetmore's claim is even more eccentric since white actors play a whole range of the non-humans, from the droid pairing of R2-D2 and C-3PO to Chewbacca, and well beyond. In what is potentially a very interesting and disruptive ideological critique, Wetmore has a tendency, like many film commentators, to self-projective eisegetical performance, to exaggerating, and to using examples that are sometimes only supportive of the claim being made when stretched very thin or on other occasions Procrusteanly remodeled to fit. In academic terms, this situation is serious. In moral terms, it is an irresponsible abuse of the material.

For a supposedly nostalgic film its moral sensibility is markedly different from the paranoid exclusion of self and Other in American science fiction cinema of the 1950s, with alien invasion movies dominating the imagination of the period. The reason for that is that what *SW* fears is not the "foreigner" as "alien" or as "monstrous" as such, nor even as insidious terrorist threat from within (Palpatine is not a foreigner to the Galactic Republic, and not influenced by the philosophies of foreign states [unless one wants to argue that the Sith are indeed foreign Others]), and in that regard *SW* has real potential to be, at least at the level of its attempted thematic, a politically hospitable text. As Booker argues, "the numerous alien invasion films and novels produced during the 1950s are quite widely regarded as allegorical responses to the fear of Soviet invasion on the part of American audiences during that period."[123] According to Peter Biskind the connection between "the red nightmare" and movies like *Invasion of the Body Snatchers* is close, thus exemplifying the movie as politically right-wing.[124] On the other hand, Booker regards this movie as being more politically interesting than that, and therefore as one that could be read as offering potential for politico-cultural resistance and even more interesting philosophical questions about the nature of agency. "While this film is particularly easy to read as an allegory about the threat of communist infiltration in the United States," Booker continues, "it is also a complex film that can be read as a commentary on a variety of domestic threats, including conformism and McCarthyism. ... The film can also be read as a commentary on concerns about the dehumanizing effects of a rapidly expanding capitalist system that was increasingly becoming a dominant factor in every aspect of human life in America."[125] Steven Sanders likewise recognizes the ambiguity of the movie's protest against social and political conformity: "nobody has established whether *Invasion* is a protest against the political and social conformity called for by right-wing anti–Communists or that demanded by pro–Soviet collectivists. ... Whether we say that the pods represent communism or McCarthyism or, indeed, the power structure that dominated Hollywood itself, their threat to autonomy and personal identity takes us well beyond the political conflicts of the day."[126]

If *Invasion of the Body Snatchers* (1956) was perhaps the most classic example of the paranoia (the Other coming unnoticed to threaten from within), another prominent movie was George Pal's version of *The War of the Worlds* (1953), a technically proficient science fiction movie for its time which falls into the trap of a generating the other as pure threat. Even in Spielberg's more interesting version, the context becomes that of the post–9/11 terrorist threat, and the alien accordingly becomes not only an intruder but a genocidal invader. According to Roz Kaveney, "The essential thing about the Malevolent Visitor or Alien Infestation movie is that they are never about anything except sensation and dread."[127] It is this that results in Susan Sontag's rather generalized complaint that science-fiction movies offer the satisfaction of "extreme moral simplification—that is to say, a morally acceptable fantasy where one can give outlet to cruel or at least amoral feelings."[128] In particular this is located in the operation of the popular mythology on the impersonal, the "us" and "it" sensibility. As Morpheus explains in *The Matrix*, "If you're not one of us you're one of them." Accordingly, for Sontag, science fiction movies satisfy the bellicose spirit. "Again and again, one detects the hunger for a 'good war,' which poses no moral problems, admits of no moral qualifications. The imagery of science fiction films will satisfy the most bellicose addict of war films, for a lot of the satisfactions of war films pass, untransformed, into science fiction films."[129] *The War of the Worlds* as invasion movie, Kaveney argues, has significantly flattened H.G. Wells' self-critique of imperialism by offering a simpler feel of America being destructively invaded by a superpower.[130] "The bacteria which undo them are clearly meant, as they are most certainly not in Wells, to act as stand-ins for the hand of God." The presence of the human-saving bacterial agent in the movie comes as a *deus ex machina* moment, a device often utilized by lazy writers unable to conceive of solving the difficulties from within the narrative arc itself, but here in Pal's movie a significant allusion to a moment of divine intervention.[131] Symbolically, the film ends with church bells ringing, a chorus of "amen," and a voice-over that proclaims that the Martian invaders have been killed by "the littlest of things, which God in His wisdom had put upon this Earth."[132]

Nonetheless, it is certainly not insignificant that critics of Lucas' *SW* can continue to ask how well these movies' visionary performs his egalitarian vision, but it is to suggest that the concerns with his saga should take a more modest form. Deis has a point when he argues that "In both the original trilogy and the *Star Wars* prequels, aliens are both 'the problem' and the 'solution' in Lucas's film imaginary."[133] The films do not develop their critical potential sufficiently far, however, and so understandably they (*ANH* most specifically) become a vehicle for the spectacular more than a re-education in value judgments and moral presuppositions. This may be no response to Othering in the vein of the unredeemable Othering evident in the jingoistic cinematic narratives *Independence Day*[134] and *Starship Troopers*, or the Other-denying identity of the assimilationist inclusivity of the cybernetic Borg in *Star Trek Next Generation* and *Star Trek Voyager*. The main problem is not that that Lucas does not generate a mode to challenge to dominant modes of race and gender exclusion, but rather that he does not often sufficiently move beyond the essentialising *symbolic* depiction of the issues. Wetmore is correct to maintain, through an appeal to Ursula K. Le Guin, "that artists have a responsibility for the worlds they create." Therefore, "there is," Le Guin continues, a "responsibility to ensure that one's work does not, even if inadvertently, employ and continue derogatory stereotypes, appropriate for selfish purposes elements of other's cultures, and present women and minorities as Other.[135]

# Chapter Notes

## Preface

1. Gilbert Perez, *The Material Ghost: Films and their Medium* (Baltimore: Johns Hopkins University Press, 1998), 3, cited in Gerard Loughlin, *Alien Sex: The Body and Desire in Cinema and Theology* (Malden: Blackwell, 2004), x.
2. George Lucas, in Tim Rayment, "Master of the Universe," *Sunday Times Magazine* (May 16, 1999), 14–24 (20).
3. Lucas, cited in Stephen Zito, "George Lucas Goes Far Out," in Sally Kline (ed.), *George Lucas: Interviews* (Jackson: University Press of Mississippi, 1999), 45–54 (53).
4. Dale Pollock, *Skywalking: The Life and Films of George Lucas, the Creator of Star Wars* (Hollywood: Samuel French, 1990), 271.
5. Carl Silvio and Tony M. Vinci, "Introduction: Moving Away From Myth: *Star Wars* as Cultural Artifact," in Carl Silvio and Tony M. Vinci (eds.), *Culture, Identities and Technology in the Star Wars Films: Essays on the Two Trilogies* (Jefferson: McFarland, 2007), 1–8 (8).
6. Grace M. Jantzen, *Foundations of Violence: Death and the Displacement of Beauty* (London: Routledge, 2004), 19.
7. Milan Kundera, *Testaments Betrayed*, trans. Linda Asher (New York: HarperCollins, 1995), 91.
8. Christine Cornea, *Science Fiction Cinema* (Edinburgh: Edinburgh University Press, 2007), 92.
9. Jonathan Rosenbaum, *Movies as Politics* (London and Berkeley: University of California Press, 1997), 106. Cf. Kevin Wetmore, Jr., *The Empire Triumphant: Race, Religion and Rebellion in the Star Wars Films* (Jefferson: McFarland, 2005), 7; Lincoln Geraghty, *American Science Fiction and Television* (Oxford: Berg, 2009), 59f.
10. See chapter 1.
11. George Steiner, *Language and Silence: Essays 1958–1967* (Harmondsworth: Penguin, 1967), 21; Paolo Freire, *Teachers as Cultural Workers: Letters to Those Who Dare Teach*, trans. Donaldo Macedo, Dale Koike, and Alexandre Oliveira (Boulder: Westview Press, 2005); Paolo Freire, *Pedagogy of the Oppressed* (New York: Continuum, 1990), 39. "The critic," Steiner argues, "lives at second-hand. He writes *about*. ... [Consequently,] criticism exists by the grace of other men's genius."
12. Jantzen, *Foundations of Violence*, 4.
13. Jantzen, *Foundations of Violence*, 19.
14. Jantzen, *Foundations of Violence*, 19.
15. Jantzen, *Foundations of Violence*, 19.
16. Jantzen, *Foundations of Violence*, 19f.
17. Stanley Aronowitz, *The Politics of Identity: Class, Culture, Social Movements* (New York: Routledge, 1992), 11.
18. Patricia Melzer, *Alien Constructions: Science Fiction and Feminist Thought* (Austin: University of Texas Press, 2006), 72, citing Ursula Le Guin, "American SF and the Other," *Science Fiction Studies* 2 (1975), 208–210 (209).
19. Cited in Rob van Scheers, *Paul Verhoeven*, trans. Aletta Stevens (London: Faber and Faber, 1997), xiii.
20. Matthew Wilhelm Kapell, "Eugenics, Racism, and the Jedi Gene Pool," in Matthew Wilhelm Kapell and John Shelton Lawrence (eds.), *Finding the Force of the Star Wars Franchise: Fans, Merchandise, and Critics* (New York: Peter Lang, 2006), 159–173 (168).
21. Henry A. Giroux, *Channel Surfing*

(New York: St. Martins, 1997), 56, cited in Wetmore, *The Empire Triumphant*, 10.

## Chapter 1

1. D. Daiches Raphael, *The Paradox of Tragedy: The Mahlon Powell Lectures 1959* (London: George Allen and Unwin, 1960), 13.
2. Dorothea Krook, *Elements of Tragedy* (New Haven: Yale University Press, 1969), 239.
3. This is Raphael's understanding of Aristotle's claim (13f.).
4. So George Steiner, *The Death of Tragedy* (Oxford: Oxford University Press, 1961), 10.
5. Terry Eagleton, *Sweet Violence: The Idea of the Tragic* (Malden: Blackwell, 2003), 25.
6. See Friedrich Nietzsche, *Birth of Tragedy*, trans. W. Kaufmann (New York: Vintage, 1967), §7; "Attempt at a Self-Criticism," in *Birth of Tragedy*, 17–27 (26).
7. George Steiner, "Tragedy, Pure and Simple," in M.S. Silk (ed.), *Tragedy and the Tragic: Greek Theatre and Beyond* (Oxford: Clarendon Press, 1996), 534–546 (545n1).
8. George Steiner, *Real Presences: Is there Anything in What we Say?* (London: Faber and Faber, 1989), 143, 144.
9. Steiner, *Real Presences*, 143.
10. Eagleton, *Sweet Violence*, 28.
11. Eagleton, *Sweet Violence*, 29.
12. Stanley Kubrick, *Sight and Sound*, February 1972, 5, cited in Aubrey Malone, *Censoring Hollywood: Sex and Violence in Film and on the Cutting Room Floor* (Jefferson: McFarland, 2011), 153. Hal Hinson, writing in *The Washington Post*, huffed, "Today, with real life violence all around us, it's harder to be sure about the cathartic function of art. We"re concerned that real violence might overwhelm us, sending us off like the Michael Douglas character in *Falling Down*: half-cocked, defeated and looking for revenge" (*Washington Post*, May 23, 1993, cited in Aubrey Malone, 191).
13. Howard Good, *Media Ethics Goes to the Movies* (Westport: Greenwood Press, 2002), 161.
14. Good, *Media Ethics Goes to the Movies*, 164f.
15. Good, *Media Ethics Goes to the Movies*, 173f.
16. Julia Kristeva, "Strangers to Ourselves," in *States of Mind: Dialogues on the European Mind* (New York: University of New York Press, 1995), 13f., cited in Richard Kearney, *Strangers, Gods and Monsters: Interpreting Otherness* (London: Routledge, 2003), 8f.
17. Rowan Williams, *Writing in the Dust: After September 11* (Grand Rapids: Eerdmans, 2002), 15.
18. Augustine, for example, argues that Rome often engages in conflict induced by injustices committed from beyond her borders (*City of God*, 3.10.98; 4.15.154).
19. Jane Mills, *The Money Shot* (Annandale: Pluto, 2001), 93, cited in Aubrey Malone, 191.
20. Ridley Scott, "The Essence of Combat: Making Black Hawk Down," http://www.imdb.com/title/tt0367710/.
21. Matthew Alford, *Reel Power: Hollywood Cinema and American Supremacy* (London: Pluto Press, 2010), 105.
22. Trevor McCrisken and Andrew Pepper, *American History and Contemporary Hollywood Film* (Edinburgh: Edinburgh University Press), 123; Susan Sontag, "The Imagination of Disaster," in *Hal in the Classroom: Science Fiction Films* (Dayton: Pflaum, 1974), 31.
23. Robin Wood, *Hollywood From Vietnam to Reagan* (New York: Columbia University Press, 1986), 163.
24. Judith Butler, *Frames of War: When is Life Grievable?* (London: Verso, 2009), 2.
25. According to Sara Mills, "Discourses structure both our sense of reality and our notion of our own identity" (*Discourse* [London: Routledge, 1997], 15).
26. Ben Agger, *Cultural Studies and Critical Theory* (Washington, D.C.: The Falmer Press, 1992), 25.
27. Margaret R. Miles and S. Brent Plate, "Hospitable Vision: Some Notes on the Ethics of Seeing Film," *Crosscurrents* (Spring 2004), 22–31 (23). Cf. John C. Lyden, *Film as Religion: Myths, Morals and Rituals* (New York: New York University Press, 2003); Tom Beaudoin, *Virtual Faith: The Irreverent Spiritual Quest of Generation X* (Chichester: Jossey-Bass, 1998); Margaret Miles, *Seeing and Believing: Religion and Values in the Movies* (Boston: Beacon,

1996). Lucas makes a similar point in interview in 1983 (Aljean Harmetz, "Burden of Dreams: George Lucas," in Sally Kline [ed.], *George Lucas: Interviews* [Jackson: University Press of Mississippi, 1999], 135–144 [143]).

28. Cited in Phillip Gourevitch, "Letter from Rwanda," *Bew Yorker* (Dec. 15, 1995), 84.

29. Carl Silvio and Tony M. Vinci, "Introduction," in Silvio and Vinci (eds.), 1–8 (3).

30. Citation from René Girard, *The Things Hidden Since the Foundation of the World* (London: Athlone, 1987), 7. On these matters see Walter Wink, *Engaging the Powers: Discernment and Resistance in a World of Domination* (Minneapolis: Fortress, 1992), ch. 1. In a revealing weblog Jason Salas admits engaging in a conversation with a Christian who admitted being unable to let her children watch sexual activity on screen while without second-thought allowing them to witness fabricated acts of murder ("On Piety, Star Wars, and Raising Your Children to be Morally Aware," http://weblogs.asp.net/jasonsalas/archive/2005/05/19/407406.aspx, consulted 08–06–05).

31. See Ariel Dorfman and Armand Mattelart, *How to Read Donald Duck: Imperialist Ideology in the Disney Comic*, trans. David Kanzle (New York: International General, 1991).

32. George Orwell, cited in Craig L. Carr, *Orwell, Politics, and Power* (New York: Continuum, 2010), 1.

33. Veronica A. Wilson, "Seduced by the Dark Side of the Force: Gender, Sexuality, and moral Agency in George Lucas's *Star Wars* Universe," in Silvio and Vinci (eds.), 134–152 (135).

34. Wetmore, *The Empire Triumphant*, 95.

35. Wilson, 136.

36. Silvio and Vinci (eds.), 3.

37. Wetmore, *The Empire Triumphant*, 48.

38. See Andrew Gordon, "*Star Wars*: A Myth for Our Time," *Literature/Film Quarterly* 6.4 (1978), 320–325; Mary Henderson, *Star Wars: The Magic of Myth* (New York: Bantam, 1997), 116–20; John Shelton Lawrence, "Joseph Campbell, George Lucas, and the Monomyth," in Kapell and Lawrence (eds.), 21–33. Cf. Leah Deyneka, "May the Myth Be with You, Always: Archetypes, Mythic Elements, and Apects of Joseph Campbell's Heroic Monomyth in the Original *Star Wars* Trilogy," in Douglas Brode and Leah Deyneka (eds.), *Myth, Media, and Culture in Star Wars: An Anthology* (Lanham: Scarecrow Press, 2012), 31–46.

39. Dan Rubey, "Not So Long Ago, Not So Far Away: New Variations on Old Themes and Questioning *Star Wars*' Revival of Heroic Archetypes," in Brode and Deyneka (eds.), 47–64 (53).

40. Silvio and Vinci (eds.), 3.

41. See Robert A. Segal, *Myth: A Very Short Introduction* (Oxford: Oxford University Press, 2004), 137f.; *Joseph Campbell: An Introduction* (New York: Garland, 1987); Beldon C. Lane, "The Power of Myth: Lessons from Joseph Campbell," *The Christian Century* (July 5–12, 1989), 652–654.

42. So Philip L. Simpson, "Thawing the Ice Princess," in Kapell and Lawrence (eds.), 115–130; Veronica A. Wilson; and Diana Dominguez, "Feminism and the Force: Empowerment and Disillusionment in a Galaxy Far, Far Away," in Silvio and Vinci (eds.), 109–133. In the third draft Lucas' hero was a woman (see Kaminski, 104, 464f., 517f.).

43. See Wetmore, *The Empire Triumphant*, chs. 4–5; Matthew Wilhelm Kapell, "Eugenics, Racism, and the Jedi Gene Pool," in Kapell and Lawrence (eds.), 159–173. There have been considerable concerns with the "racial" portrayal of the Gungans, Jar Jar Binks in particular, in *Star Wars Episode I: The Phantom Menace* (see Kaminski, 364). Robin Wood: "The war movie gave us various ethnic types (Jew, Pollack, etc.) under the leadership of a WASP American; the Lucas film substitutes fantasy figures (robots, Chewbacca) fulfilling precisely the same roles, surreptitiously permitting the same indulgence in WASP superiority" (*Hollywood from Vietnam to Reagan* [New York: Columbia University Press, 1986], 167). Cf. Wetmore, *The Empire Triumphant*, 35–39. "The people of color of the *Star Wars* universe are literally alienated—they are represented as aliens, as complete and utterly nonhuman. For the most part in the two trilogies, non-white means non-human." [Wetmore, *The Empire Triumphant*, 37] Interestingly, in the autumn of 1973 Lucas claimed of his forthcoming space-fantasy "The space

aliens are the heroes, and the Homo Sapiens naturally the villains" (cited in Kaminski, 61). Critics point to Darth Vader as a "black" character, for although the Emperor is equally garbed in black Vader's voice is that of James Earl Jones. However, Jones was not Lucas' first choice for the part, and he eventually cast Jones because of the commanding and menacing quality he could bring to the voice. Thus the casting decision was a pragmatic rather than an ideological one. "He was the best actor that I could possibly find" (Lucas in Ryder Windham and Peter Vilmus, *Star Wars: The Complete Vader* [London: Simon & Schuster, 2009], 21). Jones even requested that his name be absent from *Star Wars*' credits, claiming that David Prowse is Vader, and that Jones himself could take no major credit for the character. Moreover, Vader's racial significance becomes subverted in his identity-revelation to Luke.

44. So Carl Silvio, "The *Star Wars* Trilogies and Global Capitalism," in Silvio and Vinci (eds.), 53–73.

45. So Veronica A. Wilson; Roger Kaufman, "How the *Star Wars* Saga Evokes the Creative Promise of Homosexual Love: A Gay-Centered Psychological Perspective," in Kapell and Lawrence (eds.), 131–156.

46. So Tony M. Vinci, "The Fall of the Rebellion; or, Defiant and Obedient Heroes in a Galaxy Far, Far Away: Individualism and Intertextuality in the *Star Wars* Trilogies," in Silvio and Vinci (eds.), 11–33. While many of Lucas' own comments suggest considerable faith in the "American dream," his movies push in a different direction. After all, the ending of *THX 1138* is itself largely ambiguous, and the end of the *Star Wars* saga offers more a celebration of communitarian social difference than individualism. It is also noteworthy to consider the impact of the community of filmmakers that composed the early stages of American Zoetrope, and Lucas' own efforts to mimic that with his Skywalker Ranch.

47. See Stephanie J. Wilhelm, "Imperial Plastic, Republican Fiber: Speculating on the Post-Colonial Other," in Kapell and Lawrence (eds.), 175–183; and the fuller study of Wetmore, *The Empire Triumphant*.

48. Liam Neeson, in *Star Wars Episode I: The Phantom Menace* (2001), DVD Disc 2.

49. Dan Rubey, "Not So Long Ago, Not So Far Away: New Variations on Old Themes and Questioning *Star Wars*' Revival of Heroic Archetypes," in Brode and Deyneka (eds.), 47–64 (53).

50. Silvio and Vinci (eds.), 8.

51. Wetmore, *The Empire Triumphant*, 9f., citing Stuart Hall, "The Whites of Their Eyes: Racist Ideologies and the Media," in George Bridges and Rosalind Brunt (eds.), *Silver Linings: Some Strategies for the Eighties* (London: Lawrence and Wisehart, 1981), 37–8, and Henry A. Giroux, *Channel Surfing* (New York: St. Martins, 1997), 56.

52. Slavoj Žižek, *Violence: Six Sideways Reflections* (London: Profile, 2008), 11.

53. Walter Wink, *Engaging the Powers: Discernment and Resistance in a World of Domination* (Minneapolis: Fortress, 1992), 13; *The Powers That Be: Theology for a New Millennium* (New York: Doubleday, 1998), 42; Grace M. Jantzen, *Becoming Divine: Towards a Feminist Philosophy of Religion* (Manchester: Manchester University Press, 1998). Cf. Jantzen, *Foundations of Violence*, 8.

54. L. Gregory Jones, *Embodying Forgiveness: A Theological Analysis* (Grand Rapids: William B. Eerdmans, 1995), 77.

55. Wink, *The Powers That Be*, 42. Cf. Michelle Kinnucan, "What Star Wars Teaches Us," *CommonDreams.org*, May 10, 2002; http://commondreams.org/cgi-bin/print.cgi?file=views02/0510-06.htm; Michelle J. Kinnucan, "Pedagogy of (the) Force: The Myth of Redemptive Violence," in Kapell and Lawrence (eds.), 59–72.

56. Jonathan Wolfe, *An Introduction to Political Philosophy* (New York: Oxford University Press, 1996), 14.

57. Wink, *The Powers That Be*, 56.

58. Bryan P. Stone, *Faith and the Film: Theological Themes at the Cinema* (St. Louis: Chalice Press, 2000), 139.

59. See Stone, 139; Joey Earl Horstman, "Star Wars (Motion Picture)," *The Other Side* 33.2 (1977).

60. Robert Jewett and John Shelton Lawrence, *Captain America and the Crusade Against Evil: The Dilemma of Zealous Nationalism* (Grand Rapids: Eerdmans, 2003), xiii. Cf. George Marsden, "The American Revolution: Partisanship, 'Just Wars' and Crusades," in R.A. Wells (ed.), *The Wars of America: Christian Views*

(Grand Rapids: Eerdmans, 1981), 12; Mark A. Noll, *Christians in the American Revolution* (Grand Rapids: Eerdmans/Christian University, 1977), 72.

61. Gary Westfal, "Space Opera," in Edward James and Farah Mendelsohn (eds.), *The Cambridge Companion to Science Fiction* (Cambridge: Cambridge University Press, 2003), 197–208 (198).

62. See Lucas in interview in 1983 (Harmetz in Kline, 143]). These issues are dealt with more fully in John C. McDowell, *The Gospel According to Star Wars: Faith, Hope and the Force* (Louisville: Westminster John Knox Press, 2007).

63. Kerry O'Quinn, "The George Lucas Saga," in Kline, 98–134 (133).

64. Some thought provoking studies can be found in the likes of Silvio and Vinci and Kapell and Lawrence. Yet several of the papers are less well equipped to assess the two sets of trilogies' differences. For more on the deliberately designed parallelism see John C. McDowell, "*Star Wars*' Saving Return," *Journal of Religion and Film* 13.1 (April 2009), http://www.unomaha.edu/jrf/vol13.no1/StarWars.htm. Also, see McDowell, *The Gospel According to Star Wars*, ch. 4.

65. Jantzen, *Foundations of Violence*, 29.

66. Susanne Kappeler, *The Will to Violence: The Politics of Personal Behaviour* (Cambridge: Polity, 1995), 9.

67. Martin Luther King, Jr., *Strength to Love* (London: Collins, 1963), 31.

68. John Shelton Lawrence and Robert Jewett, *The Myth of the American Superhero* (Grand Rapids: Eerdmans, 2002), and Robert Jewett and John Shelton Lawrence, *Captain America and the Crusade Against Evil: The Dilemma of Zealous Nationalism* (Grand Rapids: Eerdmans, 2003). Cf. Lawrence, "Fascist Redemption or Democratic Hope?," in Matthew Wilhelm Kapell and William G. Doty (eds.), *Jacking into the Matrix: Cultural Reception and Interpretation* (New York: Continuum, 2004), 80–96; Jewett, *Saint Paul at the Movies: The Apostle's Dialogue with American Culture* (Louisville: Westminster John Knox, 1993), ch. 2.

69. Beaudoin, *Virtual Faith*, 21.

70. Nicholas Jackson O'Shaughnessy, *Politics and Propaganda: Weapons of Mass Seduction* (Manchester: Manchester University Press, 2004), 139.

71. O'Shaughnessy argues that "the Manichean good-evil universe ... has been a staple of Hollywood from its first beginnings" (135). This "politics of purity" which generates the "demonised other" deflects the critical moral gaze from oneself: "Enemies also freeze our conscience and assuage our guilt, nothing we do to them can possibly be bad enough" (126). Manichaean readings of *Star Wars* have been the most common way of perceiving the conceptuality of the movies (Michelle J. Kinnucan, "Pedagogy of [the] Force: The Myth of Redemptive Violence," in Kapell and Lawrence (eds.), 59–72; John Lyden, "The Apocalyptic Cosmology of *Star Wars*," *Journal of Religion and Film* 4.1 (2000), 7, http://www.unomaha.edu/jrf/LydenStWars.htm, consulted 15-05-05; Mark Rowlands, *The Philosopher at the End of the Universe* [London: Ebury Press, 2003], 209).

72. Matthew Wilhelm Kapell and John Shelton Lawrence, "Introduction: Spectacle, Merchandise, and Influence," in Kapell and Lawrence (eds.), 1–18 (9).

73. Wink, *The Powers That Be*, 42.

74. Jantzen, *Foundations of Violence*, 29.

75. See Wink, *The Powers That Be*, 54.

76. Lawrence, 82; Jewett and Lawrence, 1, 6, 8. Also, and importantly, Jewett and Lawrence explicitly use language of "redemptive violence" (27; cf. ch. 13). Cf. Lawrence, "Joseph Campbell, George Lucas, and the Monomyth," 31.

77. Wink, *The Powers That Be*, 42. Cf. Michelle Kinnucan, "What Star Wars Teaches Us," *CommonDreams.org*, May 10, 2002; http://commondreams.org/cgi-bin/print.cgi?file=views02/0510–06.htm; Kinnucan, "Pedagogy of (the) Force: The Myth of Redemptive Violence."

78. Wink, *Powers*, 48.

79. John Shelton Lawrence, "Joseph Campbell, George Lucas, and the Monomyth," in Kapell and Lawrence (eds.), 21–33.

80. Lawrence and Jewett, 268; Lawrence, 85.

81. Wink, *Powers*, 48.

82. Will Brooker, *Star Wars* (London: Palgrave Macmillian, 2009), 78f.

83. So Kinnucan, 64.

84. Butler, *Frames of War*, 14.

85. "Not So Long Ago, Not So Far Away:

New Variations on Old Themes and Questioning *Star Wars'* Revival of Heroic Archetypes," in Brode and Deyneka (eds.), 50.

86. Wetmore, *The Empire Triumphant*, 69.

87. It is this that Roz Kaveney criticises for different reasons, as a neglect of "history" in favor of "biography" (*From Alien to the Matrix: Reading Science Fiction and Film* [London: I.B. Taurus, 2005], 113). This is a strange criticism since Lucas specifically uses biography to develop symbolic figures, and to draw on mythic archetypes. At most it simply claims that Lucas' portrayal is different from that of previous space operas, and that is what renders it a failure according to Kaveney.

88. Dan Rubey, "Not So Far Away," *Jump Cut* 18 (1978), 8–14 (9); Michelle J. Kinnucan, "Pedagogy of (the) Force: The Myth of Redemptive Violence," in Kapel and Lawrence (eds.), 59–72 (64).

89. Wink, *The Powers That Be*, 53.

90. Jonathan Rosenbaum, *Movie Wars: How Hollywood and the Media Limit What Movies We Can See* (Chicago: A Capella Books, 2000), 138.

91. John Milbank, *Being Reconciled: Ontology and Pardon* (London: Routledge, 2003), 28.

92. Wink, *The Powers That Be*, 50f.

93. Wink, *Engaging the Powers*, 17.

94. Michael Pye and Linda Myles, "George Lucas," in Kline, 64–86 (85).

95. Rubey, "Not So Long Ago, Not So Far Away: New Variations on Old Themes and Questioning *Star Wars'* Revival of Heroic Archetypes," in Brode and Deyneka (eds.), 59.

96. Stephen J. Sansweet, "Foreword," in Windham and Vilmer, vii.

97. See Kaminski, 100; Rinzler, 131; Henderson, 146, 164, 189.

98. Ian McDiarmid, in *Empire* magazine (June 2005), 94.

99. Ian McDiarmid, in *Empire* magazine (June 2005), 94, and second citation in "Palpatine," http://en.wikipedia.org/wiki/Palpatine, consulted 08–06–05.

100. Rick McCallum, in "The Chosen One" Featurette, *Star Wars Episode III: The Revenge of the Sith* DVD 2 (2005).

101. Tim Rayment, "Master of the Universe," *The Sunday Times Magazine* (16 May 1999), 14–24 (20).

102. Wink, *Powers*, 53f.

103. Lucas, in Laurent Bouzereau, *Star Wars: The Annotated Screenplays* (New York: Ballantine, 1997), 180.

104. George Lucas in "The Making of Episode I" *The Phantom Menace* DVD 2 (1999).

105. The title "Lord of the Sith" comes from the fact that after "the Great Schism" outcast Jedi, who had rebelled against the Jedi Council over the use of "the dark side of the Force," came across the uncharted planet Korriban on which they discovered and conquered a race known as the Sith (see "Sith Order," http://en.wikipedia.org/wiki/Sith_Order, consulted 14–06–05).

106. *ROTS*, 213.

107. Citations from Lev, 31f.; George W. Bush, "President Holds Prime Time News Conference" (11 October 2001), http://www.whitehouse.gov/new/releases/2001/09/200109208.html; Ian Nathan, "R2D2, Where Are You?," *The Times Review* (14 May 2005), 14. Similarly, see Richard Rayner, *The Sunday Telegraph* (28 March 1999), cited in David Wilkinson, *The Power of the Force: The Spirituality of the Star Wars* (Oxford: Lion, 2000), 15.

108. Joseph Campbell, *The Hero with a Thousand Faces* (Princeton: Princeton University Press, 1949), 238.

109. Cf. Orson Scott Card, "No Faith in This Force," www.beliefnet.com/story/167/story_16700_1.html, consulted 30–05–05.

110. Hannah Pok, "The *Star Wars* Trilogy: Fantasy, Narcissism and Fear of the Other in Reagan's America," http://hannahpok.com/deepfieldspace/framesrc2c.html, consulted 18–05–05.

111. Joseph Campbell, *Myths to Live By*, cited in Wink, *The Powers That Be*.

112. John Milbank, for instance, traces an "ontology of violence" through modern liberal socio-political theory (*Theology and Social Theory: Beyond Secular Reason* [Oxford: Basil Blackwell, 1990]).

113. Wink, *Engaging*, 19.

114. Cited in Michelle Kinnucan, "What Star Wars Teaches Us," *Common Dreams.org* (10 May 2002), http://www.commondreams.org/views02/0510–06.htm, consulted 26–05–05.

115. Kinnucan, "Pedagogy of (the) Force," 65, citing Koenraad Kuiper, "*Star*

*Wars*: An Imperial Myth," *Journal of Popular Culture* 21.4 (1988), 77–86 (78).
116. Cited in Kinnucan, "What Star Wars Teaches Us."
117. Michelle Kinnucan, 'What Star Wars Teaches Us', *CommonDreams* (May 10, 2002), http://www.commondreams.org/views02/0510–06.htm, consulted 14–06-05.
118. Kaveney, 118.
119. See George Lucas, *Star Wars: From the Adventures of Luke Skywalker* (London: Sphere Books, 1977), 1.
120. On the connections with Rome see Martin M. Winkler, "*Star Wars* and the Roman Empire," in Martin M. Winkler (ed.), *Classical Myth and Culture in the Cinema* (Oxford: Oxford University Press, 2001), 272–290.
121. See Rubey, "Not So Long Ago, Not So Far Away: New Variations on Old Themes and Questioning *Star Wars*' Revival of Heroic Archetypes," in Brode and Deyneka (eds.), 61. Cf. Wetmore, 69.
122. Lawrence, 85.
123. See Michael Kaminski, *The Secret History of Star Wars: The Art of Storytelling and the Making of a Modern Epic* (Kingston: Legacy Books Press, 2008), 117f.
124. Christensen claims that the American voters "wanted a president who was sure of himself and his nation, unbothered by doubt, and unfazed by the complexities of the nation, the world, or human behaviour" (199).
125. Jonathan cf. Rosenbaum, *Movies as Politics* (Berkeley: University of California Press, 1997), 107. David Brin, "I Accuse ... Or Zola Meets Yoda," in David Brin and Matthew Woodring Stover (eds.), *Star Wars on Trial* (Dallas: Benbella, 2006), 17–48 (25).
126. Wink, *The Powers That Be*, 49.
127. See, e.g., Myles and Pye, 83; Vincent Canby, "Not Since Flash Gordon Conquers the Universe," *New York Times* (5 June 1977), §2:33; Arthur Lubow, "A Space Iliad," *Film Comment* 13 (July-August 1977), 20; Roger Banham, "Summa Galactica," *New Society* 42 (27 October 1977), 191; Anne Lancashire, "*Attack of the Clones* and the Politics of *Star Wars*," *The Dalhousie Review* 82.2 (Summer 2002), 235–253.
128. Lawrence and Jewett, *The Myth of the American Superhero*, ch. 13.

129. Dan Rubey, "Not So Long Ago, Not So Far Away: New Variations on Old Themes and Questioning *Star Wars*' Revival of Heroic Archetypes," in Brode and Deyneka (eds.), 47–64 (55).
130. Rubey, "Not So Long Ago, Not So Far Away: New Variations on Old Themes and Questioning *Star Wars*' Revival of Heroic Archetypes," in Brode and Deyneka (eds.), 55.
131. Rubey, "Not So Long Ago, Not So Far Away: New Variations on Old Themes and Questioning *Star Wars*' Revival of Heroic Archetypes," in Brode and Deyneka (eds.), 62.
132. Lucas, cited in Rinzler, 325.
133. Stephen P. McVeigh, "The Galactic Way of Warfare," in Kapell and Lawrence (eds.), 35–58 (36).
134. McVeigh, 38.
135. James W. Gibson, *Warrior Dreams: Violence and Manhood in Post-Vietnam America* (New York: Hill & Wang, 1994), 12, 14.
136. Dan Rubey, "Not So Long Ago, Not So Far Away: New Variations on Old Themes and Questioning *Star Wars*' Revival of Heroic Archetypes," in Brode and Deyneka (eds.), 49.
137. Rayment, 20.
138. Lucas, in Rayment, 20.
139. Lucas, cited in Stephen Zito, "George Lucas Goes Far Out," in Kline, 45–54 (53).
140. Matthew Stover, *Star Wars Episode III: Revenge of the Sith* (London: Century, 2005), 280.
141. See Wetmore, 5f.
142. Quentin Tarantino's movies arguably move in this morally equivocating direction—the carefully choreographed scenes of conflict and violence are orchestrated to evoke awe and fascination, dare I say it "entertainment," with the near-balletic display and thus aestheticization of violence. The dual-part revenge movie *Kill Bill* is example.
143. Rowan Williams, *The Truce of God* (London: Fount Paperbacks, 1983), 96. Even if the self is not "passive" in any simple sense, as cultural theorists rightly observe, nonetheless Williams' point is suggestive of a claim that we remain largely at the mercy of an ideology constructed and reinforced by the liberal market, so that the imagination of alternatives remains

of alternatives *within* the dominant ideology.

144. Kinnucan, "Pedagogy of (the) Force: The Myth of Redemptive Violence," 66.

145. Stover, *ROTS*, 285.

146. James B. Jordan, "Pacifism and the Old Testament," in Gary North (ed.), *The Theology of Christian Resistance* (Tyler: Geneva Divinity School Press, 1983), 92.

147. Frank Allnut, *Unlocking the Mystery of the Force: The Force of Star Wars* (Van Nuys: Bible Voice, 1997), 90.

148. Allnut, 143.

149. Allnut, 169.

150. For example, Peter Biskind, *Easy Riders, Raging Bulls: Sex-Drugs-and-Rock 'n' Roll Generation Saved Hollywood* (New York: Touchstone, 1998), 342f.; Kinnucan, "Pedagogy of (the) Force: The Myth of Redemptive Violence," 65; Mary Henderson, *Star Wars: The Magic of Myth* (New York: Bantam, 1997), 117; Wetmore, *The Empire Triumphant*, 96.

151. Hal G.P. Colebatch, *Return of the Heroes: The Lord of the Rings, Star Wars, Harry Potter, and Social Conflict*, 2d ed. (Christchurch: Cybereditions Corporation, 2003), 12.

152. Walter Wink, *Jesus and Nonviolence: A Third Way* (Minneapolis: Fortress, 2003), 72.

153. See, e.g., Miroslav Volf, *Exclusion and Embrace: A Theological Exploration of Identity, Otherness, and Reconciliation* (Nashville: Abingdon Press, 1996), 114–119.

154. Joseph Campbell, *The Hero with a Thousand Faces* (Princeton: Princeton University Press, 1949), 353.

155. Jones, *Embodying Forgiveness*, 73. "Further, the story shows the fragility of our commitment to unlearn and break our habits of sin, even when there is a desire to do so. If such commitments are to be sustained, they require supportive friendships, practices, and institutions that enable the unlearning of destructive habits and the cultivation of holy ones. The film suggests that those friendships, practices, and institutions are absent precisely because of their fragility in the face of violence and vengeance. It takes only a moment to destroy lives through violence, but it takes a lifetime to cultivate alternative patterns and practices of forgiveness, of trust, of love" (76).

156. Walter Kasper: "every attempt to alter this situation is itself subject to the conditions created by the disaster. The result is an unending satanic cycle of guilt and revenge, violence and counterviolence" (*The God of Jesus Christ*, trans. Matthew J. O"Connell [New York: Crossroad, 1984], 160).

157. Even when war is spoken of in terms of being "unavoidable," as Jon Nuttall for instance does, it quickly becomes naturalized in the imagination (Jon Nuttall, *Moral Questions: An Introduction to Ethics* [Cambridge: Polity Press, 1993], 161). The theologian Karl Barth exposes "the satanic doctrine that war is inevitable and therefore justified" shortly after calling for protest against standing armies (*Church Dogmatics*, Volume III, *The Doctrine of Creation* Part 4, trans. G.W. Bromiley and T.F. Torrance (Edinburgh: T&T Clark, 1961), III.4, 399, 400). After all, such military capabilities make the search for peace something much less strenuous, dulling and constraining the imagination to resort all too quickly to military solutions before all other options have been *honestly* exhausted.

## Chapter 2

1. M. Keith Booker, *Alternate Americas: Science Fiction Film and American Culture* (Westport: Praeger, 2006), 110.

2. Wetmore, *The Empire Triumphant*, 6.

3. Wetmore, *The Empire Triumphant*, 7.

4. Booker, 110, 114.

5. Booker, 114f.

6. Booker, 115.

7. Stephen P. McVeigh, "The Galactic Way of Warfare," in Kapell and Lawrence (eds.), 35–58 (36).

8. Booker, 13f. Cf. 115.

9. Booker, 115.

10. Booker, 115.

11. For more on Reagan's use of *SW* rhetoric see Peter Krämer, "Fighting the Evil Empire: *Star Wars*, the Strategic Defense Initiative, and the Politics of Science Fiction," in Brode and Deyneka (eds.), 63–76; Nick Desolge, "*Star Wars*: An Exhibition in cold War Politics," in Brode and Deyneka (eds.), 55–62.

12. Martin M. Winkler, "*Star Wars* and the Roman Empire," in Martin M. Winkler (ed.), *Classical Myth and Culture in the Cinema* (Oxford: Oxford University Press, 2001), 272–290 (272).

13. For Asimov's acknowledgement of Lucas' borrowing from *Foundation* see Peter Bondanella, *The Eternal City: Roman Images in the Modern World* (Chapel Hill: University of North Carolina Press, 1987), 270n11.

14. George Lucas, *Star Wars*, 1.

15. Winkler, 274.

16. Winkler, 274f.

17. Hal G.P. Colebatch, *Return of the Heroes: The Lord of the Rings, Star Wars, Harry Potter, and Social Conflict*, 2d ed. (Christchurch: Cybereditions Corporation, 2003), 30.

18. Winkler, 275.

19. Winkler, 279.

20. Winkler, 275.

21. Booker, 116, 118.

22. There is an apparent allusion to George W. Bush's "If you"re not for us you"re against us" comment in Anakin's assertion to Obi-Wan, "If you"re not for me you"re my enemy."

23. Patricia Kerslake, *Science Fiction and Empire* (Liverpool: Liverpool University Press, 2007), 29.

24. The phrase is Iain Thomson's ("Deconstructing the Hero," in Jeff McLaughlin [ed.], *Comics as Philosophy* [Jackson: University of Mississippi Press, 2005], 100–129 [103]).

25. Reinhold Niebuhr, *The Irony of American History* (London: Nisbet, 1952).

26. Cf. Slavoj Žižek, *Violence: Six Sideways Reflections* (London: Profile, 2008), 107.

27. It needs to be clarified what this *theological* comparison is and is not doing. It is *not* saying that *Star Wars* is a Christian text. This would be an odd thing to claim given the movies' eclectic borrowings. Yet there is something even stranger occurring in dividing up and hermetically sealing religious approaches neatly as if a Christian theological approach did not overlap with themes and features of non-Christian religions. Moreover, this is certainly not a way of using *Star Wars* to illustrate and demonstrate Christianity. Too much time and attention is given to understanding the saga on its own terms than is usually the case with specifically Christian writing on the saga (e.g., see Staub, Dalton, and Grimes). Yet one of the points I argue in chapter 2 of *The Gospel According to Star Wars* is that the saga has been influenced by the western Christian environment more than is usually admitted by its "readers," and that its presentation of the Force has more to do with certain western post-enlightenment theologies. Lucas claims to use *Star Wars* to, among many other things, respond critically to features of the Lutheran Christianity of some of his youth, yet he imbibes much of its imagination.

28. Mike Alsford, *Heroes and Villains* (Waco: Baylor University Press, 2006), 8.

29. Roy M. Anker, *Catching Light: Looking for God at the Movies* (Grand Rapids: Eerdmans, 2004), 230. For examples of the distinction between "warrior" and "soldier" see Robert Bly, *Iron John: A Book About Men* (New York: Vintage, 1990), 150; Dwight H. Judy, *Healing the Male Soul: Christianity and the Mythic Journey* (New York: Crossroad Publishing, 1992), 63.

30. George Lucas, in "Prime of the Jedi," *Star Wars Episode I: The Phantom Menace* (2001), DVD Disc2.

31. *Blade Runner* has a theatrical cut (1982), a Director's Cut (1992), and a Final Cut (2007).

32. See "Mace Windu," http://en.wiki pedia.org/wiki/Mace_Windu, consulted 14-06-05.

33. There are parallels here to J.R.R. Tolkien's approach to the catastrophe of mechanized warfare. In his great literary creation technology comes to play almost an archetypal role of its own in the background to the rise of the power of evil.

34. Augustine, *City of God*, trans. Henry Bettenson (Harmondsworth: Penguin, 1972), 19.7.862.

35. Chapter 31, cited in John Porter, *The Tao of Star Wars* (Atlanta: Humanics, 2003), 68.

36. It is arguable that even Tolkien's *Lord of the Rings* somewhat trades in the currency of redemptive violence, given ultimacy by the eschatological nature of the new life achieved both by the destruction of the ring of power and the violence taken to distract Sauron's eye from detecting its presence in his land of Mordor.

37. Stover, *ROTS*, 224.
38. See, e.g., Augustine, 4.15.154; Karl Barth, *Church Dogmatics Volume III The Doctrine of Creation Pt. 4*, trans. G.W. Bromiley and T.F. Torrance (Edinburgh: T&T Clark, 1961), 432.
39. Amartya Sen, *Identity and Violence: The Illusion of Destiny* (London: Penguin, 2006), xiii.
40. Stanley Hauerwas, *The Peaceable Kingdom: A Primer in Christian Ethics* (London: SCM, 1983), 79. Cf. Barth, 432.
41. According to George Weigel, "The 'presumption' has tended to give theologians and religious leaders a bloated sense of their own role in decision-making about war and peace" (Paul J. Griffiths and George Weigel, "Who Wants War? An Exchange," *First Things* 152 [2005], 10–12). This, however, painfully misses the sense in which Christian communities should be, even if it is provisional and fragile in its faithfulness, embodied expressions of God's grace to a sinful world, and therefore serious about the business of understanding and contributing interrogatively and creatively to the ongoing conversations about the common good.
42. See, e.g., Augustine, *City of God*, 4.15.154.
43. Citation from Barth, 398.
44. Roz Kaveney, it would appear, just has not paid sufficient attention when she complains that there are "too many paradoxes in Lucas' world" and then uses the Jedi as a significant example: "we are supposed to believe in the preternatural goodness of the Jedi Knights and yet at the same time watch them operating without a sense of moral incongruity in a world in which slavery is common. (To nit-pick here, it is not so much the Jedi *Knights* who are on view in the prequels as the Jedi *Masters* and particularly the Jedi *Council*.) When Obi-Wan and his mentor Qui-Gon Jinn discover the potential of young Anakin Skywalker (the future Darth Vader), they ship him off for training without bothering to free his mother from bondage" (*From Alien to the Matrix: Reading Science Fiction and Film* [London: I.B. Tauris, 2005], 116). It may not be readily apparent to the untrained eye, but the failure to liberate Shmi Skywalker was indeed one of the features in Anakin's growing resentment of his mentor Obi-Wan. It is, after all, Anakin's subsequent refusal to let his dream of another's death, that of Padmé, be realized that is an important catalyst in his "fall." Kaveney's grand claim about paradoxes and inconsistencies is predicated on substantial ignorance of some basic features of the texts themselves.
45. There can be a kind of bare "peace" involved in the subject-denying imposition of one on another, of making that other subservient to a pacifying master. This is certainly "peace," but it is "peace" in the sense that the one dominated is denied the ability to wage war. Thus what is peace to one may be violence to another, and that induces the resentment among those who feel violated. Moreover, as the conduct of the superpowers during the Cold War for example reveals, what we call "times of peace" are often really times of war conducted by other means—spying, support of governments and factions in their own struggles, and so on (see Wink, *Engaging the Powers*, 27). So Augustine speaks of a "peace" that "hates the just peace of God, and loves its own peace of injustice. ... [T]he peace of the unjust, compared with the peace of the just, is not worthy even of the name of peace" (Augustine, 19.12.868, 869).
46. Walter Wink, *Jesus and Nonviolence: A Third Way* (Minneapolis: Fortress, 2003), 5.
47. Daniel M. Bell, Jr., "Can a War Against Terror Be Just? Or, What Is Just War Good For?" *Crosscurrents* (Spring 2006), 34–45 (39).
48. Citations from Barth, 460; Jon Nuttall, *Moral Questions: An Introduction to Ethics* (Cambridge: Polity Press, 1993), 161.
49. Anker, 225.
50. Lucas, commentary on DVD of *ESB* (2004).
51. See Michael Kaminski, *The Secret History of Star Wars: The Art of Storytelling and the Making of a Modern Epic* (Kingston: Legacy Books Press, 2008), 282ff.
52. Anker, 235.
53. Citations from Martin Luther King, Jr., *Strength to Love* (London: Collins, 1963), 152.
54. Properly understood, "pacifism" is not a *negative* term indicating an *absence of action*, a *not doing*. The common misunderstanding of "pacifism" as non-action parallels the way "peace" is generally re-

garded in negative terms as the *absence of conflict*, a bare peace that is not a purposeful action as such. Luke is not "fighting" for some abstract "peace," "freedom," "sovereign autonomy," abstract notion of "civilization," or even set of principles abstracted from persons. Instead his "peace" is a *positive doing of what is just and right*, or doing that which makes for *properly peaceful relations*. His is a struggle that always "take[s] sides," resonating with a resistance that has teeth and a sharp bite, and therefore cannot trivialize or sentimentalize "peace" by imagining that all would be well if only we could act a bit nicer to each other (citation from Wink, *Jesus and Nonviolence*, 4).

55. Wink, *Jesus and Nonviolence*, 72.

56. Joseph Campbell, *The Hero with a Thousand Faces* (Princeton: Princeton University Press, 1949), 353.

57. On *Star Wars Episode III: The Revenge of the Sith* DVD 2 (2005).

58. On *Star Wars'* prequels as critique of American politics see Lawrence ("Joseph Campbell, George Lucas, and the Monomyth," 27ff.; cf. McVeigh). He continues, "First *Star Wars* was monomythic, almost by recipe, and then [in the prequels] it became a veiled commentary on American politics from which the thrilling, simplistic heroic archetypes recede" (31). The problem is that the Nazi imagery, and the fear over totalitarianism in the *"classic trilogy"* means that Lawrence overstretches his point, and Lucas has on several occasions made the connection between the politics of the earlier trilogy and Vietnam, going as far as to liken the Ewoks to the Vietcong: "I was interested in the human side of war and the fact that [in Vietnam] here was a great nation, with all this technology which was losing a war to basically tribesmen" (in John Baxter, *George Lucas: A Biography* [London: Harper Collins, 1999], 141). Moreover, arguably the Campbellian monomyth works well in the context of *ANH* but less well in the context of *ESB* and *ROTJ*. Finally, it is not so much the political that largely separates the two sets of trilogies as much as the tragic trajectory of I–III in comparison with the development of the hero in IV–VI (see McDowell, *The Gospel According to Star Wars*, ch. 4; and John C. McDowell, "*Star Wars* Saving Return," *Journal of Religion and Film* 13.1 (April 2009), http://www.unomaha.edu/jrf/vol13.no1/StarWars.htm).

59. On saying that, however, by the time of *ROTS* there is a feeling among her senatorial critics that she is turning a blind eye to the increasingly oppressive climate on Coruscant, to the loss of rights guaranteed by the Constitution, and to the growing power of Palpatine.

60. Cited in Dale Pollock, *Skywalking: The Life and Films of George Lucas, the Creator of Star Wars* (Hollywood: Samuel French, 1990), 57.

61. "George Lucas could be messing with your head," *The Guardian* (23 May 2005).

62. Can one deconstruct values such as "peace," "democracy" and "freedom" as generally reducible to little more than the rhetoric of the powerful for the maintenance of the status quo, and of the nation-state greedy for its own survival (and it should be mentioned that nations do whatever they deem necessary to secure "victory" and success)?

63. John Baxter, *George Lucas: A Biography* (London: HarperCollins, 1999), 37.

64. Lucas, cited by Judy Stone, "George Lucas," in Kline, 3–7 (3).

65. A reference to the serial drama *The Prisoner* and/or an allusion to the imprinted numerical marking of Jews by the Nazis in the concentration camps?

66. Michael Ryan and Douglas Kellner, *Camera Politica: The Politics and Ideology of Contemporary Hollywood Film* (Bloomington: Indiana University Press, 1988), 49.

67. Lucas, cited in Stone, 6f.

68. On this see, for instance, John C. McDowell, "The Force is Strong with Star Wars," *Third Way* 30.5 (2007), 22–25.

69. Stone, citing Lucas, 4.

70. Lucas, cited by Stone, 5.

71. Lucas, in Stephen Farber, "George Lucas: The Stinky Kid Hits the Big Time," in Kline, 33–44 (42).

72. Citation from Michael Pye and Lynda Myles, "George Lucas," in Kline, 64–86 (84).

73. On this see McVeigh, 38.

74. Robert A. Segal, *Joseph Campbell: An Introduction* (New York: Garland, 1987), 64.

75. Lucas, cited by Jean Valley, "*the Em-*

*pire Strikes Back* and so does Filmmaker George Lucas with his Sequel to *Star Wars*," in Kline, 87–97 (93, 96). Cf. Lucas transcribed by Sally Kline, "The *Radioland Murders* Press Conference," in Kline, 177–183 (181); Lucas in Roger Ebert and Gene Siskel (eds.), *The Future of the Movies: Interviews with Martin Scorsese, Steven Spielberg, and George Lucas* (Kansas City: Andrews and McMeel, 1991), 95.

76. Lucas, in "The Chosen One."

77. Brin, "I Accuse ... Or Zola Meets Yoda," 23. Ironically, Brin criticizes *Star Wars*, wrongly, for being Manichaean in theological outlook, and yet in 1999 had commented on what would be expected from *ROTS*: "Coruscant and a zillion other planets are gonna have to fry as the emperor takes over, since that would only happen over the dead bodies of every decent citizen with any spirit" ("What's Wrong [and Right] with 'The Phantom Menace,'" *Salon* [June 15, 1999], http://www.salon.com/ent/movies/feature/1999/06/15/brin_side/index.html). Brin seems seriously ethically confused himself and equally carelessly inattentive to the flow of the *Star Wars* movies.

78. Kaveney, on the other hand, describes *Independence Day* as irredeemably and "explicitly an anti-revisionist film about aliens" (*From Alien to the Matrix*, 47).

79. Christopher Sharrett, "The Horror Film in Neoconservative Culture," in Barry Keith Grant (ed.), *The Dread of Difference: Gender and the Horror Film* (Austin: University of Texas Press, 1996), 253–276 (269).

80. Anker, 236f.

81. The Sith Lord designation "Darth" may come from the title "*Dar*k Lord of the Si*th*."

82. Kaveney, 115.

83. Lucas, cited by Rob Waugh, "The Billion Dollar Man," in *Day and Night: The Mail on Sunday* (8 May 2005), 24–25 (25).

84. Wetmore, 20.

85. Steven M. Sanders, "An Introduction to the Philosophy of Science Fiction Film," in Steven M. Sanders (ed.), *The Philosophy of Science Fiction Film* (Lexington: University Press of Kentucky, 2008), 1–18 (16).

86. Commenting on his student days at USC associating with underground filmmakers Lucas reflects, "What we had in common is we grew up in the "60s, protesting the Vietnam War" (cited in Biskind, 317).

87. Cited in John Baxter, *George Lucas: A Biography* (London: HarperCollins, 1999), 140.

88. Stephen P. McVeigh, "The Galactic Way of Warfare," in Kapell and Lawrence (eds.), 35–58 (38).

89. Wetmore: "An audience in search of reaffirmation of a more conservative, simpler world found their needs met in *a New Hope*" (7). Yet Wetmore is not careful here to distinguish, to some degree, Lucas' text and audience reception. Ryan and Kellner regard the Rebel Alliance's values as expressing a neo-conservative ideology that supports the American ideals of individualism, elitism, antistatism, agrarianism, and anti-rationalism, and therefore of support for western capitalism.

90. See Peter Biskind, *Easy Riders, Raging Bulls: Sex-Drugs-and-Rock 'n' Roll Generation Saved Hollywood* (New York: Touchstone, 1998), 317.

91. Cited in J.W. Rinzler, *The Making of Star Wars: The Definitive Story Behind the Original Film* (Ebury Press, 2008), 65.

92. Rinzler, 4.

93. Lucas, in interview with Larry Sturhahn, 1974, in Kline, 26.

94. Lucas in interview with Stephen Farber, 1974, in Kline, 42. While there is much in this that could legitimately be criticized as naïve it is interesting to note that Lucas himself admits to not succumbing to an "all people are good" mythology. So in interview in 1980 with Jean Valley he responds to the question "how do you feel about the human condition" by admitting that "I am very cynical, and as a result, I think the defense I have against it is to be optimistic and to think people are basically good, although I know in my heart they"re not" (in Kline, 96).

95. Lucas in interview with Stephen Zito, 1977, in Kline, 53.

96. Lucas, cited in Rinzler, 12. Similarly Lucas friend and colleague Walter Murch claims that "*Star Wars* is George's version of *Apocalypse Now*, rewritten in an otherworldly context. The Rebels in *Star Wars* are the Vietnamese, and the Empire is the United States" (in Peter Crowie, *The Apocalypse Now Book* [New York: De Capo Press, 2001], 1, cited in Kaminski, 57).

97. See Rinzler, 65.
98. Cited in Rinzler, 26.
99. Cited in Rinzler, 27.
100. Lucas, *Star Wars*, 1f. "The political issues have to deal with democracies that give their countries over to a dictator because of a crisis of some kind ... this was a very big issue when I was writing the first *Star Wars* because it was soon after Nixon's presidency, and there was a point, right before he was thrown out of office, where he suggested that they change a constitutional amendment so that he could run for a third term. Even when he started getting into trouble, he was saying, 'If the military will back me, I'll stay in office.' His idea was 'to hell with Congress and potential impeachment. I'll go directly to the army, and between the army and myself, I'll continue to be president.' This is what happens here. An emergency in the Republic leads the Senate to make Palpatine, essentially, 'dictator for life'" (cited in Jody Duncan, *Mythmaking: Behind the Scenes of Star Wars: Episode 2: Attack of the Clones* [New York: Ballantine Books, 2002], 101–103).
101. Andrew Gordon, "*Star Wars*: A Myth for Our Time," *Literature/Film Quarterly* 6.4 (1978), 320–325.
102. Rinzler, 15.
103. *Star Wars Episode VI: The Return of the Jedi*, dir. Richard Marquand (1983).
104. See Biskind, 342.
105. See Kaminski, 67.
106. Lawrence, 27.
107. The implication of my reading is that Lawrence and Jewett are mistaken in regarding Reagan's move to be a natural consequence of *Star Wars'* fascist politics (282).
108. For details on the latter see McDowell, *The Gospel According to Star Wars*, 92–108.
109. Lucas, cited in Kaminski, 140.
110. Lucas, cited in Kaminski, 140f.
111. Biskind, 336.
112. On this, see McDowell, "*Star Wars* Saving Return." It is true that there are significant aesthetic, conceptual, narrative, and other differences between the two sets of trilogies, particularly differences in ethos (and I have highlighted that on several occasions in this paper, noting, for instance, the "darkening" hermeneutical effect of the "tragic drama" (I–III) on IV–VI. Yet it would be a deep mistake to miss the quite deliberate parallelisms.
113. See McDowell, *The Gospel According to Star Wars*, ch. 7.
114. *Catechism of the Catholic Church* (1997), § 2304, cited in James Turner Johnson, "Just War, As It was and Is," *First Things* 149 (2005), 14–24.
115. Henry A. Giroux, "Reclaiming the social: Pedagogy, Resistance, and Politics in Celluloid Culture," in Jim Collins, Hilary Radner, and Ava Preacher Collins (eds.), *Film Theory Goes to the Movies* (London: Routledge, 1993), 37–55 (39).
116. O'Shaughnessy, 25.
117. On a relevant personal note, as a child I never created scenarios of peacemaking or non-violent resistance when playing with my *Star Wars* figures; and as an adult, I have always found the option to fight as a Sith-lord or as the Empire to be more interesting and appealing than it should [in games such as *Star Wars Battlefront* and *Battlefront II*, and *Star Wars Galactic Battlegrounds*]. That, of course, probably says more about me.
118. See Neil Postman, *Amusing Ourselves to Death: Public Discourse in the Age of Show Business* (New York: Viking Penguin, 1985), 3f.
119. Neil Postman, *Amusing Ourselves to Death: Public Discourse in the Age of Show Business* (New York: Viking Penguin, 1985.), 16.
120. Lucas, in Rayment, 16.
121. Carl Freedman, *Critical Theory and Science Fiction* (Hanover: Wesleyan University Press, 2000).
122. Martin M. Winkler, "*Star Wars* and the Roman Empire," in Martin M. Winkler (ed.), *Classical Myth and Culture in the Cinema* (Oxford: Oxford University Press, 2001), 272–290 (280).
123. J.P. Telotte, *Science Fiction Film* (Cambridge: Cambridge University Press, 2001), 128.
124. Cited in Jack Nelson-Pallmyer, *Saving Christianity From Empire* (New York: Continuum, 2005), 1.

## Chapter 3

1. Claudia Card, in *Feminist Ethics*, ed. Claudia Card (Lawrence: University

Press of Kansas, 1991), 4, cited in Elizabeth Kamarck Minnich, "Can Virtue Be Taught? A Feminist Reconsiders," in Barbara Darling-Smith (ed.), *Can Virtue Be Taught?* (Notre Dame: University of Notre Dame Press, 1993), 69–85 (70).

2. Elizabeth Kamarck Minnich, 70.

3. Margaret R. Miles and Brent S. Plate, "Hospitable Vision: Some Notes on the Ethics of Seeing Film," *Crosscurrents* 54.1 (2004), 22–31 (25).

4. Patricia Melzer, *Alien Constructions: Science Fiction and Feminist Thought* (Austin: University of Texas Press, 2006), 11.

5. See Dale Pollock for Pauline Kael's suggestion of sexism in the ending of Lucas' *American Graffiti* (1973), and Lucas' response (*Skywalking: The Life and Films of George Lucas, the Creator of Star Wars* [Hollywood: Samuel French, 1990], 147).

6. Rubey, "Not So Long Ago, Not So Far Away: New Variations on Old Themes and Questioning *Star Wars'* Revival of Heroic Archetypes," in Brode and Deyneka (eds.), 52. Cf. Peter Lev, "Whose Future? Star Wars, Alien and Blade Runner," *Literature/Film Quarterly* 26.1 (1998), 30–37; Diana Dominguez, "Feminism and the Force: Empowerment and Disillusionment in a Galaxy Far, Far Away," in Silvio and Vinci (eds.), 109–133; Philip L. Simpson, "Thawing the Ice Princess," in Kapell and Lawrence (eds.), 115–130 (115f.); Veronica A. Wilson, "Seduced by the Dark Side of the Force: Gender, Sexuality, and moral Agency in George Lucas's *Star Wars* Universe," in Silvio and Vinci (eds.), 134–152 (134); Ray Merlock and Kathy Merlock Jackson, "Lightsabers, Political Arenas, and Marriages for Princess Leia and Queen Amidala," in Brode and Deyneka (eds.), 77–88; Jeanne Cavelos, "Stop Her, She's Got a Gun! How the Rebel Princess and the Virgin Queen Became Marginalized and Powerless in George Lucas's Fairy Tale," in Jeanne Cavelos and Bill Spangler (eds.), *Star Wars on Trial: Science Fiction and Fantasy Writers Debate the Most Popular Science Fiction Films of All Time* (Dallas: Benbella, 2006), 305–322; Roz Kaveney, *From Alien to the Matrix: Reading Science Fiction Film* (London: I.B. Tauris, 2005), 116. These issues are only very briefly addressed in McDowell, *The Gospel According to Star Wars*, 88–92. Cf. Lucas in Clare Clouzot, "The Morning of the Magician: George Lucas and *Star Wars*," in Kline, 55–63 (57f.).

7. Anne Cranny-Francis, "Feminist Futures: A Generic Study," in Annette Kuhn (ed.), *Alien Zone: Cultural Theory and Contemporary Science Fiction Cinema* (London: Verso, 1990), 219–227 (223).

8. Robert Stam and Louise Spence, "Colonialism, Racism and Representation," *Screen* 24.2 (1983), 3, cited in Jude Davies and Carol R. Smith, *Gender, Ethnicity and Sexuality in Contemporary American Film* (New York: Routledge, 2000), 1.

9. Henry A. Giroux, *The Mouse that Roared: Disney and the End of Innocence* (Lanham: Rowman & Littlefield, 1999), 27. Giroux cites Jack Japes on Disney: this company provides theatrical animations that reproduce "a type of gender stereotyping.... Parents think they"re essentially harmless—and they're not harmless" (*The Mouse That Roared*, 103).

10. Minnich, 71.

11. Cavelos, 325.

12. Davies and Smith, 8, citing Manning Marable, *Beyond Black and White: Transforming African American Politics* (London: Verso, 1993), xii.

13. Jantzen, *Foundations of Violence*, 16.

14. Cavelos, 305.

15. Hanson and Kay, 250.

16. Lev, 34; Wilson, 143. Wilson needs to be asked in what ways Leia is unimportant or expendable. Moreover, Padmé is only expendable because Lucas has to explain how she dies some time prior to *ANH*.

17. Wetmore, *The Empire Triumphant*, 141.

18. Campbell, *The Hero with a Thousand Faces*, 109–120.

19. Dominguez, 116.

20. Lev, 33, 34, 36, citing Robin Wood, *Hollywood From Vietnam to Reagan* (New York: Columbia University Press, 1986).

21. There are suggestions that Han Solo was originally conceived as a Lando, and therefore black, figure. "Still smarting from criticism that *Star Wars* was racist, George conceived of Lando as a suave, dashing black man in his thirties/ and specified in his script that half of the Cloud City residents and troops were to be black" (Pollock, 213).

22. The *Clone Wars* introduce Asajj

Ventress as a student of Count Dooku, although there is a clear reference by Tyrannus to her not being Sith, and other moments of the Expanded Universe have Mara Jade as the Emperor's Hand.

23. Kathleen Ellis, "New World, Old Habits: Patriarchal Ideology in *Star Wars: A New Hope*," *Australian Screen Education* 30 (Spring 2002), 135–138 (135). Cf. Lev, "Whose Future?" 31.

24. Dominguez, 110.

25. Merlock and Jackson, 80.

26. Lucas, cited in Pollock, 165.

27. Carrie Fisher, cited in Bill Spangler, "Fighting Princesses and Other Distressing Damsels," in Jeanne Cavelos and Bill Spangler (eds.), *Star Wars on Trial: Science Fiction and fantasy Writers Debate the Most Popular Science Fiction Films of All Time* (Dallas: Benbella, 2006), 329–338 (331).

28. Cavelos, 325.

29. Sherrie Inness, *Tough Girls: Women Warriors and Wonder Women in Popular Culture* (Philadelphia: University of Pennsylvania Press, 1999), cited in Carla Kungl, "'Long Live Stardoe!' Can a Female Starbuck Survive?" in Potter and Marshall, 198–209 (202). Brian Attebery: "When women, too, can be adventurous, autonomous, and audacious, then the carefully constructed masculine self loses its foundation" (*Decoding Gender in Science Fiction* [New York: Routledge, 2002], cited in Kungl, 202).

30. Dominguez, 113.

31. See Jim Smith, *George Lucas* (London: Virgin Books, 2003), 131.

32. Cavelos, 324.

33. Henry Giroux, *The Mouse that Roared: Disney and the End of Innocence* (Lanham: Rowman & Littlefield, 1999), 103.

34. Segal, 14.

35. Rubey, "Not So Long Ago, Not So Far Away: New Variations on Old Themes and Questioning *Star Wars'* Revival of Heroic Archetypes," in Brode and Deyneka (eds.), 57.

36. And yet, here again, there is some ambiguity—by retroactively connecting the revelation of Leia's parentage in *ROTJ* and Yoda's response to Obi-Wan's comment concerning Luke "That boy is our last hope" by announcing that "No, there is another" we can see that suddenly Leia herself becomes a symbol of hope and redemption.

37. Rubey, "Not So Long Ago, Not So Far Away: New Variations on Old Themes and Questioning *Star Wars'* Revival of Heroic Archetypes," in Brode and Deyneka (eds.), 63.

38. Simpson, 115f.

39. Simpson, 115f.

40. Seyla Benhabib, *Situating the Self: Gender, Community and Postmodernism in Contemporary Ethics* (Cambridge: Polity Press, 2002), 14.

41. Robin Wood, *Hollywood from Vietnam to Reagan* (New York: Columbia University Press, 1986), 166.

42. Davies and Smith, 24.

43. Merlock and Jackson, 82.

44. Elizabeth Stuart, "Sacramental Flesh," in Gerard Loughlin (ed.), *Queer Theology: Rethinking the Western Body* (Malden: Blackwell, 2007), 65–75 (65).

45. Luce Irigaray, *To Be Two*, trans. Monique Rhodes and Marco Cocito-Monoc (London: Athlone Press, 2000), 25.

46. Irigaray, 27.

47. Irigaray, 30.

48. Simone de Beauvoir, *The Second Sex*, trans. H.M. Parshley (New York: Vintage, 1974), xxii.

49. Benhabib, 149.

50. Jantzen, *Becoming Divine*, 70.

51. Terry Eagleton reasons that a constructivist account of human autonomy or "self-authorship is the bourgeois myth of self-origination. Denying that our freedom thrives only within the context of a more fundamental dependency lies at the root of a good deal of historical disaster" (*Reason, Faith and Revolution: Reflections on the God Debate* [New Haven: Yale University Press, 2009], 16).

52. Simpson, 121.

53. Wetmore, *The Empire Triumphant*, 72.

54. Benhabib, 198.

55. Dominguez, 117.

56. Cornea, 150.

57. See Barbara Creed, "Alien and the Monstrous-Feminine," in Annette Kuhn (ed.), *Alien Zone: Cultural Theory and Science Fiction Cinema* (London: Verso, 1990), 128–141 (140). In an application of Julia Kristeva's ideas concerning the representation of the feminine as abject, Creed explicates *Alien* in terms of "monstrous femininity." She observes that the monstrous

one emits fluids, is associated with maternality and reproductivity, and is to be excluded as the threatening and wholly "other" who cannot be integrated. "Although women are not unique in having bodies, their bodies have unique features that render them especially problematic in the context of managing fears associated with mortality. They menstruate, lactate, and carry and bear the labor to deliver children. Though men can also invest a great deal in the caring for offspring, their obligatory, bodily investment is relatively minimal" (R.L. Trivers, *Parental Investment and Sexual Selection*, in B. Campbell [ed.], *Sexual Selection and the Descent of Man* [Chicago: Aldine, 1972], 136–179). Therefore, according to Cornea, "*Alien* articulates a masculine fear of gender dissolution, a dissolution that is initially presented under the guise of a progressive futurism and then quickly undercut with the introduction of the alien" (150).

58. Kaveney, *From Alien to the Matrix*, 133.
59. Dawson, 76.
60. Gerard Loughlin, *Alien Sex: The Body and Desire in Cinema and Theology* (Malden: Blackwell, 2004), 107.
61. Kungl, 208, referring to Innes' reading.
62. Cornea, 161.
63. Cornea, 161.
64. See Julia Kristeva, "La femme, ce n'est jamais ca," *Tel Quel* 59 (Autumn 1974).
65. Cornea, 160.
66. Doherty, 194.
67. Doherty, 194.
68. Merlock and Jackson, 85.
69. Doherty, 194.
70. Loughlin, 119f.
71. Doherty, 194.
72. Cornea, 150.
73. Cornea, 150: "Upon learning of her replicated status, Rachel looks to Deckard for a sense of identity and acceptance—she is seen to acquiesce to Deckard's suggestions and appears eager to become what he wants her to be. Likewise, Deckard looks to Rachel in order to assert his own masculinity and to provide himself with a secure identity and future outside of his role as a killer."
74. Cavelos, in "the Courtroom," in Cavelos and Spangler, 323–327 (323).

75. Kaveney, 134.
76. Simpson, 121.
77. Andrew Gordon, "The Power of the Force: Sex in the *Star Wars* Trilogy," in Donald Palumbo (ed.), *Eros in the Mind's Eye: Sexuality and the Fantastic in Art and Film* (New York: Greenwood Press, 1986), 193–207; Martin Miller and Robert Sprich, "The Appeal of *Star Wars*: An Archetypal-Psychoanalytic View," *American Imago* 38.2 (Summer 1981), 203–220; Roger Kaufman, "How the *Star Wars* Saga Evokes the Creative Promise of Homosexual Love: A Gay-Centered Psychological Perspective," in Kapell and Lawrence (eds.), 131–156.
78. Lucas, cited in Pollock, 165.
79. Dominguez, 111.
80. Merlock and Jackson, 85.
81. Amartya Sen, *Identity and Violence: The Illusion of Destiny* (London: Penguin, 2006), 13, 10.
82. Sen, 21.
83. Jantzen, *Becoming Divine*, 114. Jantzen's particular worry is that it refers to "something that happens to a clearly understood self, or something that such a self does. In much philosophy of religion [for instance,] selfhood or subjectivity is treated as conceptually straightforward: a self just *is* a unified subject, a subject of attributes, experiences, actions" (115).
84. Cited in James H. Cone, *For My People: Black Theology and the Black Church* (Maryknoll, NY: Orbis, 1984), 124.
85. Benhabib, 164.
86. Beatrice Hanssen, *Critique of Violence: Between Poststructuralism and Critical Theory* (London: Routledge, 2000), 241, citing Monique Wittig.
87. Hanssen, 212.
88. Teresa de Luretis, cited in Hanssen, 215.
89. Foucault, *Madness and Civilization*, in Hanssen, 215.
90. Hanssen, 215.
91. Melzer, 15.
92. Margaret D. Kamitsuka, *Feminist Theology and the Challenge of Difference* (Oxford: Oxford University Press, 2007), 27.
93. On Wollstonecraft's "liberal feminism," see Wendy Brown, *Regulating Aversion: Tolerance in the Age of Identity and Empire* (Princeton: Princeton University Press, 2006), 62f.

94. Hanssen, 188.

95. The importance of the female Jedi in the Order is revealed more in the literature covering the period. In *TPM* the following female are on the Jedi High Council: Depa Billaba, Adi Gallia, and Yaddle (admittedly that is a paltry three of the twelve members); in *ATOC*: Depa Billaba, Adi Gallia, and Shaak Ti; added to these are the further prominent Jedi Aayla Secura, and Luminara Unduli with her Padawan Barriss Offee. Featuring in significant roles in the Lucas-endorsed *Clone Wars* short animations are Shaak Ti, Luminara Unduli, and Padawan Barriss Offee. These three feature in *ROTS* along with Stass Allie.

96. George Lucas, "The Beginning: The Making of Episode I," *TPM* DVD 2 (1999).

97. See Judith Butler, *Gender Trouble: Feminism and the Subversion of Identity* (New York: Routledge, 1990), 7.

98. Grace M. Jantzen, *Foundations of Violence: Death and the Displacement of Beauty* (London: Routledge, 2004), 27.

99. On saying that, however, by the time of *ROTS* there is a feeling among critics that she is turning a blind eye to the increasingly oppressive climate on Coruscant, to the loss of rights guaranteed by the Constitution, and to the growing power of Palpatine.

100. Mary Wollstonecraft, *A Vindication of the Rights of Women*, ed. Carol H. Poston, 2d ed. (New York: Norton, 1998), 33, 34, 39. Cf. Brown, 62.

101. Cited in Pollock, 57. As John Sutherland writes, "He shaped Star Wars as anti-Vietnam allegory" ("George Lucas could be messing with your head," *The Guardian* [23 May 2005]).

102. Dominguez, 110, 111.
103. Wilson, 139.
104. Dominguez, 110.
105. Dominguez, 111.

106. On the prequel trilogy as a tragic drama see McDowell, *The Politics of Big Fantasy*, ch. 2.

107. Wilson, 140.
108. Wilson, 140.
109. Wilson, 140.
110. Wilson, 137.

111. "George Lucas: Mapping the Mythology," *CNN* (May 8, 2002), www.archives.cnn.com/2002/SHOWBIZ/Movies/05/07/ca.s02.george.lucas/index.html, consulted 08–05–05.

112. Lucas, in *Time Magazine*, cited http://boards.theforce.net/The_Star_Wars_Saga/b104556/13106765/p2, consulted 08–05–05.

113. Wilson, 138.
114. Wilson, 141f.
115. Wilson, 139.
116. Irigaray, 18.
117. Irigaray, 40.

118. See Ryder Windham, *Star Wars: The Ultimate Visual Guide* (London: Dorling Kindersley, 2005), 110.

119. Ian McDiarmid, in "The Chosen One."

120. Jeffrey Overstreet, "Star Wars: Episode III—Revenge of the Sith," *Christianity Today* (18 May 2005), www.christianitytoday.com/movies/reviews/starwars3.html, consulted 1–06–05.

121. Wilson, 140.
122. Wilson, 140f.
123. Dominguez, 127.
124. Wilson, 143.
125. Wilson, 145.
126. Dominguez, 127.
127. Wilson, 142.

128. Vivian Sobchack, *Screening Space: The American Science Fiction Film* (New Brunswick: Rutgers University Press, 1998), 277.

129. Melzer, 1.
130. See Pollock, 106.
131. Pollock, 147.

132. Clare Clouzot, "The Morning of the Magician: George Lucas and *Star Wars*," in Kline, 55–63 (57f.).

133. See Edith Wyschogrod, *Saints and Postmodernism: Revisioning Moral Philosophy* (Chicago: University of Chicago Press, 1990).

134. Cavelos, 311.
135. Merlock and Jackson, 78.
136. Cavelos, 306.

137. Geoff King, *New Hollywood Cinema: An Introduction* (London: I.B. Tauris, 2002), 135.

138. Booker, 115.

139. The worry is that of the moral questionability of the instrumentalizing of life, the denial of otherness for self-aggrandizing purposes. While *THX 1138* earlier movie in its turn presents no obvious controllers of the politico-economic system and its economic reduction of persons to biomechanical working units, it too is animated by the

tension between (corporate) systems that induce conformity and the nature of embodied selfhood-in-relation (such as is explored in THX's moment of erotic discovery of human relationality in the mutual caress with LUH). In the *SW* saga, the ruthless instrumentalization in the political sphere is removed from the progressive goals of creating conditions for critical agency, ethical responsibility and accountability, and the obligations of democratic public life.

140. Booker, 117.

141. Peter Krämer, "Fighting the Evil Empire: *Star Wars*, the Strategic Defense Initiative, and the Politics of Science Fiction," in Brode and Deyneka (eds.), 63–76 (70), referring to Michael Ryan and Douglas Kellner, *Camera Politica: The Politics and Ideology of Contemporary Hollywood Film* (Bloomington: Indiana University Press, 1988), 234–5, 303–5, 308.

## Chapter 4

1. In a distinctly limited and limiting claim for science fiction Jerold J. Abrams announces that "for anyone living in the late twentieth and early twenty-first centuries, science fiction cinema is one of the few art forms that attempts to predict the future of human nature and civilization—a future filled with space travel, nanotechnology, genetic engineering, and widespread surveillance" (The Dialectic of Enlightenment in *Metropolis*," in Steven M. Sanders [ed.], *The Philosophy of Science Fiction Film* [Lexington: University Press of Kentucky, 2008], 153–170 [153]).

2. H.G. Wells, cited in Patricia Kerslake, *Science Fiction and Empire* (Liverpool: Liverpool University Press, 2007), 2.

3. Penley, 198.

4. Pyle, 233.

5. Booker, 266.

6. See Susan Sontag, "The Imagination of Disaster," in Sean Redmond (ed.), *Liquid Metal: The Science Fiction Film Reader* (London: Wallflower Press, 2004), 40–47 (40).

7. Scott Bukatman, *Blade Runner* (London: BFI, 1997), 8, citing Frederic Jameson, *Postmodernism, or the Cultural Logic of Late Capitalism* (Durham: Duke University Press, 1991), 285.

8. John C. McDowell, *The Politics of Big Fantasy: The Ideologies of Star Wars, The Matrix and The Avengers* (Jefferson: McFarland, 2014), ch. 3.

9. Wetmore, *The Empire Triumphant*, 185.

10. Kenneth Surin, *Freedom Not Yet: Liberation and the Next World Order* (Durham: Duke University Press, 2009), 6.

11. Heidi Kaye and I.Q. Hunter, "Introduction—Alien Identities: Exploring Difference in Film and Fiction," in Deborah Cartmell, I.Q. Hunter, Heidi Kaye, and Imelda Whelehan (eds.), *Alien Identities: Exploring Difference in Film and Fiction* (London: Pluto Press, 1999), 1–10 (1).

12. Kaye and Hunter, 2.

13. Kaye and Hunter, 2.

14. Cited in Rob van Scheers, *Paul Verhoeven*, trans. Aletta Stevens (London: Faber and Faber, 1997), xiii.

15. Aubrey Malone, *Censoring Hollywood: Sex and Violence in Film and on the Cutting Room Floor* (Jefferson: McFarland, 2011), 7.

16. Davies and Smith, 53.

17. Matthew Wilhelm Kapell, "Eugenics, Racism, and the Jedi Gene Pool," in Kapell and Lawrence (eds.), 159–173 (168).

18. Booker, 117.

19. Sanders, 16.

20. Christopher Deis, "Erasing Difference," "Erasing Difference: The Cylons as Racial Other," in Tiffany Porter and C.W. Marshall (eds.), *Cylons in America: Critical Studies in Battlestar Galactica* (New York: Continuum, 2008), 156–168 (160).

21. Wetmore, *The Empire Triumphant*, 128.

22. Andrew Howe, "*Star Wars* in Black and White: Race and Racism in a Galaxy Not So Far Away," in Brode and Deyneka (eds.), 11–23 (14).

23. Wetmore, *The Empire Triumphant*, 127.

24. Wetmore, *The Empire Triumphant*, 128.

25. Christopher Deis, "May the Force (Not) Be with You: "'Race Critical' Readings and the *Star Wars* Universe," in in Silvio and Vinci (eds.), 77–108 (80).

26. Howe, 17.

27. Stuart Hall, "What Is the 'Black' in Popular Culture?" in Gina Dent (ed.), *Black Popular Culture* (Seattle: Bay Press, 1992),

cited in Giroux, *The Mouse That Roared*, 126.
28. This is a theme important to Boulle's source novel for the first film in the series. See Booker, 99f.
29. Cornea, 181.
30. Eric Greene, *Planet of the Apes as American Myth: Race, Politics, and Popular Culture* (Middletown: Wesleyan University Press, 1996), 9.
31. Cornea, 181.
32. Cornea, 181f.
33. Davies and Smith, 53.
34. Lincoln Geraghty, *American Science Fiction and Television* (Oxford: Berg, 2009), 41.
35. Darko Suvin, *Metamorphoses of Science Fiction: On the Poetics and History of a Literary Genre* (New Haven: Yale University Press, 1979), 63.
36. Deis, "Erasing Difference," 157.
37. Deis, "Erasing Difference," 167.
38. Deis, "Erasing Difference," 160.
39. Deis, "Erasing Difference," 161.
40. Cornea, 176.
41. Tzvetan Todorov, *The Fantastic: A Structural Approach to a Literary Genre* (Ithaca: Cornell University Press, 1975), 56. According to Jenny Wolmark, the alien functions as a device since "it enables difference to be constructed in terms of binary oppositions which reinforce relations of dominance and subordination.... [The alien can] explore the way in which the deeply divisive dichotomies of race and gender are embedded in the repressive structures and relations of dominance and subordination" (*Aliens and Others: Science Fiction, Feminism and Postmodernism* [Iowa City: University of Iowa Press, 1994], 2, 27).
42. Kerslake, 16. Cf. Isaiah Lavender III, *Race in American Science Fiction* (Bloomington: Indiana University Press, 2011), 8: "In my estimation there is nowhere better than sf to examine the fear and excitement generated through alien encounters with race and racism. ... With concepts of otherhood, we can examine degrees of black marginalization in sf (i.e., blackground)."
43. Wetmore, *The Empire Triumphant*, 131.
44. Daniel Leonard Bernardi, *Star Trek and History: Race-ing Toward a White Future* (New Brunswick: Rutgers University Press, 1998), 80.
45. Deis, 77.
46. Elvis Mitchell, "Works Every Time," in Glenn Kenny (ed.), *A Galaxy Not So Far Away* (New York: Henry Holt, 2002), 77–85 (78). Cf. Pollock, 213; Chris Salewicz, *George Lucas Close Up: The Making of His Movies* (London: Orion, 1998), 80.
47. Mitchell, 80.
48. Wetmore, *The Empire Triumphant*, 133.
49. Wetmore, *The Empire Triumphant*, 135.
50. Wetmore, *The Empire Triumphant*, 132.
51. Howe, 14.
52. Richard H. Dees, "Moral Ambiguity in a Black-and-White Universe," in Kevin S. Decker and Jason T. Eberl (eds.), *Star Wars and Philosophy: More Powerful Than You Can Possibly Imagine* (Chicago: Open Court, 2005), 39–53 (45f.).
53. Dees, 46.
54. *ESB* DVD commentary.
55. Wetmore, *The Empire Triumphant*, 17.
56. Howe, 20.
57. Wetmore, *The Empire Triumphant*, 134. Cf. Donald Bogle, *Toms, Coons, Mulattoes, Mammies and Bucks: An Interpretive History of Blacks in American Film*, 4th ed. (New York: Continuum, 2002), 422.
58. Howe, 17.
59. Wetmore, *The Empire Triumphant*, 17.
60. See Greg Grewell, cited in Deis, "May the Force (Not) Be with You," 94; Wetmore, *The Empire Triumphant*, ch. 5; Deis, "May the Force (Not) Be with You," 94ff.; Kapell, 168f.
61. Howe, 20.
62. Howe, 18.
63. Melzer, 44.
64. McDowell, *The Gospel According to Star Wars*, 90.
65. Lucas, *Star Wars*, 95.
66. Howe, 12. Deis: "the Other of droids and robots challenges narrow visions of humanity and the value of difference" ("May the Force (Not) Be with You," 95).
67. Kerslake, 20.
68. John W. Wright, "Levinasian Ethics of Alterity: The Face of the Other in Spielberg's Cinematic Language," in Dean A. Kowalski (ed.), *Steven Spielberg and Philosophy: We"re Gonna Need a Bigger Book*

(Lexington: University of Kentucky, 2008), 50–68 (56, 58).
69. Booker, 117.
70. Booker, 117f.
71. Carl Silvio, "The *Star Wars* Trilogies and Global Capitalism," in Silvio and Vinci (eds.), 53–73 (58).
72. Wilson, 143.
73. Howe, 13.
74. Pollock, 213.
75. Richard Kearney, *Strangers, Gods and Monsters: Interpreting Otherness* (London: Routledge, 2003), 5.
76. Deis, "May the Force (Not) Be with You," 81. Deis draws attention to an important allusion to Dooku's aspirations for humanocentric hygenization of governance in the novelization of *ROTS* (see Stover, 83). "The warm, primary colors that typified democracy are increasingly replaced by colors that are symbolic of the rise of Nazi-like, militaristic, fascist State Accordingly, as the narrative advances from a time of peace to one of perpetual war and conflict, the color plate of the chancellor's office begins to feature the color red—a color that symbolizes violence and bloodshed—with the blue Senatorial Guards that were fixtures of *The* Republic being replaced in *Attack of the Clones* by the Emperor's iconic, red Imperial Guards" (Deis, 81). This is evident already in *TPM* with regard to the contrast between the lush landscape and flowing garments of an aesthetically developed Naboo culture and the cold and militaristic grey of the Federation Starships, and the moral sterility of the technomechanistic fetishization of the Trade Federation.
77. Wetmore, *The Empire Triumphant*, 139.
78. See, e.g., John Harlow, "And Now, the End is Near...," *The Sunday Times Culture* (8 May 2005), 10–11 (11).
79. Howe, 18.
80. George Lucas, "*Star Wars*: Lucas Strikes Back," news.bbc.co.uk/2/hi/entertainment/394542.stm, cited in Howe, 18.
81. Howe, 18.
82. Wetmore, *The Empire Triumphant*, 144.
83. Citation from Wetmore, *The Empire Triumphant*, 143.
84. Wetmore, *The Empire Triumphant*, 144.

85. David West Reynolds, in David West Reynolds, James Luceno, and Ryder Windham, *Star Wars: The Complete Visual Dictionary* (London: Dorling Kindersley, 2006), 46.
86. Michael J. Hanson and Max S. Kay, *Star Wars: The New Myth* (Xlibris, 2001), 382.
87. See David West Reynolds, *Star Wars: Attack of the Clones. The Visual Dictionary* (London: Dorling Kindersley, 2002), 39.
88. Wetmore, *The Empire Triumphant*, 141.
89. Wetmore, *The Empire Triumphant*, 154f.
90. Peter Lev, "Whose Future? Star Wars, Alien, and Blade Runner," *Literature/Film Quarterly* 26.1 (1998), 30–37 (31f.). For broadly dualistic readings see Mark Rowlands, *The Philosopher at the End of the Universe* (London: Ebury Press, 2003); Dick Staub, *Christian Wisdom of the Jedi* (San Francisco: Jossey-Bass, 2005). Cf. Hannah Pok, "The *Star Wars* Trilogy: Fantasy, Narcissism and Fear of the Other in Reagan's America," http://hannahpok.com/deepfieldspace/framesrc2c.html, consulted 18–05–05; Terry Christensen, *Reel Movies: American Political Movies from The Birth of a Nation to Platoon* (New York and Oxford: Basil Blackwell, 1987).
91. For further elaboration of this point see John C. McDowell, *The Gospel According to Star Wars: Faith, Hope and the Force* (Louisville: Westminster John Knox Press, 2007), ch. 3.
92. Kapell, 169.
93. Kapell, 169.
94. Ryder Wyndham, *Star Wars: The Ultimate Visual Guide* (London: Dorling Kindersley, 2005), 31.
95. Lev, *American Films of the 70s*, 165f.
96. Kaveney, *From Alien to the Matrix*, 133.
97. Kaveney, *From Alien to the Matrix*, 136.
98. In important ways, with the romantic theme *King Kong* is not straightforwardly describable as a monster drama. The *Jurassic Park* series is more interested in critiquing the monstrousness of corporate interests than in representing the animals as the focus of monstrous Otherness. *The Sea Horse* presents the prehistoric animal in a different, and less threatening, way again.

99. Kaveney, *From Alien to the Matrix*, 159.
100. Kaveney, *From Alien to the Matrix*, 133.
101. Kaveney, *From Alien to the Matrix*, 138.
102. Kaveney, *From Alien to the Matrix*, 138f.
103. Doherty, 195.
104. Doherty, 195.
105. Kearney, *Strangers, Gods and Monsters*, 49f.
106. See Creed. Through a psychoanalytic reading, Creed construes the movies as subverting the feminine.
107. Kearney, *Strangers, Gods and Monsters*, 50.
108. Kaveney, *From Alien to the Matrix*, 134.
109. Kaveney, *From Alien to the Matrix*, 134.
110. Kaveney, *From Alien to the Matrix*, 144.
111. Thomas Doherty, "Gene, Gender, and the *Aliens* Trilogy," in Barry Keith Grant (ed.), *Dread of Difference: Gender and the Horror Film* (Austin: University of Texas Press, 1996), 181–199 (192).
112. In Kearney, *Strangers, Gods and Monsters*, 52.
113. Amy Taubin, "Invading Bodies: *Alien3* and the Trilogy," *Sight and Sounds* 2.3 (July 1992), 8–10 (9).
114. Judith Newton, "Feminism and Anxiety in *Alien*," in Annette Kuhn (ed.), *Alien Zone: Cultural Theory and Science Fiction Cinema* (London: Verso, 1990), 82–87 (82).
115. Howe, 11.
116. Lola Young, *Fear of the Dark: "Race," Gender and Sexuality in the Cinema* (New York: Routledge, 1996), 40.
117. Cornea, 176.
118. Cornel West, "New Cultural Politics," 69, cited in Davies and Smith, 61. "What West's argument offers is the possibility of contesting the demeaning effects of white supremacist stereotypes and the marginalisation of black representations but also the transactional uses of images of African Americans. The implication ... is that racism has to be understood not simply as a cause but also as an effect, and in this case as fulfilling a strategic function, the securing of alliances among whites of different geographical, cultural, and political affiliations" (Davies and Smith, 62).
119. Cornea, 216.
120. Melzer, 45.
121. Lev, 34.
122. Wetmore, *The Empire Triumphant*, 152, citing Carson, 168.
123. Booker, 35.
124. Peter Biskind, *Seeing Is Believing* (New York: Pantheon, 1983), 111. Cf. "Pods, Blobs, and Ideology in American Films of the Fifties," in Al LaValley (ed.), *Invasion, Invasion of the Body Snatchers* (New Brunswick: Rutgers University Press, 1989), 194.
125. Booker, 8, 59. "Star Kevin McCarthy (whose shared surname with Senator McCarthy provides an additional irony) has stated in an interview that he himself felt that the pod people were reminiscent of the heartless capitalists who work on Madison Avenue. Indeed, if communism was perceived by many Americans of the 1950s as a threat to their cherished individuality, capitalism itself was often perceived in much the same way. While the burgeoning capitalist system of the 1950s produced unprecedented opportunities for upward mobility in America, this highly complex system also required, for its operation, an unprecedented level of efficiency and standardization. Thus, if the 1950s represented a sort of Golden Age of science fiction film, the decade was also the Golden Age of American homogenization, as efficiency-oriented mass production techniques pioneered by industrialists such as Henry Ford reached new heights of sophistication and new levels of penetration into every aspect of American life. While television helped to homogenize the thoughts and dreams of the rapidly expanding American population, General Motors, the great industrial power of the decade, achieved unprecedented success in the business in which Ford's techniques had originally been developed. At the same time, Bill Levitt's Long Island suburb of Levittown brought mass production to the housing industry, ushering in the great age of suburbanization, perhaps the single most important step in the commodification of the American dream. The 1950s were also the Golden Age of branding and franchising, as standard brands, aided by television advertising, in-

stalled themselves in the collective American consciousness, while chain franchises spread across the nation, informed by the central driving idea of homogeneity—selling identical products in identical ways at thousands of identical franchises across the country. Thus, if Levitt's vision helped to homogenize the American home, Kemmons Wilson's Holiday Inn chain made identical lodgings available to Americans wherever they drove on the nation's rapidly expanding (and more and more homogeneous) highway system in their increasingly powerful, standardized automobiles. Similarly, Ray Kroc made homogeneous food available on the road when he took the fast-food production techniques pioneered by Ray Kroc and the McDonald brothers and made standardized hamburgers an indispensable part of everyday cuisine in America" (66f.).

126. Steven M. Sanders, "Picturing Paranoia: Interpreting *Invasion of the Body Snatchers*," in Steven M. Sanders (ed.), *The Philosophy of Science Fiction Film* (Lexington: University Press of Kentucky, 2008), 55–72 (59).

127. Kaveney, *From Alien to the Matrix*, 44.

128. Susan Sontag, "The Imagination of Disaster," in Sean Redmond (ed.), *Liquid Metal: The Science Fiction Film Reader* (London: Wallflower Press, 2004), 40–47 (42).

129. Sontag, 44.

130. Kaveney, *From Alien to the Matrix*, 39.

131. One lazy version is a moment in *TPM* when the Gungan Bongo on the way to Theed City is saved from its deadly aquatic pursuer, to which Qui Gon Jinn responds, "There is always a bigger fish."

132. See Booker, 7.

133. Deis, "May the Force (Not) Be with You," 95.

134. The political effect is evident in the movie—the flag, country, president rushing into battle. It is a celebration less of the independence of the nation from British imperialism as the freedom of the nation from all that is utterly destructive and colonizing. As a consequence, the nation basks on a purer hue than it might otherwise.

135. Wetmore, *The Empire Triumphant*, 10.

# Bibliography

Abrams, Jerold J. "A Technological Galaxy: Heidegger and the Philosophy of Technology in *Star Wars*." In *Star Wars and Philosophy: More Powerful Than You Can Possibly Imagine*, eds. Kevin S. Decker and Jason T. Eberl. Chicago: Open Court, 2005, 107–119.

Adorno, Theodor W. *The Culture industry: Selected Essays on Mass Culture*, ed. J.M. Bernstein. London: Routledge, 1991.

Adorno, Theodor W., and Max Horkheimer. *Dialectic of Enlightenment*, trans. John Cumming. London: Verso, 1979.

Agger, Ben. *Cultural Studies and Critical Theory*. Washington, D.C.: The Falmer Press, 1992.

Ahrensdorf, Peter J. *Tragedy and Political Philosophy: Rationalism and Religion in Sophocles" Theban Plays*. Cambridge: Cambridge University Press, 2009.

Alfonsi, Alice. *Star Wars: The Skywalker Family Album*. London: Scholastic, 2002.

Alford, Matthew. *Reel Power: Hollywood Cinema and American Supremacy*. London: Pluto Press, 2010.

Alsford, Mike. *Heroes and Villains*. Waco: Baylor University Press, 2006.

Andrae, Thomas. "From Menace to Messiah: The History and Historicity of Superman." In *American Media and Mass Culture: Left Perspectives*, ed. Donald Lazere. Berkeley: University of California Press, 1987, 124–138.

Anker, Roy M. *Catching Light: Looking for God at the Movies*. Grand Rapids: Eerdmans, 2004.

Aperlo, Peter. *Watchmen: The Film Companion*. London: Titan Books, 2009.

Aristotle. *Poetics*, trans. I. Bywater. In *The Complete Works of Aristotle Volume Two*, ed. Jonathan Barnes. Princeton: Princeton University Press, 1984.

Aronowitz, Stanley. *The Politics of Identity: Class, Culture, Social Movements*. New York: Routledge, 1992.

Augustine. *City of God*, trans. Henry Bettenson. Harmondsworth: Penguin, 1972.

Baccolini, Raffaella, and Tom Moylan, eds. *Dark Horizons: Science Fiction and the Dystopian Imagination*. New York: Routledge, 2003.

Barth, Karl. *Church Dogmatics*, Volume III. *The Doctrine of Creation* Part 4, trans. G.W. Bromiley and T.F. Torrance. Edinburgh: T&T Clark, 1961.

Bassham, Gregory. "The Religion of *The Matrix* and the Problems of Pluralism." In *The Matrix and Philosophy*, ed. William Irwin. Chicago: Open Court, 2002, 111–125.

Bassom, David. *Battlestar Galactica: The Official Companion*. London: Titan Books, 2005.

_____. *Battlestar Galactica: The Official Companion: Season Two*. London: Titan Books, 2006.

_____. *Battlestar Galactica: The Official Companion: Season Three*. London: Titan Books, 2007.

Battis, Jes. *Investigating Farscape: Uncharted Territories of Sex and Science Fiction*. London: I.B. Tauris, 2007.

Bauman, Zygmunt. *Globalization: The Human Consequences*. New York: Columbia University Press, 1998.

_____. *Intimations of Postmodernity*. London: Routledge, 1992.

Baxter, John. *George Lucas: A Biography*. London: HarperCollins, 1999.

Beaudoin, Tom. *Virtual Faith: The Irreverent Spiritual Quest of Generation X*. San Francisco: Jossey-Bass, 1998.

Bell, Daniel M., Jr. "Can a War Against Terror Be Just? Or, What Is Just War Good For?" *Crosscurrents*, Spring 2006, 34–45.

Benhabib, Seyla. *Situating the Self: Gender, Community and Postmodernism in Contemporary Ethics*. Cambridge: Polity Press, 2002.

Bercovitch, Sacvan. *The Puritan Origins of the American Self*. New Haven: Yale University Press, 1975.

Bernardi, Daniel Leonard. *Star Trek and History: Race-ing Toward a White Future*. New Brunswick: Rutgers University Press, 1998.

Bernstein, J.M. "Introduction." In Theodor Adorno, *The Culture Industry: Selected Essays on Mass Culture*, ed. J.M. Bernstein. London: Routledge, 1991, 1–28.

Beauvoir, Simone de. *The Second Sex*, trans. H.M. Parshley. New York: Vintage, 1974.

Birzer, Bradley J. *J.R.R. Tolkien's Sanctifying Myth*. Wilmington, DE: ISI Books, 2003.

Biskind, Peter. *Easy Riders, Raging Bulls: Sex-Drugs-and-Rock 'n' Roll Generation Saved Hollywood*. New York: Touchstone, 1998.

\_\_\_\_. *Seeing Is Believing*. New York: Pantheon, 1983.

Bly, Robert. *Iron John: A Book about Men*. New York: Vintage, 1990.

Bogle, Donald. *Toms, Coons, Mulattoes, Mammies and Bucks: An interpretive History of Blacks in American Film*, 4th ed. New York: Continuum, 2002.

Bondanella, Peter. *The Eternal City: Roman Images in the Modern World*. Chapel Hill: University of North Carolina Press, 1987.

Booker, M. Keith. *Alternate Americas: Science Fiction Film and American Culture*. Westport: Praeger, 2006.

Boozer, Jack, Jr. "Crashing the Gates of Insight: *Blade Runner*." In *Retrofitting Blade Runner: Issues In Ridley Scott's Blade Runner and Philip K. Dick's Do Androids Dream of Electric Sheep?*, ed. Judith B. Kerman. Madison: University of Wisconsin Press, 1991, 212–228.

Bortolin, Matthew. *The Dharma of Star Wars*. Boston: Wisdom Publications, 2005.

Bouzereau, Laurent. *Star Wars: The Annotated Screenplays*. New York: Ballantine, 1997.

Brin, David. "I Accuse ... Or Zola Meets Yoda." In *Star Wars on Trial*, eds. David Brin and Matthew Woodring Stover. Dallas: Benbella, 2006, 17–48.

Brooker, Will. *Star Wars*. London: Palgrave Macmillan, 2009.

\_\_\_\_. *Using the Force: Creativity, Community and Star Wars Fans*. New York: Continuum, 2002.

\_\_\_\_, ed. *The Blade Runner Experience: The Legacy of a Science Fiction Classic*. London: Wallflower Press, 2005.

Brooks, Terry. *Star Wars Episode I: The Phantom Menace*. London: Century, 1999.

Bukatman, Scott. *Blade Runner*. London: BFI, 1997.

\_\_\_\_. "Who Programs You? The Science Fiction of the Spectacle." In *Alien Zone: Cultural Theory and Contemporary Science Fiction Cinema*, ed. Annette Kuhn. London: Verso, 1990, 196–213.

Bush, George W. "President Delivers State of the Union." www.whitehouse.gov/news/releases/2003/01/20030128-19.html, accessed 30–06–2005.

Butler, Judith. *Frames of War: When Is Life Grievable?* London: Verso, 2009.

\_\_\_\_. *Gender Trouble: Feminism and the Subversion of Identity*. New York: Routledge, 1990.

Campbell, Joseph. *The Hero with a Thousand Faces*. Princeton: Princeton University Press, 1949.

Caputo, John D. *On Religion*. London: Routledge, 2001.

Card, Orson Scott. "'Star Wars' Our Public Religion." *USA Today*, 17 March 1997, 13A.

Carpenter, Stanford W. "Truth Be Told: Authorship and the Creation of the Black Captain America." In *Comics as Philosophy*, ed. Jeff McLaughlin. Jackson: University of Mississippi Press, 2005, 46–62.

Carr, Craig L. *Orwell, Politics, and Power*. New York: Continuum, 2010.

Cartmell, Deborah, Heidi Kaye, I.Q. Hunter, and Imelda Whelehan, eds. *Alien Identities: Exploring Differences in Film and Fiction*. London: Pluto Press, 1999.

Cavelos, Jeanne. "Stop Her, She's Got a Gun! How the Rebel Princess and the Virgin Queen Became Marginalized and Powerless In George Lucas's Fairy Tale." In

*Star Wars on Trial: Science Fiction and Fantasy Writers Debate the Most Popular Science Fiction Films of All Time*, eds. Jeanne Cavelos and Bill Spangler. Dallas: Benbella, 2006, 305–322.

Champlin, Charles. *George Lucas: The Creative Impulse*, rev. ed. London: Virgin, 1997.

Chattaway, Peter T. "Star Wars: Episode III—Revenge of the Sith." http://canadianchristianity.com/cgi-bIn/na.cgi?film/starwars3, consulted 30-06-05.

Christensen, Terry. *Reel Movies: American Political Movies from The Birth of a Nation to Platoon*. New York: Basil Blackwell, 1987.

Clarke, James. *Ridley Scott*. London: Virgin, 2002.

\_\_\_\_\_. *The Pocket Essential George Lucas*. Harpenden: Pocket Essentials, 2002.

Colebatch, Hal G.P. *Return of the Heroes: The Lord of the Rings, Star Wars, Harry Potter, and Social Conflict*, 2d ed. Christchurch: Cybereditions Corporation, 2003.

Collins, Jim, Hilary Radner, and Ava Preacher Collins, eds. *Film Theory Goes to the Movies*. London: Routledge, 1993.

Collins, Robert G. "*Star Wars*: The Pastiche of Myth and the Yearning for a Past Future." *Journal of Popular Culture* 11.1 (1977), 1–10.

Cone, James H. *For My People: Black Theology and the Black Church*. Maryknoll: Orbis, 1984.

Copper, Marc. "A Year Later: What the Right and Left Haven't Learned." In *The Iraq War: History, Documents, Opinions*, eds. Micah L. Sifry and Christopher Cerf. New York: Touchstone, 2003, 225–228.

Corliss, Richard and Cagie, Jess. "Dark Victory." *Time*, http://www.time.com.time/covers/1101020429/story.html, consulted 30-07-02.

Cornea, Christine. *Science Fiction Cinema*. Edinburgh: Edinburgh University Press, 2007.

Cranny-Francis, Anne. "Feminist Futures: A Generic Study." In *Alien Zone: Cultural Theory and Contemporary Science Fiction Cinema*, ed. Annette Kuhn. London: Verso, 1990, 219–227.

Creed, Barbara. "Alien and the Monstrous-Feminine." In *Alien Zone: Cultural Theory and Science Fiction Cinema*, ed. Annette Kuhn. London: Verso, 1990, 128–141.

Dalton, Russell W. *Faith Journey Through Fantasy Lands: A Christian Dialogue With Harry Potter, Star Wars, and the Lord of the Rings*. Minneapolis: Augsburg Books, 2003.

Davies, Jude, and Carol R. Smith. *Gender, Ethnicity and Sexuality in Contemporary American Film*. New York: Routledge, 2000.

Decker, Kevin S., and Jason T. Eberl, eds. *Star Wars and Philosophy: More Powerful Than You Can Possibly Imagine*. Chicago: Open Court, 2005.

Dees, Richard H. "Moral Ambiguity in a Black-and-White Universe." In *Star Wars and Philosophy: More Powerful Than You Can Possibly Imagine*, eds. Kevin S. Decker and Jason T. Eberl. Chicago: Open Court, 2005, 39–53.

Deis, Christopher. "Erasing Difference: The Cylons as Racial Other." In *Cylons in America: Critical Studies in Battlestar Galactica*, eds. Tiffany Porter and C.W. Marshall. New York: Continuum, 2008, 156–168.

\_\_\_\_\_. "May the Force Not Be with You: "Race Critical" Readings and the *Star Wars* Universe." In *Culture, Identities and Technology in the Star Wars Films: Essays on the Two Trilogies*, eds. Carl Silvio and Tony M. Vinci. Jefferson, McFarland, 2007, 77–108.

Desolge, Nick. "*Star Wars*: An Exhibition in Cold War Politics." In *Sex, Politics, and Religion in Star Wars: An Anthology*, eds. Douglas Brode and Leah Deyneka. Lanham: Scarecrow Press, 2012, 55–62.

Desser, David. "Race, Space and Class: The Politics of the SF Film from *Metropolis* to *Blade Runner*." In *Retrofitting Blade Runner: Issues in Ridley Scott's Blade Runner and Philip K. Dick's Do Androids Dream of Electric Sheep?*, 2d ed., ed. Judith B. Kerman. Madison: University of Wisconsin Press, 1997, 110–123.

Devlin, William J. "Some Paradoxes of Time Travel in *the Terminator* and *12 Monkeys*." In *The Philosophy of Science Fiction Film*, ed. Steven M. Sanders. Lexington: University Press of Kentucky, 2008, 103–117.

Deyneka, Leah. "May the Myth Be With You, Always: Archetypes, Mythic Elements, and Aspects of Joseph Campbell's Heroic Monomyth in the Original *Star Wars* Trilogy." In *Myth, Media, and Culture In Star Wars: An Anthology*, eds. Douglas Brode and Leah Deyneka. Lanham: Scarecrow Press, 2012, 31–46.

Dinello, Daniel. *Technophobia! Science Fiction Visions of Posthuman Technology*. Austin: University of Texas Press, 2005.

\_\_\_\_\_. "The Wretched of New Caprica." In *Battlestar Galactica and Philosophy: Mission Accomplished or Mission Frakked Up?*, eds. J. Steiff and T.D. Tamplin. Chicago: Open Court, 2008, 185–200.

Dominguez, Diana. "Feminism and the Force: Empowerment and Disillusionment in a Galaxy Far, Far Away." In *Culture, Identities and Technology in the Star Wars Films: Essays on the Two Trilogies*, eds. Carl Silvio and Tony M. Vinci. Jefferson: McFarland, 2007, 109–133.

Donald, James, ed. *Fantasy and the Cinema*. London: BFI, 1989.

Dorfman, Ariel, and Armand Mattelart. *How to Read Donald Duck: Imperialist Ideology in the Disney Comic*, trans. David Kanzle. New York: International General, 1991.

Duncan, Jody. *Mythmaking: Behind the Scenes of Star Wars: Episode 2: Attack of the Clones*. New York: Ballantine, 2002.

Eagleton, Terry. *Holy Terror*. Oxford: Oxford University Press, 2005.

\_\_\_\_\_. *Reason, Faith and Revolution: Reflections on the God Debate*. New Haven: Yale University Press, 2009.

\_\_\_\_\_. *Sweet Violence: The Idea of the Tragic*. Malden: Blackwell Publishing, 2003.

\_\_\_\_\_. "Tragedy and Revolution." In *Theology and the Political: The New Debate*, eds. Creston Davis, John Milbank, and Slavoj Žižek. Durham: Duke University Press, 2005, 7–21.

Ebrel, Jason T., ed. *Battlestar Galactica and Philosophy: Knowledge Here Begins Out There*. Malden: Blackwell, 2008.

Eick, David. "Battlestar Expands Horizons: Sci-fi References to Middle East Impress Critics." *Calgary Herald*, 7 October 2006, D4.

Ellis, Kathleen. "New World, Old Habits: Patriarchal Ideology in *Star Wars: A New Hope*." *Australian Screen Education* 30 (Spring 2002), 135–138

Ellul, Jacques. *Propaganda: The Formation of Men's Attitudes*, trans. Konrad Kellen and Jean Lerner. New York: Random House, 1973.

Falzon, Christopher. "The Limits of Film as Philosophy." Unpublished paper delivered to the Philosophy Society. University of Newcastle, NSW, October 2013.

\_\_\_\_\_. *Philosophy Goes to the Movies: An Introduction to Philosophy*. London: Routledge, 2002.

Fitting, Peter. "Unmasking the Real? Critique and Utopia in Recent SF Films." In *Dark Horizons: Science Fiction and the Dystopian Imagination*, eds. Raffaella Baccolini and Tom Moylan. New York: Routledge, 2003, 155–166.

Francavilla, Joseph. "The Android as *Doppelgänger*." In *Retrofitting Blade Runner: Issues in Ridley Scott's Blade Runner and Philip K. Dick's Do Androids Dream of Electric Sheep?*, 2d ed., ed. Judith B. Kerman. Madison: University of Wisconsin Press, 1997, 4–15.

Freeden, Michael. *Ideology: A Very Short Introduction*. Oxford: Oxford University Press, 2003.

Freedman, Carl. *Critical Theory and Science Fictions*. Hannover: Wesleyan University Press, 2000.

Freire, Paolo. *Pedagogy of the Oppressed*, trans. Myra Bergman. London: Penguin, 1996.

\_\_\_\_\_. *Teachers as Cultural Workers: Letters to Those Who Dare Teach*, trans. Donaldo Macedo, Dale Koike, and Alexandre Oliveira. Boulder: Westview Press, 2005.

Geraghty, Lincoln. *American Science Fiction and Television*. Oxford: Berg, 2009.

Gibson, James W. *Warrior Dreams: Violence and Manhood in Post-Vietnam America*. New York: Hill & Wang, 1994.

Giddens, Anthony. *The Nation-State and Violence*. Berkley: University of California Press, 1987.

Gilmore, Richard A. *Doing Philosophy at the Movies*. New York: State University of New York Press, 2005.

Girard, René. *The Things Hidden Since the Foundation of the World*. London: Athlone, 1987.

Giroux, Henry A. *Channel Surfing*. New York: St. Martins, 1997.

\_\_\_\_\_. *The Mouse That Roared: Disney and*

the End of Innocence. Lanham: Rowman & Littlefield, 1999.

_____. "Reclaiming the Social: Pedagogy, Resistance, and Politics in Celluloid Culture." In *Film Theory Goes to the Movies*, eds. Jim Collins, Hilary Radner, and Ava Preacher Collins. London: Routledge, 1993, 37–55.

Glut, Donald F. *Star Wars Episode V: The Empire Strikes Back*. London: Sphere Books, 1980.

Good, Howard. *Media Ethics Goes to the Movies*. Westport: Greenwood Press, 2002.

Gordon, Andrew. "The Power of the Force: Sex in the *Star Wars* Trilogy." In *Eros In the Mind's Eye: Sexuality and the Fantastic in Art and Film*, ed. Donald Palumbo. New York: Greenwood Press, 1986, 193–207.

_____. "*Star Wars*: A Myth for Our Time." *Literature/Film Quarterly* 6.4 (1978), 320–5.

Gorringe, Timothy J. *Furthering Humanity: A Theology of Culture*. Surrey: Ashgate, 2004.

Gourevitch, Phillip. "Letter from Rwanda." *New Yorker*, December 15, 1995, 84.

Gowland, Rohan. "The Phantom Menace of Idealism: Film Review." *The Guardian*, 16 June 1999, www.zipworld.com.au/~cpa/garchive/958star.htm, consulted 30-05-05.

Graham, Elaine L. *Representations of the Post/Human: Monsters, Aliens and Others in Popular Culture*. Manchester: Manchester University Press, 2002.

Grant, Barry Keith, ed. *The Dread of Difference: Gender and the Horror Film*. Austin: University of Texas Press, 1996.

Gray, John Scott. "They Evolved, but Do They Deserve Consideration?" In *Battlestar Galactica and Philosophy: Mission Accomplished or Mission Frakked Up?*, eds. J. Steiff and T. D. Tamplin. Chicago: Open Court, 2008 163–170.

Greene, Eric. *Planet of the Apes as American Myth: Race, Politics, and Popular Culture*. Middletown: Wesleyan University Press, 1996.

Grenier, Richard. "Celebrating Defeat." *Commentary* 70.2 (1980), 58.

Griffiths, Paul J., and George Weigel. "Who Wants War? An Exchange." *First Things* 152 (2005), 10–12.

Grimes, Caleb. *Star Wars Jesus*. Enumclaw: Winepress, 2007.

Grob, Gerald N., and George Athan Billias, eds. *Interpretations of American History: Patterns and Perspectives*, 6th ed. New York: Macmillan, 1992.

Hanley, Richard. "Send in the Clones: The Ethics of Future Wars." In *Star Wars and Philosophy: More Powerful Than You Can Possibly Imagine*, eds. Kevin S. Decker and John T. Eberl. Chicago: Open Court, 2005, 93–103.

Hanson, Michael J., and Max S. Kay. *Star Wars: The New Myth*. Xlibris, 2001.

Hanssen, Beatrice. *Critique of Violence: Between Poststructuralism and Critical Theory*. London: Routledge, 2000.

Harlow, John. "And Now, the End is Near...." *The Sunday Times Culture*, 8 May 2005, 10–11.

Hart, Hugh. "Flaws in a Good Heart." *LA Times.com*, January 20, 2002, www.latimes.com, consulted 08–05–05.

Hatch, Richard, ed. *So Say We All*. Dallas: Benbella, 2006.

Hauerwas, Stanley. *The Peaceable Kingdom: A Primer in Christian Ethics*. London: SCM, 1983.

_____. *With the Grain of the Universe: The Church's Witness and Natural Theology*. London: SCM Press, 2001.

Hauerwas, Stanley, and William H. Willimon. *Resident Aliens: Life in the Christian Colony*. Nashville: Abingdon Press, 1989.

Hawk, Julie. "*Objec 8* and the Cylon Remainder: Posthuman Subjectivization in *Battlestar Galactica*." *The Journal of Popular Culture* 44.1 (2011), 3–15.

Held, Jacob M. "Can We Steer this Rudderless World? Kant, Rorschach, Retributivism, and Honor." In *The Watchmen and Philosophy: A Rorschach Test*, ed. Mark D. White. Hoboken: John Wiley & Sons, 2009, 19–31.

Henderson, Mary. *Star Wars: The Magic of Myth*. New York: Bantam, 1997.

Higgins, Charlotte. "Final Star Wars Bears Message for America." *The Guardian*, 16 May, 2005, http://film.guardian.co.uk/cannes2005/story/0,15927,1484795,00.html#article_continue, consulted 26-05-05.

Horton, Scott. "*Star Wars* and the American Empire." www.antiwar.com/orig/

horton.php?articleid=6041, consulted 26-05-05.
Horstman, Joey Earl. "Star Wars. Motion Picture." *The Other Side* 33.2 (1977).
Howe, Andrew. "*Star Wars* in Black and White: Race and Racism in a Galaxy Not So Far Away." In *Sex, Politics, and Religion In Star Wars: An Anthology*, eds. Douglas Brode and Leah Deyneka. Lanham: Scarecrow Press, 2012, 11–23.
Irigaray, Luce. *To Be Two*, trans. Monique Rhodes and Marco Cocito-Monoc. London: Athlone Press, 2000.
Jaeger, Werner. *Paedeia Volume 1*, trans. Gilbert Highet. Oxford: Blackwell, 1939.
Jameson, Frederic. *Archaeologies of the Future: The Desire Called Utopia and Other Science Fictions*. London: Verso, 2005.
\_\_\_\_\_. "Progress Versus Utopia, Or Can We Imagine the Future." *Science Fiction Studies* 9 (1982). In *Fantasy and the Cinema*, ed. James McDonald. London: BFI, 1989, 197–212.
Jantzen, Grace M. *Becoming Divine: Towards a Feminist Philosophy of Religion*. Manchester: Manchester University Press, 1998.
\_\_\_\_\_. *Foundations of Violence: Death and the Displacement of Beauty*. London: Routledge, 2004.
Jenkins, Garry. *Empire Building: The Remarkable Real Life Story of Star Wars*. London: Simon & Schuster, 1997.
Jewett, Robert. *Saint Paul at the Movies: The Apostle's Dialogue with American Culture*. Louisville: Westminster John Knox, 1993.
Jewett, Robert, and John Shelton Lawrence. *Captain America and the Crusade Against Evil: The Dilemma of Zealous Nationalism*. Grand Rapids: Eerdmans, 2003.
Johnson, James Turner. "Just War, as It Was and Is." *First Things* 149 (2005), 14–24.
Johnson-Lewis, Erika. "Torture, Terrorism, and Other Aspects of Human Nature." In *Cylons in America: Critical Studies in Battlestar Galactica*, eds. Tiffany Potter and C.W. Marshall. New York: Continuum, 2008, 27–39.
Johnston, Robert K. *Reel Spirituality: Theology and Film in Dialogue*. Grand Rapids: Baker Academic, 2000.
Jones, L. Gregory. *Embodying Forgiveness: A Theological Analysis*. Grand Rapids: Eerdmans, 1995.
Jowett, Lorna. "Mad, Bad, and Dangerous to Know? Negotiating Stereotypes in Science." In *Cylons in America: Critical Studies in Battlestar Galactica*, eds. Tiffany Potter and C.W. Marshall. London: Continuum, 2008, 64–75.
Judy, Dwight H. *Healing the Male Soul: Christianity and the Mythic Journey*. New York: Crossroad, 1992.
Jung, Carl Gustav. "On the Nature of Dreams." *The Collected Works of C.G. Jung*, vol. 8, 293. 1974. Reprinted in Jung, Carl Gustav. *Dreams*. London: Routledge, 2001, 69–84.
Kahn, James. *Star Wars Episode VI: Return of the Jedi*. London & Sydney: Futura, 1983.
Kaminski, Michael. *The Secret History of Star Wars: The Art of Storytelling and the Making of a Modern Epic*. Kingston: Legacy Books Press, 2008.
Kamitsuka, Margaret D. *Feminist Theology and the Challenge of Difference*. Oxford: Oxford University Press, 2007.
Kapell, Matthew Wilhelm. "Eugenics, Racism, and the Jedi Gene Pool." In *Finding the Force of the Star Wars Franchise: Fans, Merchandise, and Critics*, eds. Matthew Wilhelm Kapell and John Shelton Lawrence. New York: Peter Lang, 2006, 159–173.
Kapell, Matthew Wilhelm, and John Shelton Lawrence, eds. *Finding the Force of the Star Wars Franchise: Fans, Merchandise, and Critics*. New York: Peter Lang, 2006.
Kappeler, Susanne. *The Will to Violence: The Politics of Personal Behaviour*. Cambridge: Polity, 1995.
Kasper, Walter. *The God of Jesus Christ*, trans. Matthew J. O'Connell. New York: Crossroad, 1984.
Kaufman, Roger. "How the *Star Wars* Saga Evokes the Creative Promise of Homosexual Love: A Gay-Centered Psychological Perspective." In *Finding the Force of the Star Wars Franchise: Fans, Merchandise, and Critics*, eds. Matthew Wilhelm Kapell and John Shelton Lawrence. New York: Peter Lang, 2006, 131–156.
Kaveney, Roz. *From Alien to the Matrix: Reading Science Fiction and Film*. London: I.B. Tauris, 2005.
Kaye, Heidi and I.Q. Hunter. "Introduc-

tion—Alien Identities: Exploring Difference in Film and Fiction." In *Alien Identities: Exploring Difference in Film and Fiction*, eds. Deborah Cartmell, I.Q. Hunter, Heidi Kaye, and Imelda Whelehan. London: Pluto Press, 1999, 1–10.

Kearney, Richard. *On Stories*. London and New York: Routledge, 2002.

\_\_\_\_\_. *Strangers, Gods and Monsters: Interpreting Otherness*. London: Routledge, 2003.

Kerman, Judith B. ed., *Retrofitting Blade Runner: Issues In Ridley Scott's Blade Runner and Philip K. Dick's Do Androids Dream of Electric Sheep?* Madison: University of Wisconsin Press, 1991.

Kershaw, Ian. *The "Hitler Myth": Image and Reality in the Third Reich*. Oxford: Oxford University Press, 1989.

Kerslake, Patricia. *Science Fiction and Empire*. Liverpool: Liverpool University Press, 2007.

King, Geoff. *New Hollywood Cinema: An Introduction*. London: I.B. Tauris, 2002.

King, Martin Luther, Jr. *Strength to Love*. London and Glasgow: Collins, 1963.

Kinnucan, Michelle J. "Pedagogy of the Force: The Myth of Redemptive Violence." In *Finding the Force of the Star Wars Franchise: Fans, Merchandise, and Critics*, eds. Matthew Wilhelm Kapell and John Shelton Lawrence. New York: Peter Lang, 2006, 59–72.

\_\_\_\_\_. "What Star Wars Teaches Us." *CommonDreams.org*, May 10, 2002, http://commondreams.org/cgi-bIn/print.cgi?file=views02/0510-06.htm.

Kline, Sally, ed. *George Lucas: interviews*. Jackson: University Press of Mississippi, 1999.

Knight, Deborah, and George McKnight. "What Is It to Be Human? *Blade Runner* and *Dark City*." In *The Philosophy of Science Fiction Film*, ed. Steven M. Sanders. Lexington: University Press of Kentucky, 2008, 21–37.

Krämer, Peter. "Fighting the Evil Empire: Star Wars, the Strategic Defense Initiative, and the Politics of Science Fiction." In *Sex, Politics, and Religion In Star Wars: An Anthology*, eds. Douglas Brode and Leah Deyneka. Lanham: Scarecrow Press, 2012, 63–76.

\_\_\_\_\_. "*Star Wars*: Peter Krämer Tells How the Popularity of the Sci-Fi Epic Proved Timely for Ronald Reagan and the Strategic Defense initiative." *History Today*, March 199, 41–47.

Krook, Dorothea. *Elements of Tragedy*. New Haven: Yale University Press, 1969.

Kuhn, Annette, ed. *Alien Zone: Cultural Theory and Science Fiction Cinema*. London a: Verso, 1990.

Kundera, Milan. *Testaments Betrayed*, trans. Linda Asher. New York: HarperCollins, 1995.

Kungl, Carla. "'Long Live Stardoe!' Can a Female Starbuck Survive?" In *Cylons in America: Critical Studies in Battlestar Galactica*, eds. Tiffany Potter and Christopher Marshall. London: Continuum, 2007, 198–209.

Kupfer, Joseph. *Feminist Ethics in Film: Reconfiguring Care Through Cinema*. Bristol: intellect, 2012.

Lancashire, Anne. "*Attack of the Clones* and the Politics of *Star Wars*." *The Dalhousie Review* 82.2 (Summer 2002), 235–253.

Landon, Brooks. "'There's Some of Me in You': *Blade Runner* and the Adaptation of Science Fiction Literature into Film." In *Retrofitting Blade Runner: Issues in Ridley Scott's Blade Runner and Philip K. Dick's Do Androids Dream of Electric Sheep?* 2d ed., ed. Judith B. Kerman. Madison: University of Wisconsin Press, 1997, 90–102.

Landsberg, Alison. "Prosthetic Memory: *Total Recall* and *Blade Runner*." In *Liquid Metal: The Science Fiction Film Reader*, ed. Sean Redmond. London: Wallflower Press, 2004, 239–248.

Lane, Beldon C. "The Power of Myth: Lessons from Joseph Campbell." *The Christian Century*, July 5–12, 1989, 652–654.

Larsen, S., and R. Larsen. *A Fire in the Mind: The Life of Joseph Campbell*. New York: Doubleday, 1991.

Lasch, Christopher. *The Culture of Narcissism: American Life in an Age of Diminishing Expectations*. New York: W.W. Norton, 1979.

\_\_\_\_\_. *The Minimal Self: Psychic Survival in Troubled Times*. New York: W.W. Norton, 1984.

Last, Jonathan V. "The Case for the Empire: Everything You Know about Star Wars Is Wrong." *Daily Standard*, 16 May 2002, http://www.weeklystandard.com/Utilities/printer_preview.asp?idArticle=1248&R=C5, consulted 08-06-05.

Lavender III, Isiah. *Race in American Science Fiction*. Bloomington: Indiana University Press, 2011.

Lawrence, John Shelton. "Fascist Redemption of Democratic Hope?" In *Jacking into the Matrix: Cultural Reception and interpretation*, eds. Matthew Wilhelm Kapell and William G. Doty. New York: Continuum, 2004, 80–96.

_____. "Joseph Campbell, George Lucas, and the Monomyth." In *Finding the Force of the Star Wars Franchise: Fans, Merchandise, and Critics*, eds. Matthew Wilhelm Kapell and John Shelton Lawrence. New York: Peter Lang, 2006, 21–33.

Lawrence, John Shelton, and Robert Jewett. *The Myth of the American Superhero*. Grand Rapids: Eerdmans, 2002.

Lev, Peter. *American Films of the 70s: Conflicting Visions*. Austin: University of Texas Press, 2000.

_____. "Whose Future? Star Wars, Alien, and Blade Runner." *Literature/Film Quarterly* 26.1 (1998), 30–37.

Livingston, Paisley, and Carl Plantinga, eds. *The Routledge Companion to Philosophy and Film*. London: Routledge, 2009.

Loughlin, Gerard. *Alien Sex: The Body and Desire in Cinema and Theology*. Malden: Blackwell, 2004.

Lucas, George. "George Lucas Interview—The Story Comes First." January 15, 2002, www.starwars.com/episode-ii/bts/profile/f20020115/indexp2.html, consulted 4/4/06.

_____. Interview on www.supershadow.com. 21 May 2005, consulted 26–05–05.

_____. Interview with Bill Moyers, "Of Myth and Men: A Conversation between Bill Moyer and George Lucas on the Meaning of the Force and the True Theology of Star Wars." *Time* 153.16 (26 April 1999), 90–94, http://www.time.com/time/magazine/article/0,9171,990820,00.html, consulted 4/4/06.

_____. *Star Wars: From the Adventures of Luke Skywalker*. London: Sphere Books, 1977.

Luceno, James. *The Labyrinth of Evil*. New York: Del Ray, 2005.

_____. *Star Wars: Revenge of the Sith. The Visual Dictionary*. London: Dorling Kindersley, 2005.

Lyden, John C. *Film as Religion: Myths, Morals, and Rituals*. New York: New York University Press, 2003.

Lynch, Gordon. *Understanding Theology and Popular Culture*. Malden: Blackwell, 2005.

Malone, Aubrey. *Censoring Hollywood: Sex and Violence in Film and on the Cutting Room Floor*. Jefferson: McFarland, 2011.

Marsden, George. "The American Revolution: Partisanship, 'Just Wars' and Crusades." In *The Wars of America: Christian Views*, ed. R.A. Wells. Grand Rapids: Eerdmans, 1981.

Marsh, Clive. *Theology Goes to the Movies*. London: Routledge, 2007.

Marshall, C.W., and Tiffany Potter. "'I See the Patterns': Battlestar Galactica and the Things That Matter." In *Cylons in America: Critical Studies in Battlestar Galactica*, eds. Tiffany Potter and C.W. Marshall. London: Continuum, 2008, 1–10.

Marshall, C.W., and M. Wheeland. "The Cylons, the Singularity, and God." In *Cylons in America: Critical Studies in Battlestar Galactica*, eds. Tiffany Potter and C.W. Marshall. London: Continuum, 2008, 91–104.

Martin, Joel W., and Ostwalt, Conrad E., eds. *Screening the Sacred: Religion, Myth, and Ideology in Popular American Film*. Boulder: Westview Press, 1995.

Martin, Judith. "The Second *Star Wars*." *Washington Post*, Friday, May 23, 1980, 17.

Maxwell, Howard. *George Lucas Companion*. London: B.T. Batsford, 1999.

McCrisken, Trevor, and Andrew Pepper. *American History and Contemporary Hollywood Film*. Edinburgh: Edinburgh University Press, 2005.

McDowell, John C. *The Gospel According to Star Wars: Faith, Hope and the Force*. Louisville: Westminster John Knox Press, 2007.

_____. *The Politics of Big Fantasy: The Ideologies of Star Wars, The Matrix and The Avengers*. Jefferson: McFarland, 2014.

_____. "*Star Wars*' Saving Return." *Journal of Religion and Film* 13.1 (April 2009), http://www.unomaha.edu/jrf/vol13.no1/StarWars.htm.

_____. "'Unlearn What You Have Learned' [Yoda]: The Critical Study of the Myth of *Star Wars*." In *Understanding Religion and Popular Culture*, eds. Terry R. Ryan and Dan W. Clayton. London: Routledge, 2012, 104–117.

———. "'Wars Not Make One Great': Redeeming the *Star Wars* Mythos from Redemptive Violence." *Journal of Religion and Popular Culture* 22.1 (2010), http://www.usask.ca/relst/jrpc/art22(1-Wars NotGreat.html.

McNeilly, Kevin. "'This Might be Hard for You to Watch': Salvage Humanity in 'Final Cut.'" In *Cylons in America: Critical Studies in Battlestar Galactica*, eds. Tiffany Potter and C.W. Marshall. London: Continuum, 2008, 185–197.

McVeigh, Stephen P. "The Galactic Way of Warfare." In *Finding the Force of Star Wars: Fans, Merchandise, and Critics*, eds. Matthew Wilhelm Kapell and John Shelton Lawrence. New York: Peter Lang, 2006, 35–58.

Melzer, Patricia. *Alien Constructions: Science Fiction and Feminist Thought*. Austin: University of Texas Press, 2006.

Merlock, Ray, and Kathy Merlock Jackson. "Lightsabers, Political Arenas, and Marriages for Princess Leia and Queen Amidala." In *Sex, Politics, and Religion In Star Wars: An Anthology*, eds. Douglas Brode and Leah Deyneka. Lanham: Scarecrow Press, 2012, 77–88.

Milbank, John. *Being Reconciled: Ontology and Pardon*. London: Routledge, 2003.

———. *Theology and Social Theory: Beyond Secular Reason*. Oxford: Basil Blackwell, 1990.

Miles, Margaret R. *Seeing and Believing: Religion and Values in the Movies*. Boston: Beacon, 1996.

Miles, Margaret R., and Brent S. Plate. "Hospitable Vision: Some Notes on the Ethics of Seeing Film." *Crosscurrents* 54.1 (2004), 22–31.

Miller, Martin, and Robert Sprich. "The Appeal of *Star Wars*: An Archetypal-Psychoanalytic View." *American Imago* 38.2 (Summer 1981), 203–220.

Mills, Anthony R. "From Rugged to Real: Stan Lee and the Subversion of the American Monomyth in Theological Anthropology and American Comics and Films." Doctoral dissertation. Fuller Theological Seminary, 2010.

Mills, Sarah. *Discourse*. London: Routledge, 1997.

Minnich, Elizabeth Kamarck. "Can Virtue Be Taught? A Feminist Reconsiders." In *Can Virtue Be Taught?* ed. Barbara Darling-Smith. Notre Dame: University of Notre Dame Press, 1993, 69–85.

Mitchell, Elvis. "Works Every Time." In *A Galaxy Not So Far Away*, ed. Glenn Kenny. New York: Henry Holt, 2002, 77–85.

Monaco, James. *American Film Now*. New York: Oxford University Press, 1979.

Montieth, Sharon. *American Culture in the 1960s*. Edinburgh: Edinburgh University Press, 2008.

Mulhal, Stephen. *On Film*. London: Routledge, 2002.

Myers, Thomas B. "Commodity Futures." In *Alien Zone: Cultural Theory and Contemporary Science Fiction Cinema*, ed. Annette Kuhn. London: Verso, 1990, 39–50.

Nathan, Ian. "R2D2, Where Are You?" *The Times Review*, 14 May 2005, 14.

Neale, Stephen. "Issues of Difference: *Alien* and *Blade Runner*." In *Fantasy and the Cinema*, ed. James McDonald. London: BFI, 1989, 213–223.

Nelson-Pallmeyer, Jack. *Saving Christianity from Empire*. New York: Continuum, 2005.

Newton, Judith. "Feminism and Anxiety in *Alien*." In *Alien Zone: Cultural Theory and Science Fiction Cinema*, ed. Annette Kuhn. London: Verso, 1990, 82–87.

Niebhur, Reinhold. *The Irony of American History*. London: Nisbet, 1952.

Nietzsche, Friedrich. *Birth of Tragedy*, trans. W. Kaufmann. New York: Vintage, 1967.

Noll, Mark A. *Christians in the American Revolution*. Grand Rapids: Eerdmans/Christian University, 1977.

Nuttall, Jon. *Moral Questions: An Introduction to Ethics*. Cambridge: Polity Press, 1993.

O'Shaughnessy, Nicholas Jackson. *Politics and Propaganda: Weapons of Mass Seduction*. Manchester: Manchester University Press, 2004.

Ott, Brian L. "(Re)Framing Fear: Equipment for Living in a Post-9/11 World." In *Cylons in America: Critical Studies in Battlestar Galactica*, eds. Tiffany Potter and C.W. Marshall. New York: Continuum, 2008, 13–26.

Overstreet, Jeffrey. "Star Wars: Episode III—Revenge of the Sith." *Christianity Today*, 18 May 2005, www.christianitytoday.com/movies/reviews/starwars3.html, consulted 1–06–05.

Palmer, R. Barton. "Imagining the Future, Contemplating the Past: The Screen Versions of *1984*." In *The Philosophy of Science Fiction Film*, ed. Steven M. Sanders. Lexington: University Press of Kentucky, 2008, 171–190.

Pearce, Joseph. *Tolkien: Man and Myth*. San Francisco: Ignatius, 1998.

Penley, Constance. "Time Travel, Prime Scene and the Critical Dystopia." In *Fantasy and the Cinema*, ed. James McDonald. London: BFI, 1989, 197–212.

Plate, S. Brent. "Filmmaking and World Making: Re-Creating Time and Space in Myth and Film." In *Teaching Religion and Film*, ed. Gregory J. Watkins. Oxford: Oxford University Press, 2008, 219–231.

Pok, Hannah. "The *Star Wars* Trilogy: Fantasy, Narcissism and Fear of the Other in Reagan's America." http://hannahpok.com/deepfieldspace/framesrc2c.html, consulted 18–05–05.

Pollock, Dale. *Skywalking: The Life and Films of George Lucas, the Creator of Star Wars*. Hollywood: Samuel French, 1990.

Porter, John. *The Tao of Star Wars*. Atlanta: Humanics, 2003.

Postman, Neil. *Amusing Ourselves to Death: Public Discourse in the Age of Show Business*. New York: Viking Penguin, 1985.

\_\_\_\_\_. *The End of Education: Redefining the Value of School*. New York: Vintage, 1995.

Potter, Tiffany, and Christopher Marshall, eds. *Cylons in America*. London: Continuum, 2007.

Probst, Christopher. "Welcome to the Machine." *American Cinematographer* 80.4 (1999), 32–36.

Pyle, Forest. "Making Cyborgs, Making Humans: Of Terminators and Blade Runners." In *Film Theory Goes to the Movies*, eds. Jim Collins, Hilary Radner, and Ava Preacher Collins. London: Routledge, 1993, 227–241.

Rapaport, David. "Some General Observations on Religion and Violence." In *Violence and the Sacred In the Modern World*, ed. Mark Juergensmeyer. London: Frank Cass, 1992, 118–140.

Raphael, D. Daiches. *The Paradox of Tragedy: The Mahlon Powell Lectures 1959*. London: George Allen & Unwin, 1960.

Rayment, Tim. "Master of the Universe." *Sunday Times Magazine*, May 16, 1999, 14–24.

Redmond, Sean. *Studying Blade Runner*, rev. ed. Leighton Buzzard: Auteur, 2008.

\_\_\_\_\_, ed. *Liquid Metal: The Science Fiction Film Reader*. London: Wallflower Press, 2004.

Reynolds, David West. *Star Wars: Attack of the Clones. The Visual Dictionary*. London: Dorling Kindersley, 2002.

\_\_\_\_\_. *Star Wars Episode I: The Visual Dictionary*. London: Dorling Kindersley, 1999.

Reynolds, David West, James Luceno, and Ryder Windham. *Star Wars: The Complete Visual Dictionary*. London: Dorling Kindersley, 2006.

Rinzler, J.W. *The Making of Star Wars: The Definitive Story Behind the Original Film*. London: Ebury Press, 2008.

Roberts, Adam. *Science Fiction*, 2d ed. London: Routledge, 2006.

Rose, Mark. *Alien Encounters*. Cambridge: Harvard University Press, 1981.

Rosenbaum, Jonathan. *Movie Wars: How Hollywood and the Media Limit What Movies We Can See*. Chicago: A Capella, 2000.

\_\_\_\_\_. *Movies as Politics*. Berkeley: University of California Press, 1997.

Rowlands, Mark. *The Philosopher at the End of the Universe*. London: Ebury Press, 2003.

Rubey, Dan. "Not So Far Away." *Jump Cut* 18 (1978), 8–14.

\_\_\_\_\_. "Not So Long Ago, Not So Far Away." *Jump Cut* 41 (1997), 2–12.

\_\_\_\_\_. "Not So Long Ago, Not So Far Away: New Variations on Old Themes and Questioning *Star Wars*' Revival of Heroic Archetypes." In *Myth, Media, and Culture in Star Wars: An Anthology*, eds. Douglas Brode and Leah Deyneka. Lanham: Scarecrow Press, 2012, 47–64.

Ryan, Michael, and Kellner, Douglas. *Camera Politica: The Politics and Ideology of Contemporary Hollywood Film*. Bloomington: Indiana University Press, 1988.

Ryn, Claes G. *America the Virtuous*. New Brunswick: Transaction, 2003.

Said, Edward W. *Culture and Imperialism*. New York: Vintage, 1993.

———. *Orientalism: Western Conceptions of the Orient*. London: Penguin, 1978.

———. *The Pen and the Sword: Conversations with David Barsamian*. Edinburgh: AK Press, 1994.

Salas, Jason. "On Piety, Star Wars, and Raising Your Children to Be Morally Aware." http://weblogs.asp.net/jasonsalas/archive/2005/05/19/407406.aspx, consulted 08-06-05.

Salewicz, Chris. *George Lucas Close Up: The Making of His Movies*. London: Orion, 1998.

Salvatore, R.A. *Star Wars Episode II: Attack of the Clones*. London: Century, 2002.

Sanders, Steven M. "Picturing Paranoia: Interpreting *Invasion of the Body Snatchers*." In *The Philosophy of Science Fiction Film*, ed. Steven M. Sanders. Lexington: University Press of Kentucky, 2008, 55–72.

———, ed. *The Philosophy of Science Fiction Film*. Lexington: University Press of Kentucky, 2008.

Scheers, Rob van. *Paul Verhoeven*, trans. Aletta Stevens. London: Faber and Faber, 1997.

Schwarzmantel, John. *The Age of Ideology: Political Ideologies from the American Revolution to Post-Modern Times*. London: Macmillan, 1998.

Scott, Bernard Brandon. *Hollywood Dreams and Biblical Stories*. Minneapolis: Fortress, 1994.

Scott, Ridley. "The Essence of Combat: Making Black Hawk Down." http://www.imdb.com/title/tt0367710/.

Seabrook, John. *Nobrow: The Culture of Marketing—The Marketing of Culture*. New York: Knopf, 2000.

Segal, Robert A. *Joseph Campbell: An Introduction*. New York: Garland, 1987.

———. *Myth: A Very Short Introduction*. Oxford: Oxford University Press, 2004.

Sen, Amartya. *Identity and Violence: The Illusion of Destiny*. London: Penguin, 2006.

Shakespeare, William. *King Lear*, ed. G.K. Hunter. Harmondsworth: Penguin, 1972.

Sharrett, Christopher. "The Horror Film in Neoconservative Culture." In *The Dread of Difference: Gender and the Horror Film*, ed. Barry Keith Grant. Austin: University of Texas Press, 1996, 253–276.

Sheehan, Henry. "Star Wars: Episode III Revenge of the Sith." www.henrysheehan.com/reviews/stuv/star-wars-3.html, consulted, 26-05-05.

Shipman, Hal. "Some Cylons are More Equal than Others." In *Battlestar Galactica and Philosophy: Mission Accomplished or Mission Frakked Up?* eds. J. Steiff and T.D. Tamplin. Chicago: Open Court, 2008, 155–170.

Silvio, Carl. "The *Star Wars* Trilogies and Global Capitalism." In Carl Silvio and Tony M. Vinci. eds., *Culture, Identities and Technology in the Star Wars Films: Essays on the Two Trilogies*. Jefferson: McFarland, 2007, 53–73.

Silvio, Carl, and Tony M. Vinci. "Introduction. Moving Away From Myth: *Star Wars* as Cultural Artifact." In *Culture, Identities and Technology in the Star Wars Films: Essays on the Two Trilogies*, eds. Carl Silvio and Tony M. Vinci. Jefferson: McFarland, 2007, 1–8.

Silvio, Carl, and Tony M. Vinci, eds. *Culture, Identities and Technology in the Star Wars Films: Essays on the Two Trilogies*. Jefferson: McFarland, 2007.

Simpson, Philip L. "Thawing the Ice Princess." In *Finding the Force of the Star Wars Franchise: Fans, Merchandise, and Critics*, eds. Matthew Wilhelm Kapell and John Shelton Lawrence. New York: Peter Lang, 2006, 115–130.

Skidmore, Max J., and Joey Skidmore. "More Than Mere Fantasy: Political Themes in Contemporary Comic Books." *Journal of Popular Culture* 17.1 (Summer 1983), 83–92.

Slotkin, Richard. *Regeneration Through Violence: The Mythology of the American Frontier, 1600–1860*. Middletown: Wesleyan University Press, 1973.

Slusser, George E., and Eric S. Rabkin. "Introduction: The Anthropology of the Alien." In *Aliens: The Anthropology of Science Fiction*, eds. George E. Slusser and Eric S. Rabkin. Carbondale: Southern Illinois University Press, 1987, 6–14.

Smith, Jim. *George Lucas*. London: Virgin, 2003.

Sobchack, Vivian. *Screening Space: The American Science Fiction Film*. New Brunswick: Rutgers University Press, 1998.

Sontag, Susan. "The Imagination of Disaster." In *Liquid Metal: The Science Fiction*

*Film Reader*, ed. Sean Redmond. London: Wallflower Press, 2004, 40–47.

Spangler, Bill. "Fighting Princesses and Other Distressing Damsels." In *Star Wars on Trial: Science Fiction and Fantasy Writers Debate the Most Popular Science Fiction Films of All Time*, eds. Jeanne Cavelos and Bill Spangler. Dallas: Benbella, 2006, 329–338.

Staub, Dick. *Christian Wisdom of the Jedi Masters*. San Francisco: Jossey-Bass, 2005.

_____. "On the Star Wars Myth." *Christianity Today*, 16 May, 2005, http://www.christianitytoday.com/ct/2005/120/22.0.html, consulted 26–05–05.

Steiner, George. *Language and Silence: Essays 1958–1967*. Harmondsworth: Penguin, 1967.

_____. *Real Presences: Is there Anything in What We Say?* London: Faber and Faber, 1989.

_____. *The Death of Tragedy*. Oxford: Oxford University Press, 1961.

Stone, Bryan P. *Faith and the Film: Theological Themes at the Cinema*. St. Louis: Chalice Press, 2000.

Stover, Matthew. *Star Wars Episode III: Revenge of the Sith*. London: Century, 2005.

Stoy, Jennifer. "Of Great Zeitgeist and Bad Faith: An Introduction to *Battlestar Galactica*." In *Battlestar Galactica: Investigating Flesh, Spirit and Steel*, eds. Roz Kaveney and Jennifer Stoy. London: I.B. Tauris, 2010, 1–36.

Stuart, Elizabeth. "Sacramental Flesh." In *Queer Theology: Rethinking the Western Body*, ed. Gerard Loughlin. Malden: Blackwell, 2007, 65–75.

Surin, Kenneth. *Freedom Not Yet: Liberation and the Next World Order*. Durham: Duke University Press, 2009.

Suvin, Darko. *Metamorphoses of Science Fiction: On the Poetics and History of a Literary Genre*. New Haven: Yale University Press, 1979.

Taubin, Amy. "Invading Bodies: *Alien3* and the Trilogy." *Sight and Sounds* 2.3 (July 1992), 8–10.

Telotte, J.P. *Science Fiction Film*. Cambridge: Cambridge University Press, 2001.

Thomson, Iain. "Deconstructing the Hero." In *Comics as Philosophy*, Jeff McLaughlin. Jackson: University of Mississippi Press, 2005, 100–129.

Tiffin, Jessica. "Digitally Remythicised: Star Wars, Modern Popular Mythology, and *Madam and Eve*." In *Inter Action 6: Proceedings of the Fourth Postgraduate Conference*, eds. Hermann Wittenberg, G. Baderoon and Y. Steenkamp. Bellville: UWC Press, 1998, 99–114.

Tindall, George Brown, and David E. Shi. *America: A Narrative History, Volume Two*, 4th ed. New York: W.W. Norton, 1996.

Todorov, Tzvetan. *The Fantastic: A Structural Approach to a Literary Genre*. Ithaca: Cornell University Press, 1975.

Trivers, R.L. "Parental Investment and Sexual Selection." In *Sexual Selection and the Descent of Man*, ed. B. Campbell. Chicago: Aldine, 1972, 136–179.

Tylor, E.B. *Primitive Culture: Researches into the Development of Mythology, Philosophy, Religion, Art, and Custom*, 2 vols. London: Murray, 1871.

Vidal, Gore. *Perpetual War for Perpetual Peace: How We Got to Be So Hated*. New York: Thunder's Mouth Press/Nation's Books, 2002.

Vinci, Tony M. "The Fall of the Rebellion; or, Defiant and Obedient Heroes in a Galaxy Far, Far Away: Individualism and intertextuality in the *Star Wars* Trilogies." In *Culture, Identities and Technology In the Star Wars Films: Essays on the Two Trilogies*, eds. Carl Silvio and Tony M. Vinci. Jefferson: McFarland, 2007, 11–33.

Vint, Sherryl. *Bodies of Tomorrow: Technology, Subjectivity, Science Fiction*. Toronto: University of Toronto Press, 2007.

Volf, Miroslav. *Exclusion and Embrace: A Theological Exploration of Identity, Otherness, and Reconciliation*. Nashville: Abingdon Press, 1996.

Watkins, Gregory J. "Introduction: Teaching Religion and Film." In *Teaching Religion and Film*, ed. Gregory J. Watkins. Oxford: Oxford University Press, 2008, 3–14.

Waugh, Rob. "The Billion Dollar Man." In *Day and Night: The Mail on Sunday*, 8 May 2005, 24–25.

Westfahl, Gary. "Space Opera." In *The Cambridge Companion to Science Fiction*, eds. Edward James and Farah Mendlesohn. Cambridge: Cambridge University Press, 2003, 197–208.

Wetmore, Kevin J., Jr. *The Empire Triumphant: Race, Religion and Rebellion in the Star Wars Films. Jefferson: McFarland, 2005.

_____. The Theology of Battlestar Galactica: American Christianity in the 2004–2009 Television Series. Jefferson: McFarland, 2012.

White, Mark D. "Introduction: A Rorschach Test." In The Watchmen and Philosophy: A Rorschach Test, ed. Mark D. White. Hoboken: John Wiley & Sons, 2009, 1–4.

_____, ed. Watchmen and Philosophy: A Rorschach Test. Hoboken: John Wiley & Sons, 2009.

Wilhelm, Stephanie J. "Imperial Plastic, Republican Fiber: Speculating on the Post-Colonial Other." In Finding the Force of the Star Wars Franchise: Fans, Merchandise, and Critics, eds. Matthew Wilhelm Kapell and John Shelton Lawrence. New York: Peter Lang, 2006, 175–183.

Wilkinson, David. The Power of the Force: The Spirituality of the Star Wars. Oxford: Lion, 2000.

Williame, J-P. "Religion in Ultramodernity." In Theorising Religion: Classical and Contemporary Debates, eds. J.A. Beckford and J. Wallis. Aldershot: Ashgate, 2006, 77–89.

Williams, Rowan. The Truce of God. London: Collins, 1983.

_____. Writing in the Dust After September 11. Grand Rapids: William B. Eerdmans, 2002.

Willis, Garry. Under God: Religion and American Politics. New York: Simon & Schuster, 1990.

Wilson, Veronica A. "Seduced by the Dark Side of the Force: Gender, Sexuality, and Moral Agency in George Lucas's Star Wars Universe." In Culture, Identities and Technology in the Star Wars Films: Essays on the Two Trilogies, eds. Carl Silvio and Tony M. Vinci. Jefferson: McFarland, 2007, 134–152.

Windham, Ryder. Star Wars: Revenge of the Sith Scrapbook. London: Scholastic, 2005.

Windham, Ryder, and Peter Vilmus. Star Wars: The Complete Vader. London: Simon & Schuster, 2009.

Wink, Walter, Engaging the Powers: Discernment and Resistance in a World of Domination. Minneapolis: Fortress, 1992.

_____. Jesus and Nonviolence: A Third Way. Minneapolis: Fortress, 2003.

_____. The Powers That Be: Theology for a New Millennium. New York: Doubleday, 1998.

Winkler, Martin M. "Star Wars and the Roman Empire." In Classical Myth and Culture in the Cinema, ed. Martin M. Winkler. Oxford and New York: Oxford University Press, 2001, 272–290.

Winter, Karen. "The Politics of Star Wars." http://belladonna.org/Karen/politicsofstarwars.html, consulted 30-05-05.

Wolfe, Jonathan. An Introduction to Political Philosophy. New York: Oxford University Press, 1996.

Wollstonecraft, Mary. A Vindication of the Rights of Women, ed. Carol H. Poston, 2d ed. New York: Norton, 1998.

Wolmark, Jenny. Aliens and Others: Science Fiction, Feminism and Postmodernism. Iowa City: University of Iowa Press, 1994.

Wood, Robin. Hollywood from Vietnam to Reagan. New York: Columbia University Press, 1986.

Woodman, Tom. "Science Fiction, Religion and Transcendence." In Science Fiction: A Critical Guide, ed. Patrick Parrinder. New York: Longman, 1979, 110–130.

Wright, John W. "Levinasian Ethics of Alterity: The Face of the Other in Spielberg's Cinematic Language." In Steven Spielberg and Philosophy: We're Gonna Need a Bigger Book, ed. Dean A. Kowalski. Lexington: University of Kentucky, 2008, 50–68.

Wyschogrod, Edith. Saints and Postmodernism: Revisioning Moral Philosophy. Chicago: University of Chicago Press, 1990.

_____. Spirit in Ashes: Hegel, Heidegger, and Man-Made Mass Death. New Haven: Yale University Press, 1985.

Young, Lola. Fear of the Dark: "Race," Gender and Sexuality in the Cinema. New York: Routledge, 1996.

Žižek, Slavoj. Violence: Six Sideways Reflections. New York: Picador, 2008.

_____. Welcome to the Desert of the Real! Five Essays on September 11 and Related Dates. London: Verso, 2002.

Zynda, Lyle. "Was Cypher Right? Part II: The Nature of Reality and Why It Matters." In Taking the Red Pill: Science, Philosophy, and Religion in the Matrix, ed. Glenn Yeffeth. Dallas: Benbella, 2003, 43–55.

# Index

Abrams, Jerold J. 172*n*1
Ackbar, Adm. Gial 82, 135, 140
Adorno, Theodor 3, 16, 117, 118
Agger, Ben 16
Alba, Jessica 91
Alderaan 35, 59, 80, 85, 136
Alford, Mathew 14
*Alien* 52, 67, 81, 91–93, 95, 100, 118, 144–147, 148, 169–170*n*57
*Alien Abduction* 118
*Alien Autopsy* 118
*Aliens* 52, 92, 95, 145, 147, 148
*All Quiet on the Western Front* 13
Allie, Stass 171*n*95
Allnut, Frank 39
Alsford, Mike 49
*American Graffiti* 43, 64, 65, 71, 74, 111
American Revolution 45
American supremacism 18
Amidala, Padmé 58, 62, 63, 68, 69, 79, 80, 87, 99–111, 112–113, 138–139, 140, 141, 164*n*44, 165*n*59, 168*n*16
*The Andromeda Strain* 44
Anker, Roy 50, 59, 61, 67
*Apocalypse Now* 13, 14, 23, 64, 65, 70, 71, 166*n*96
Apocalyptic 67
*Apollo 13* 118
Aragorn 94
Ardala, Princess 96
*Area 51* 118
Arendt, Hannah 2, 90
Aristotle 11, 156*n*3
Aronowitz, Stanley 5
Arthurian legends 112
Arwen 94
Asimov, Isaac 35, 44, 163*n*13
Attebery, Brian 169*n*29
Augustine 53, 54, 55, 56, 57, 74, 156*n*18, 164*n*38, 164*n*42, 164*n*45
*Avatar* 94
*Avengers* 119

Baba, Ponda 139, 149
*Bambi* 27

Banham, Roger 161*n*127
*Barbarella* 91, 95
Barth, Karl 1, 55, 56, 58, 162*n*157, 164*n*38, 164*n*40, 164*n*43, 164*n*48
Batgirl 96
*Batman Begins* 14
*Battlefield Los Angeles* 67, 118
*Battlestar Galactica* 121, 126
Beaudoin, Tom 23, 156*n*27
Beauvoir, Simone de 89
Bell, Daniel, Jr. 57
Benhabib, Seyla 88, 90, 98
Bergman, Ingmar 30, 110
Bernardi, Daniel 127
Bespin 88, 128, 129, 130, 168*n*21
Bible 39
Billalba, Depa 52, 81, 136, 171*n*95
Binks, Jar Jar 137, 138, 157*n*43
*The Birth of a Nation* 120, 125
Biskind, Peter 74, 151, 162*n*150, 167*n*104
*Blade Runner* 32, 52, 95, 118, 144, 163*n*31, 170*n*73
Bly, Robert 163*n*29
Bogle, Donald 173*n*57
Bondanella, Peter 163*n*13
Booker, Keith 42–44, 46, 113–114, 116, 117, 120–121, 134, 151, 173*n*28, 175*n*125, 176*n*132
Bossk 140
Boulle, Pierre 124
Boussh 86
Branagh, Kenneth 116
*Brazil* 65
Brin, David 67, 166*n*77
Brooker, Will 36–37
*The Brothers Grimm* 83
Brown, Wendy 170*n*93
*Buck Rogers* 14
*Buck Rogers in the 25th Century* 96
*Buffy the Vampire Slayer* 94
Bukatman, Scott 118
Bulq, Sora 52
Bush, George W. 47, 63, 163*n*22
Butler, Judith 15, 26, 89

C-3PO  26, 83, 85, 130, 133, 151
Calrissian, Lando  62, 64, 82, 128–130, 140, 142, 149, 168n21
Cameron, James  95, 116, 145, 147
Campbell, Joseph  17, 18–19, 28, 31, 32, 40, 49, 62, 65, 72, 81, 86, 96, 165n58
Canby, Vincent  161n127
Capitalism  18, 64–65, 90, 131–132, 148, 151
Card, Claudia  78
Card, Orson  32, 160n109
Carson, Tom  150
Catwoman  96
Cavelos, Jeanne  80, 84, 85, 95, 112, 168n6
Chewbacca  26, 88, 121, 122, 128, 134, 136, 139, 140, 150, 151, 157n43
Christensen, Terry  174n90
*Chronicle*  75
the Church  38, 163n27, 164n41
Cicero  77
*Clerks*  36
*A Clockwork Orange*  44
Clone Army  33, 54, 141
Clone Wars  51, 55, 58, 61, 168–169n22
*Close Encounters of the Third Kind*  133, 134
*Cloverfield*  145
Coakley, Sarah  89
Cold War  44, 46, 48, 164n45
*Commando*  50
The Company  147
*Conan the Barbarian*  50
Confederacy of Independent Systems  61, 62, 100, 101, 141
Connor, Sarah  93–94, 117
Conrad, Joseph  145, 148
*Contact*  118
Coppola, Francis  64, 70, 71
Cornea, Christine  3, 91, 92, 93, 95, 124, 125, 127, 150, 170n57, 170n73
Coruscant  101, 103, 131, 165n59, 171n99
*Cowboys Versus Aliens*  118
Cranny-Francis, Anne  79
Creed, Barbara  92, 146, 169–170n57
Cyberdyne  147

Dagobah  49–50, 74
*The Darkest Hour*  118
Darklighter, Biggs  26
Darkseid  30
Darth Maul  29, 113, 141
Darth Plagueis the Wise  113
Darth Sidious  29–30, 33, 34–35, 37, 39, 44–45, 46, 53, 56, 59–62, 72, 73, 101, 103, 106, 108, 109, 113, 137, 138, 140, 151, 165n59, 167n100, 171n99, 174n76
Darth Tyrannus *see* Dooku, Count
Darth Vader  26, 29–30, 33, 35, 39, 50, 51, 54, 59–62, 66–69, 73, 75, 83, 105, 106, 109, 113, 122, 124, 127–128, 129, 131, 135, 138, 140, 141–142, 158n43
Davies, Jude  80, 88, 125, 175n118
Dawson, Anna  92

*The Day the Earth Stood Still*  118
Dearing, Col. Wilma  96
Death Star  32, 33, 35, 39, 49, 53, 83, 84, 85, 90, 99
Death Star, the second  36, 59, 86, 129, 140
Dees, Richard  130
Deis, Christopher  121, 123, 126, 127, 137, 173n66
*Demolition Man*  50
Dengar  140
Descartes, René  90, 98, 99
Desolge, Nick  162n11
Dick, Philip K.  65, 76
Disney  7, 83, 168n9
*District 9*  133–134
*Do Androids Dream of Electric Sheep?*  65
Doctor Doom  30
*Dr. Strangelove*  126
Dodonna, Gen. Jan  85
Doherty, Thomas  94, 145, 147
Dominguez, Diana  81, 83, 84, 85, 91, 96, 101–102, 109–110, 112, 157n42, 168n6
Dooku, Count  51, 54, 56, 100, 109, 113, 141, 144, 169n22, 174n76
Douglas, Michael  156n12
*The Dukes of Hazzard*  91
Dylan, Bob  25

Eagleton, Terry  12, 169n51
*Earth to Echo*  119, 133
Eastwood, Clint  40
Ellis, Kathleen  82
The Emperor *see* Darth Sidious
Endor  59, 86, 128
*E.T.*  133
Evazan, Dr.  140, 149
Ewoks  72, 121, 134, 140, 148, 165n58
Expanded Universe  7, 52, 61, 96, 108, 169n22

*Falling Down*  156n12
*Falling Skies*  119
*Fantastic Voyage*  94
Feminism  78, 89, 98
Fett, Boba  140
Fett, Jango  130, 141
Fincher, David  146
Fisher, Carrie  84, 100
*Flash Gordon*  3, 14, 42, 112
Fonda, Jane  91, 95
the Force  39, 49, 50, 54, 57, 61, 68, 75, 103, 163n27
Fortuna, Bib  140
*The 4400*  119
4-Lom  140
Fox, Megan  91
*Frankenstein*  116
Freedman, Carl  76
*Freiheit*  101
Freire, Paolo  4
Frodo  56, 148

# Index

Galactic Basic 137
Galactic Empire 34–35, 42, 51, 54, 59, 63, 72, 73, 80, 82, 94, 115, 121, 123, 128, 134, 135, 136, 137, 142, 166n96
Gallia, Adi 81, 136, 171n95
Gandalf 56
*Gandhi* 76
Geonosis 100, 130
Geraghty, Lincoln 126, 155n9
*G.I. Jane* 94, 100
Gibbon, Edward 44
Gibson, James 37
Giger, H.R. 144
Gilliam, Terry 65
Girard, René 16, 157n30
Giroux, Henry 19, 75, 79, 85
*Gladiator* 46, 50
*God Bless America* 14
*Godzilla* 145
Good, Howard 12
Gordon, Andrew 18, 72, 96
Greedo 51–52
Greene, Eric 124
Grendel 149
Grievous, General 33, 39, 54, 141
Griffith, D.W. 120, 125, 126
Gungans 82, 131, 137, 138–139, 140
Gunray, Nute 131

Hall, Stuart 19, 124
Hamill, Mark 60, 111
*Hamlet* 104
Hanson, Michael 81
Hanssen, Beatrice 98
Hauerwas, Stanley 41, 55
Henderson, Mary 18, 32, 160n97, 162n150
the Hero 20–21, 24–25, 36, 40, 49–51, 59, 62, 65, 66, 69, 76, 84, 89
Hett, Sharad 143
*Hidden Fortress* 82–83, 133
*High Noon* 28
Hinson, Hal 156n12
Hiroshima 35
Hitler, Adolf 34, 45
Hobbes, Thomas 20
*The Hobbit* 149
*Homeland* 119
Homer 2, 38
Homophobia 18
Horkheimer, Max 117
Horstman, Joey 158n49
*Hotel Rwanda* 13, 19
Hoth 86
How, Tey 131
Howe, Andrew 122, 123–124, 129, 131, 132, 136, 137, 148
Hunter, I.Q. 118, 119

IG-88 140
*Independence Day* 67, 119, 153, 166n78
Individualism 18, 79

Inness, Sherrie 84
Instrumentalization 106, 107, 137, 147, 171–172n139
*Invaders from Mars* 14
*Invasion* 119
*Invasion of the Body Snatchers* 144, 151–152, 175n125
Irigaray, Luce 107

Jabba the Hutt 86, 88, 90–91, 120, 128, 129, 134, 139, 140, 149
Jackson, Kathy Merlock 83, 88, 94, 96, 112, 168n6
Jackson, Peter 148
Jackson, Samuel L. 130–131
Jade, Mara 169n22
Jameson, Frederic 118
Jantzen, Grace 2, 4–5, 20, 22, 24, 80, 85, 90, 170n83
Jawas 120, 134, 141
*Jaws* 145, 146
Jedi 34, 38, 39, 51, 53, 56, 58, 61, 62, 73, 74, 86, 105, 106, 107, 108, 109, 111, 113, 123, 130, 141, 142, 143, 160n105, 171n95
Jesus 39, 57, 64–65
Jettster, Dexter 141
Jeunet, Jean-Pierre 146
Jewett, Robert 3, 21, 23, 24, 25, 69, 70, 74, 159n68, 159n76, 167n107
Jinn, Qui-Gon 19, 27, 55, 138, 140, 164n44
*John Carter on Mars* 118
Jones, James Earl 122, 127, 158n43
Jones, L. Gregory 20, 40
Judy, Dwight 163n29
Jung, Carl 17
Julius Caesar 44
*Jurassic Park* 174n98
Just war 6, 15, 21, 48, 55–58

Kael, Pauline 111
Kamino 130
Kaminski, Michael 157n42, 160n97, 161n123, 164n53, 167n105
Kamitsuka, Margaret 98
Kant, Immanuel 89
Kapell, Matthew 7, 24, 120, 142, 157n43, 159n64
Kappeler, Susanne 22
Kashyyk 122, 136
Kasper, Walter 162n156
Kaufman, Roger 96, 158n45
Kaveney, Roz 34, 69, 92, 144, 145, 152, 160n87, 164n44, 166n78, 168n6
Kay, Max 81
Kaye, Heidi 118, 119
Kazanjian, Howard 60
Kearney, Richard 136, 146
Kellner, Douglas 64, 114
Kenobi, Obi-Wan 20, 26, 29, 31, 33, 39, 49, 52, 53, 54, 55, 59, 61, 62, 66, 67, 83, 103, 105, 107, 109, 128, 130, 134, 136, 139, 140, 141–142, 143, 163n22, 164n44

Kershner, Irvin 59
Kerslake, Patricia 47, 127, 133
King, Martin Luther, Jr. 22, 164*n*53
*King Kong* 174*n*98
*King Lear* 68, 102, 104
Kinnucan, Michelle 27, 32–33, 39, 159*n*71, 159*n*77, 159*n*83, 162*n*150
Kirby, Jack 30
Kissinger, Henry 46
*Kitsch* 12
Kleiser, Randall 63, 101
Korriban 160*n*105
Koth, Eeth 136, 143
Krämer, Peter 114, 162*n*11
Kristeva, Julia 13, 169*n*57
Ku Klux Klan 125
Kubrick, Stanley 12
Kuiper, Koenraad 32
Kundera, Milan 3
Kurosawa, Akira 82, 133
Kurtz, Gary 14

Lama Su 33
Lancashire, Anne 161*n*127
Lane, Beldon 157*n*41
Lars, Beru 26, 59
Lars, Cliegg 143
Lars, Owen 26, 59
Lawrence, John 3, 18, 21, 23, 24, 25, 35, 69, 70, 74, 159*n*64, 159*n*68, 159*n*76, 165*n*58, 167*n*107
Le Guin, Ursula 153, 155*n*18
Lev, Peter 81, 82, 141, 150, 168*n*6
Lightsaber 49, 52–53, 60
Lloyd, Jake 68
*The Lord of the Rings* 148
Loughlin, Gerard 93
Lubow, Arthur 161*n*127
Lucas, George 2, 3, 4, 7, 18–19, 21, 31, 32, 34, 36, 37–38, 46, 51, 53, 58, 59, 61, 63, 64, 65, 66, 67, 69, 70, 71–72, 73, 74, 75, 76, 78, 79, 80, 82, 83–84, 85, 86, 87, 89, 94, 99, 100, 101, 104, 105, 108, 110, 111, 118, 121, 122, 124, 131, 136, 137, 138, 141, 143, 148–149, 153, 157*n*27, 157–158*n*43, 158*n*46, 159*n*62, 160*n*87, 163*n*27, 166*n*75, 166*n*86, 166*n*94, 167*n*100, 168*n*16
Lucas, George, Sr. 70
Lucas, Marcia 87
Lucasfilm 7, 42
Luretis, Teresa de 98
Lydon, John 156*n*27, 159*n*71

Magna Guards 39
*Maleficent* 83
Malone, Aubrey 120
Manichaeanism 3, 24, 31, 40, 43, 47, 67, 68–69, 73, 114, 120, 141, 146, 159*n*71
Manifest Destiny 29
Mann, Anthony 44
Marquand, Richard 58–59
*Mars Attacks* 67, 119

Marsden, George 158–159*n*60
*The Matrix* 35, 94, 118, 152
McCallum, Rick 30, 63
McCarthy, Sen. Joseph 151–152
McCrisken, Trevor 14–15
McDiarmid, Ian 30, 108
McDowell, John C. 1, 7, 21–22, 51–52, 60, 132, 159*n*62, 159*n*64, 163*n*27, 165*n*58, 165*n*68, 167*n*108, 167*n*112, 167*n*113, 167*n*117, 168*n*6, 171*n*106, 172*n*8, 173*n*64, 174*n*76, 174*n*91
McVeigh, Stephen 37, 43, 70
Melzer, Patricia 6, 78, 98, 111, 132, 150
*Men in Black* 118
Merlock, Ray 83, 88, 94, 96, 112, 168*n*6
*Metropolis* 64
Milbank, John 28
Miles, Margaret 16, 78, 123, 124, 156*n*27
Millennium Falcon 86, 88, 121, 129
Miller, Frank 13
Miller, Martin 96
Mills, Sarah 156*n*25
Minnich, Elizabeth 78, 79
*Mirror Mirror* 83
Mitchell, Elvis 128
Mollica, Richard 16
*Monsters* 67, 118
Mos Eisley 51, 132, 140
Mothma, Mon 80, 81, 86, 110, 140
*Mulan* 85
Mundi, Ki-Adi 150
Murch, Walter 166*n*96
Mustafar 103
Myles, Linda 29, 161*n*127
Mythology 2, 3, 15–16, 18–19, 160*n*87, 165*n*58

Naboo 34, 53, 81, 86, 99, 100, 107, 131, 139, 140, 143
Nagasaki 35
Nass, Boss 137
Natality 2
Nazism 30, 34–37, 44–45, 66, 73, 119, 123, 165*n*58, 165*n*65, 174*n*76
Necrophilia 2
Neesen, Liam 19
Neoconservatism 3
Neytiri 94
Niebuhr, Reinhold 48
Nietzsche, Friedrich 11
Nixon, Richard 3, 6, 46, 72, 167*n*100
Nolan, Christopher 14
Noll, Mark 159*n*60
Nonviolence 21, 62, 164–165*n*54
*Nothing* 3
Nunb, Nien 140
Nuremburg Rally 37
Nuttall, Jon 162*n*157, 164*n*48

Obi-Wan Kenobi 20, 26, 29, 31, 33, 39, 49, 52, 53, 54, 55, 59, 61, 62, 66, 67, 83, 103, 105, 107, 109, 128, 130, 134, 136, 139, 140, 141–142, 143, 163*n*22, 164*n*44

Offee, Barriss 171*n*95
*The Omega Man* 44
*Once Upon a Time* 83
*1 Million Years B.C.* 91
Organa, Bail 135, 141
Organa, Leia 26, 39, 64, 68, 76, 78, 79, 80–91, 94–100, 104, 112, 121, 128–130, 135, 139–141, 168*n*6, 168*n*16, 169*n*36, 185
Orwell, George 17
O'Shaughnessy, Nicholas 23–24, 75, 159*n*71
the Other 2, 6, 47, 78, 89, 117, 118, 120, 126, 127, 131, 133, 142, 143, 144, 145, 148, 150, 151–153, 159*n*71, 174–175*n*98
Overstreet, Jeffrey 108

Pacifism *see* Nonviolence
Pal, George 152
Palpatine *see* Darth Sidious
Panaka, Capt. Quarsh 139, 149
Patriarchalism 18, 79, 85, 90, 93, 112, 135
*Paul* 118
Pedagogy 2, 4, 5, 72
Penley, Constance 117
Pepper, Andrew 14–15
Perez, Gilbert 1
Piell, Evan 150
*Planet of the Apes* 124–125, 126
Plate, S. Brent 16, 78
Plato 64
Pok, Hannah 160*n*110, 174*n*90
Pollock, Dale 2, 63, 83, 101, 111, 136, 171*n*130
Postman, Neil 76, 167*n*118
Powergirl 96
*Predator* 67, 118
*Pretty Woman* 91
Princess Leia *see* Organa, Leia
*The Prisoner* 165*n*65
*Prometheus* 118
Prowse, David 158*n*43
*The Punisher* 40
Puritans 67
Pye, Michael 29, 123, 124, 161*n*127
Pyle, Forest 117

R2-D2 26, 83, 133, 151, 160*n*107, 185
Racism 18, 19, 22, 79, 127, 132, 137, 150, 168*n*21, 173*n*42, 175*n*118
*Rambo* 50, 94
Raphael, D. Daiches 11
Rayment, Tim 30
Rayner, Richard 160*n*107
Reagan, Ronald 35–36, 44, 72, 167*n*107
Rebel Alliance 33, 35, 36–37, 39, 46, 60, 72, 82, 83, 85, 86, 87, 100, 110, 123, 128, 134, 135, 139, 141, 166*n*96
Republic (Old) 39, 44–45, 51, 54, 62, 101, 103, 122, 123, 137, 141, 151, 167*n*100, 174*n*76
*The Return of the King* 94
Revenge 36
Rex, Captain 109
Reynolds, David West 138

Riefenstahl, Leni 37, 73
Rinzler, J.W. 72, 160*n*97
Ripley, Ellen 91–93, 95, 145, 147, 148
*Rise of the Planet of the Apes* 124
Roberts, Julia 91
*Robocop* 67
*Robot Overlords* 118
Roman Empire 35, 44–46
Rosenbaum, Jonathan 3, 28, 36
Rowlands, Mark 174*n*90
Rowling, J.K. 142
Rubey, Dan 18, 19, 27, 29, 78, 81, 86, 87, 161*n*121
Rutledge, Gregory 126
Ryan, Michael 64, 114

The Sand People *see* Tusken Raiders
Sanders, Stephen 69–70, 121, 151
Sarlaac 128
*Schindler's List* 13, 19
Scott, Ridley 14, 93, 95, 118, 144, 146–147
*The Sea Horse* 174*n*98
Secura, Aayla 171*n*95
Segal, Robert 157*n*41
Sen, Amartya 55, 97
Seneca 12, 13
Shakespeare, William 68
*Shane* 124
Sharrett, Christopher 67
Shelley, Mary 116
*Shooting Dogs* 13, 19
*Shrek* 83
*The Siege* 119
Sifo-Dyas 33
*Silent Running* 44
Silvio, Carl 2, 16, 18, 19, 135, 158*n*44, 159*n*64
Simpson, Jessica 91
Simpson, Philip 87, 88, 90, 157*n*42, 168*n*6
*Sin City* 91
Sith 34, 39, 60, 63, 106, 113, 141, 142, 144, 151, 160*n*105, 166*n*81, 169*n*22
Skywalker, Anakin 27, 34, 38, 52, 56, 66–69, 73, 74, 75, 80, 99, 101, 102, 103, 104–109, 128, 131, 140, 141, 142, 144, 163*n*22, 164*n*44
Skywalker, Luke 20, 26, 34, 35, 49–54, 59–62, 64, 66, 73, 74, 75, 76, 79, 80, 81, 83, 84, 86, 87, 88, 90, 91, 96, 97, 99, 111, 128, 129, 135, 139, 140, 141–142, 158*n*43, 165*n*54, 169*n*36
Skywalker, Leia *see* Organa, Leia
Skywalker, Shmi 68, 104, 105, 106, 164*n*44
Smith, Carol 80, 88, 125, 175*n*118
Smith, Kevin 36
Smits, Jimmy 135
*Snow White and the Huntsman* 83
Sobchack, Vivian 111
Solo, Han 26, 28–29, 51–52, 64, 76, 80, 81, 86, 87, 88, 90, 91, 104, 121, 122, 123, 128, 129, 131, 134, 136, 139, 140, 141, 142, 168*n*21
Sontag, Susan 15, 152, 172*n*6
Soviet Communism 35, 64, 72, 114, 119, 151–152

*Soylent Green* 44
*Spartacus* 13, 46
Spence, Louise 79
Spielberg, Steven 119, 133, 152
*Spooks* 119
Sprich, Robert 96
Stam, Robert 79
*Star Trek* 111, 126–127, 150, 153
*Star Wars Clone Wars* 14
*Star Wars Episode VII: The Force Awakens* 4, 7
*Star Wars Rebels* 14
Starkiller, Luke 51
*Starship Troopers* 67, 119, 153
Staub, Dick 174$n$90
Steiner, George 4, 11–12, 155$n$11
Stone, Bryan 20, 158$n$49
Stuart, Elizabeth 89
Sully, Jake 94
Surin, Kenneth 118
Sutherland, John 171$n$101
Suvin, Darko 112, 117, 126

*Taken* 119
*Tangled* 83
Tano, Ashoka 109
Tantive IV 42, 50
Tao 53
Tarantino, Quentin 13, 67, 161$n$142
Tarkin, Grand Moff Wilhuff 29, 45, 83, 140
Tarpals, Captain 137
Tatooine 42, 49, 103, 106, 136, 137, 143
Taubin, Amy 148
Telotte, J.P. 77
*The Terminator* 67, 116–117, 147
*Terminator 2: Judgment Day* 93–94, 100
*The Thing* 67
Thomson, Iain 163$n$24
*Thor* 116
*300* 13, 50
*THX 1138* 4, 6, 64–65, 70, 71, 72, 77, 118, 158$n$46, 171–172$n$139
Ti, Shaak 81, 171$n$95
Todorov, Tzvetan 127
Tolkien, J.R.R. 30, 34, 148, 163$n$33, 163$n$36
Trade Federation 28, 54, 55, 99, 131, 139, 144
Tragic drama 1, 11–12, 56, 66, 68, 75, 102, 142, 171$n$106
Trandoshan Slavers 136
*Transformers* 91, 118
*The Triumph of the Will* 37, 73
*Troll Hunter* 144
*Troy* 50
Truth, Sojourner 97–98
Tusken Raiders 120, 123, 134, 139, 143, 144, 150
20th Century–Fox 73
Typho, Captain 141

Unduli, Luminara 171$n$95
*The Unforgiven* 40

*V* 119
*V for Vendetta* 14
Vaapad Combat-Form III 52
Valorum, Chancellor Finis 34, 135
Ventress, Asajj 168–169$n$22
Verhoeven, Paul 6–7, 119
Vietnam 2, 3, 6, 23, 37–38, 43, 46, 48, 63, 64, 65, 70–71, 147–148, 165$n$58, 166$n$86, 166$n$96
Villa, Pancho 81
Vinci, Tony 2, 16, 18, 19, 158$n$46, 159$n$64
Violence 2, 6, 11–77, 97, 146, 162$n$155
Volf, Miroslav 162$n$153

Wampa 49
*War of the Worlds* 14, 67, 119, 152
Watergate 3, 43, 70, 72
Watto 131, 132
Weigel, George 164$n$41
Welch, Raquel 91, 94
Wells, H.G. 116, 152
West, Cornel 149, 175$n$118
Westerns 2, 28–29, 38, 40, 124
Westfal, Gary 159$n$61
Wetmore, Kevin 17, 18, 19, 43, 69, 81, 90, 118, 120, 122–123, 126, 128, 131, 132, 137–138, 139, 150, 151, 153, 155$n$9, 157$n$43, 158$n$47, 161$n$141, 162$n$150
*The Whispers* 119
*The Wild Bunch* 70
Wilhelm, Stephanie 158$n$47
Williams, Billy Dee 128
Williams, John 42
Williams, Rowan 161–162$n$143
Wilson, Veronica 17, 81, 102, 103, 104, 106, 107, 108, 110, 112, 135, 157$n$42, 158$n$45, 168$n$6, 168$n$16
Windham, Ryder 171$n$118
Windu, Mace 31, 52, 53, 54, 56, 103, 105, 130–131, 140, 149
Wink, Walter 20, 24–25, 28, 29, 30, 36, 40, 57, 62, 159$n$75, 165$n$54
Winkler, Martin 44–46, 76, 161$n$120
Wolfe, Jonathan 20
Wollstonecraft, Mary 101
Wolmark, Jenny 173$n$41
Wonder Woman 96
Wood, Robin 15, 88, 157$n$43
Wookies 136, 141
*The World's End* 118
Wright, John 134
Wyschogrod, Edith 171$n$133

*The X-Files* 119
*Xena: The Warrior Princess* 94

Yaddle 81, 171$n$95
Yavin, Battle of 26, 85
Yoda 20, 31, 34, 49–51, 53–56, 59, 61, 68, 73, 74, 82, 105, 128, 135, 140, 141, 169$n$36

Žižek, Slavoj 20, 163$n$26

www.ingramcontent.com/pod-product-compliance
Ingram Content Group UK Ltd.
Pitfield, Milton Keynes, MK11 3LW, UK
UKHW042007140426
5217IPUK00015B/1026